WILLIAM PENN'S LEGACY

THE JOHNS HOPKINS UNIVERSITY STUDIES
IN HISTORICAL AND POLITICAL SCIENCE

Ninety-Fifth Series (1977)

1. The Military Coup d'Etat as a Political Process:
   Ecuador, 1948–1966   *by John Samuel Fitch*

2. William Penn's Legacy: Politics and Social Structure
   in Provincial Pennsylvania, 1726–1755   *by Alan Tully*

William Penn's Legacy

POLITICS AND SOCIAL STRUCTURE

IN PROVINCIAL PENNSYLVANIA,

1726-1755 § *by Alan Tully*

THE JOHNS HOPKINS UNIVERSITY PRESS

Baltimore and London

This book has been brought to publication with the generous assistance of the Andrew W. Mellon Foundation.

The Johns Hopkins University Press, Baltimore, Maryland 21218
The Johns Hopkins Press Ltd., London

Library of Congress Catalog Card Number 77-4548
ISBN 0-8018-1932-6
Library of Congress Cataloging in Publication data will be found on the last printed page of this book.

For Betty

CONTENTS

APPENDICES

FIGURES

ACKNOWLEDGMENTS

§

During the lean years in which I researched and wrote this book, a number of agencies extended me financial aid. The Canada Council gave me support both as a graduate student and as a faculty member, the Colonial Dames of America awarded me scholarships that I invested in the early stages of this project, and the American Council of Learned Societies and the President's Committee on Research at the University of British Columbia provided funds that allowed me to finish up my research and rewriting. To all of these agencies, I am grateful.

I am also deeply indebted, for giving me access to manuscripts in their possession, to the American Philosophical Society; the Bucks County Historical Society; the Chester County Historical Society; the Friends Historical Library; the Haverford College Library–Quaker Collection; the Historical Society of Pennsylvania; the Lancaster County Historical Society; the Library Company of Philadelphia; officials of the Bucks, Chester, and Lancaster County Court Houses; the Presbyterian Historical Society; and the Philadelphia City Archives. The staff at all of these archives were unfailingly helpful, and to them I extend my thanks. At the two depositories that I most consider home, the Historical Society of Pennsylvania and the Chester County Historical Society, there are some special friends. At the former Peter Parker and Linda Stanley did all they could to help me—and at the same time we laughed a lot. At the latter, Dorothy Lapp put her vast knowledge of Chester County events, families, and sources at my disposal and encouraged me to use the material there the way an archives should be used.

There are, of course, many others who have contributed a great deal to this effort, in one form or another. They are Andre Arpin, Margaret Boyler, Fred DeKuyper, Eli Hofstetter, Eugenia Calvert

Holland, Ruth Keen, Jackie Livesay, Mrs. Charles Lundgren, Mrs. Willard Rouse, Margery Tippie, Henry Y. K. Tom, Heather Troche, and various members of my own and my wife's families. Leslie Upton, Jack Marietta, Ted Cook, and Barry Levy read earlier versions of the text and have helped me with their criticisms. Harold Livesay heard all of the ideas in this book—endlessly—and has had much to do with its final form. Ken Lockridge offered me a rescuing hand at a time when I was tired of the whole project, and his insightful suggestions and enthusiasm helped me through an important last revision. In addition, there are two scholars who, although they had nothing to do with this book, do bear some responsibility for my historical stabbings. A long time ago, Fred Somkin first awakened me to the excitement of historical inquiry and Bill Nelson pointed out by his example what the historian's work really entailed.

My greatest debt, however, is to you, Jack Greene—for taking a chance on a retread when hotshot graduate students were easy to come by, for constantly sharing your delight in finding new ways to look at old questions, for being tough when it mattered, and for leaving me alone as much as you did. All of that and one thing more—your willingness to take a jibe. That's what made it fun, Jack.

PROLOGUE

§

What was the political world of America's eighteenth-century colonists really like? For decades historians have been trying to answer this question. In the late nineteenth century whig historians traced out the path the colonists took to liberty and self-government; in the early twentieth the imperial historians emphasized the growing powers of the colonial Assemblies as the most important fact of political life; simultaneously, and with a vigor that kept their influence strong until the 1950s, the so-called progressive historians pronounced that the essence of the colonial political experience was the ever-present conflict between the disadvantaged many and the privileged few.[1] In each of these basic interpretations there was some major feature of colonial politics which advocates of that view argued was crucial for an understanding of the early American political experience and which, apparently, changed little over time. Whether the arena was a southern or a New England colony, there were important common threads—a sameness about political affairs. Thus, no matter what the exact trend or division these early historians saw, they all testified to the existence of regular patterns of political behavior in the colonies.

Of the large number of revisionist historians who have written about colonial politics in the past twenty years, only a few have offered general interpretations. Of those, the most like his predecessors is Jack P. Greene. In a series of pieces written since 1961, Greene has taken the findings of the imperial school as a starting point and demonstrated in sophisticated fashion the central place of the assemblymen's fight against the executive's perogative powers in colonial political life.[2] Others have been more concerned with the problem of contexture. Reacting to the progressives' description of colonial politics as "oligarchical," Robert E. Brown argued that political relationships in pre-revolutionary America were essentially "democratic" in nature, while

J. R. Pole and Richard Buel, Jr., described them as "deferential" and Michael Zuckerman pronounced them "consensual."[3] Others, some of whom found inspiration in the old progressive literature, have stressed the restrictive and oppressive nature of political power in the colonies.[4] Although these recent historians differ in their conclusions, they, like their forerunners, do share one thing in common: they all stress some widespread and enduring pattern of political relationships that tends to lend coherence to early American politics.

As noteworthy as all of these recent interpretations are, however, they have, in a very real sense, been of secondary importance—for the last ten years have really belonged to Bernard Bailyn. It is his writings that have radically changed the modern historian's conception of eighteenth-century politics.

In order to understand Bailyn's view of colonial politics and to see why it has been so dominant, it is necessary to go back slightly in time. Between the mid-1930s and the 1960s a plethora of monographic literature appeared, analyzing the peculiarities of political behavior in the different colonies. Gradually, the clear-cut patterns that the progressive historians had seen in colonial politics were obliterated beneath the welter of personality conflicts, family disputes, ethnic and national group antipathies, religious differences, sectional tensions, economic rivalries, and social divisions that the revisionist historians apparently found.[5] It was to this confusing array of evidence that Bailyn brought some semblance of order when, in 1965, he suggested that a Madisonian insight into the structure of revolutionary and confederation politics might be used to illuminate the pre-revolutionary experience. In his *Origins of American Politics*, Bailyn argued that the distinguishing feature of colonial American politics was the multifaceted factional conflicts of competing interest groups that, at times, "reduced the politics of certain colonies to an almost unchartable chaos."[6] Because these competing groups were constantly shifting and reforming, and because they were so aggressive in their pursuit of power, colonial politics were inherently unstable—an instability that was reflected in the roar of contention that inevitably accompanied open political confrontation. Moreover, this kind of political environment predisposed colonial politicians to adopt a type of English radical-whig ideology that in turn tended to encourage divisiveness and thereby intensify factional behavior.[7]

Because of his feat of finding some meaning in the disparate and confusing monographic literature, because of his emphasis on conflict (even though for Bailyn it was what might best be described as a kind of pre-industrial pluralistic conflict) at a time when American historians were moving back in droves to conflict models of social analysis, and because of the truly exciting way he used his conception of eighteenth-century politics to explain the anxieties of American politicians during the revolutionary crisis,[8] Bailyn has had a great impact both on the questions American political historians have asked and on the design of their work. Since 1965 a whole series of new colonial studies have confirmed Bailyn's judgment that the form of colonial politics was milling factionalism, the character of political relationships that of constant strife and chronic instability, and the mental state of eighteenth-century politicians one of virtual paranoia.[9]

There can be no doubt that Bailyn's work deserves all the accolades it has received, but at the same time there is reason for dissatisfaction among those who want to grasp the real political world of the eighteenth-century colonist. For, like that of his predecessors, Bailyn's political history is single-strand history; what he describes is there all right, but it is only one strand. Like all such one-dimensional history, it cannot capture the rich texture of colonial politics because it excludes or at least reduces to marginal significance those facets of political life which are outside the predominant mode. To be faithful to the shape and detail of colonial political life, it is necessary to take Bailyn's factionalism into account, yet not be limited by it. One must, as it were, push beyond it.

Hopes of accomplishing this were what prompted this study of Pennsylvania. What I wanted to do was to find the political world of mid-eighteenth-century colonials and, without any initial imposition of categories, to enter into it and to explore it thoroughly. Then, having found the concerns and perspectives of politically aware colonials, I wanted to recreate their world in its full variety and proper proportion. Of course, it was impractical to try to do this for more than one colony, and after looking at several I chose Pennsylvania. Here was a major colony, the political history of which had been used to illustrate, not just Bailyn's, but all of the other major interpretations of colonial politics.[10] Moreover, there was one largely ignored span of thirty years, beginning immediately after the well-known political factionalism and economic dislocation of the early 1720s and ending with the well-studied Quaker "withdrawal" from government in the mid-1750s, which seemed suited to such a project.

What struck me as soon as I began to look closely at Pennsylvania was the relative peacefulness of political relationships in the province. There was little of the overt contention that is widely accepted as the most reliable indicator of factional activity. The years that exhibited no open political strife far outnumbered those that did. A spate of overt political conflict in the late 1720s, a two-and-a-half-year period of angry politics in the early 1740s, and a new round of executive-legislative conflict in 1754–55—that was the extent of the contention. The politics of peace filled the remaining years. As for the active politicians and the politically aware, they most often desired political peace, expected it, and worked for it. When contention arose, they both consciously and unconsciously assigned well-worn parameters to that conflict and thus made it both intelligible and familiar. And in cases of long standing personal antipathies there quickly appeared a sense of ennui rather than of unpredictability. Only on the rare occasion when events conspired to force a change in the roles political enemies played was there the kind of uncertainty that the term "factionalism" implies.

Beyond the prevalence of peaceful political relationships, what impressed me most about Pennsylvania society was the existence of a whole series of widely shared social experiences, informal relationships, lines of influence, institutional arrangements, divisions of power, and forms of legislative behavior that worked to order political affairs, regularize decision making, and resolve conflict. Instead of being a constant source of acute political differences, the peculiar economic and social structure of the Pennsylvania community very often fulfilled needs, satisfied expectations, and circumscribed the very conflict it did engender; instead of being distinguished by the kinds of ill-defined categories of governmental authority that encouraged the formation of factional groups, government affairs were characterized by the existence of well-established procedures and by political habits that elicited widespread respect and compliance; instead of giving free rein to their occasional anger, and paranoic fears, Pennsylvanians demonstrated a willingness to blunt their differences, to avoid the kinds of confrontations that could only lead to prolonged disagreement, and to work within the established framework of government for the kind of political harmony they deemed intrinsically good. Thus, the desire for political peace and the traditional ways of ensuring that peace were mutually reinforcing.

Judging from the evidence, then, the only sensible starting place for any attempt to reconstruct the political world of mid-eighteenth-century Pennsylvanians was with the stability so clearly present and so eagerly sought after by many provincial residents. To attempt to describe it, to explore its sources, and in the end to reflect briefly on the implications of it for the study of early American politics—that, obviously, was the historian's task.

PART ONE

CONFIGURATIONS

§

The political world of mid-eighteenth-century Pennsylvania had many facets. The politician's concerns and those of his knowledgeable constituents included myriad questions about public policy, questions that ranged from matters of political right to those of patronage. But as always there were some issues and concerns that loomed above others. These—and both the way in which prominent personalities handled them and the ways in which the undistinguished reacted to them—gave shape and dimension to political affairs. While overall the politics of peace predominated in Pennsylvania, there were some times that were more tense than others, and there were moments when outright contention carried the day. Yet, throughout the entire thirty years, provincial residents lived in a known political world. Even the contention and faction that occurred were understood features that blended easily into the familiar, and predominantly tranquil, political landscape that was Pennsylvania's.

CHAPTER 1

PROPRIETARY POLICIES
AND PROVINCIAL POLITICS,
1726–1739[1]

§

During the years 1726 to 1739, public affairs in Pennsylvania encompassed both the unfolding of, and interplay between, proprietary policies and provincial politics. In the late 1720s members of the proprietary family attempted to clear up the disputed provincial title that William Penn had left behind, to comprehend what policies their Pennsylvania deputies had followed in the absence of a firm proprietary hand, and to end the Baltimore family's claim to parts of southern Pennsylvania. Once he arrived in Pennsylvania in the early 1730s, the proprietary's chief spokesman, Thomas Penn, had to deal directly with an attempt by Marylanders to occupy western Pennsylvania and to try, under difficult circumstances, to implement an effective land policy. In provincial politics the late 1720s brought the end of the Keithian disruptions and the beginning of a relatively long-lasting period of peace. Largely through the good offices of Andrew Hamilton, and because of the threat that Maryland posed to all Pennsylvanians, proprietor and provincial politicians worked together harmoniously throughout the 1730s. As the decade closed, however, it was clear that rather than strengthen the proprietary's political interest, Thomas Penn's policies and his politics had done much to weaken it.

§

Throughout the 1720s, proprietary control of land settlement was at a minimum in Pennsylvania. The reason for this laxity was simple

3

enough: no one knew where authority lay. When William Penn died in 1718 he left all of his lands in America, with the exception of a number of specific bequests, to his three sons—John, Thomas, and Richard—by his second wife, Hannah Callowhill, "in such proportion and for such estates" as she should "think fit." The validity of the will, however, was questioned by the offspring of Penn's first marriage, the Springett branch of the family, and a long chancery suit ensued. In the summer of 1727 the court established the legality of the will, but the title that was then vested in John, Thomas, and Richard was still encumbered by a heavy mortgage their father had contracted, and, in addition, Springett Penn, William senior's grandson, still had some vaguely defined claims to the power of government in Pennsylvania.

During the next four years, these obstacles were eliminated. By January 1730 the mortgage had been discharged, and in September 1731 William Penn 3d, having inherited his brother's claims when Springett died in the winter of 1730-31, relinquished his rights in exchange for £5,500. Agreement, too, had been reached within the Callowhill branch of the family. After Hannah's death in 1727, the exact terms of the disposition of the Pennsylvania estate were worked out and formally agreed to by her three surviving sons. Finally, in May 1732 the descent of the property was established among Pennsylvania's three young proprietors—John, Thomas, and Richard Penn.[2]

The fourteen years of uncertainty within the Penn family were mirrored by public affairs in Pennsylvania. In his will William Penn left the management of his colonial estate to five Pennsylvania trustees. These men interpreted their trust as an obligation to manage the proprietary lands until the mortgage against the estate could be discharged. But although the contesting of Penn's will meant that the duties of the trustees, qua trustees, went into abeyance, four of them were still responsible for managing the Penn family affairs in the interim. As commissioners of property they had the unenviable task of overseeing the operations of the Pennsylvania Land Office.[3]

The main function of the Land Office was to grant land titles to those who wanted to purchase land.[4] With William Penn's death, however, clear title was exactly what no commissioner of property could provide. Because no one knew where the proprietary power resided, no deputy could conclude a contract on the proprietary behalf. Had there been little demand for such transactions an effective expedient might have been found, but it was the future proprietors' misfortune to be thus paralyzed at a time when land-hungry immigrants were arriving in growing numbers. Between 1720 and 1730 Pennsylvania's population shot up from approximately 35,000 to

50,000. No matter whether the newcomers were English, Scotch-Irish, or German, most of them wanted land.[5]

In response to this demand, Secretary of the Land Office James Logan devised what expedients he could.[6] For those few who would risk it and pay a price "better than common," Logan granted title by the authority delegated to the commissioners of property by William Penn.[7] Most prospective purchasers, however, hearing of the confusion in proprietary affairs, did not even apply for a warrant—an application for purchase that in normal circumstances was followed by a Land Office survey and the granting of title.[8] Yet it was inconceivable that the proprietary men should merely step aside and allow the immigrants to sit down at will on land of their choice. Logan reasoned rightly that the new arrivals, settling in groups as they did, would form a "general combination" and prove "unmanageable" at a later date.[9] To establish some leverage on these groups, Logan made tacit agreements with "those who made the best appearance."[10] In such a situation, "tho' we would never by any means mention a price, yet they expect it must be £10 per 100 acres and perhaps interest from the time of settlement."[11] Many of those who were party to such understandings were successful in pressing the Land Office to survey their land; thus the survey alone came to represent a legitimate property right.[12]

As a short-term expedient this plan was realistic, but over a period of fourteen years it had severe limitations. Many of the poorer settlers were deliberately excluded from participation, others refused to come into any sort of understanding, and still others were either ignorant of, or indifferent to, the formal arrangements. Such men marked out the bounds of their claims and "resolutely" sat down "without any manner of right or pretence to it."[13] Although Logan undoubtedly exaggerated when he wrote to Hannah Penn that a hundred thousand acres had been taken up "in such a fashion," his assertion that in newly organized Lancaster County "settling without leave" was the "common practice" might well have been true.[14]

By the mid 1720s there were several different kinds of property rights—warrant, warrant and survey, survey, and quiet possession—all of which were known as "improvements."[15] Such rights were protected by law and capable of being alienated.[16] The settlers who lived on them "pay[ed] taxes maintained roads as well as [did] freeholders."[17] Of course, the Land Office officials tried to protect from excessive exploitation the proprietary land on which these rights were located: Receiver-General James Steel pursued those who settled for a short time "without any grant or license . . . dispose[d] of the same under the name of improvements" and then "remove[d] to another place with the same design";[18] James Logan demanded foreknowledge of the sale of any approved settlement, suggested that those allowed to settle should post a bond against permanent damage to the plantation, and attempted to stop the despoiling of any unsettled land. These efforts, however, were usually ineffective.[19]

The long period of delay in settling William Penn's estate was not the only factor that prohibited orderly land settlement in Pennsylvania. The boundary line between Pennsylvania and Maryland had never been drawn, and after William Penn's death the proprietary family of Maryland, the Baltimores, pressed their claims with renewed vigor.[20] The Maryland charter of 1632 placed that colony's northern boundary at forty degrees latitude, a line that in 1714 was rumored to be approximately ten miles *north* of Philadelphia.[21] Although Charles Calvert, the fifth Baron Baltimore, publicly claimed that he should have all the land south of that line, custom dictated otherwise. In the seventeenth century all parties to the dispute had been satisfied that the line lay about twenty miles *south* of Philadelphia. In 1682 the third Lord Baltimore had run a boundary line from the mouth of the Octorara River to the coast, and the commissioners of property for Pennsylvania, having accepted "Lord Baltimore's line" as valid, had taken possession down to that line by settling land that far south in the early 1700s.[22] In the 1720s the Pennsylvania commissioners continued to recognize that boundary; they agreed to settlements north of those early "Nottingham lots" and refused to allow settlements below that point.[23] Yet, as Logan recognized, the Baltimore claims to such a large section of Pennsylvania was the "deeper cause" of the proprietary paralysis;[24] for, even when the family dispute was settled, new land titles had to be conditional on the conclusion of a boundary settlement.[25]

Given the uncertain state of the proprietary title, the reaction of many Pennsylvania residents was both predictable and sensible: they refused to pay quitrents. If the commissioners of property did not have the power to grant titles, how could the receiver-general have authority to collect their rents? If quitrents were paid to one representative of the Penn family, might not others demand the same as arrears once the succession had been settled? If Baltimore was to be their proprietor in the future, what could be gained by paying rent to the Penns?[26]

Throughout the late 1720s and early 1730s, Logan bombarded the Penns with complaints and suggestions. Little could be expected in the way of revenue, methods of making even modest remittances were few, and the trustees had never been given any commission or instrument that would publicly designate them as proprietary agents.[27] The proprietary interest was swiftly "bleeding" away, and only resolute action could prevent its destruction.[28] The family dispute had to be resolved, an agreement concluded with Lord Baltimore, and above all one of the proprietors, preferably elder brother John who owned one-half of the proprietary interest, had to come to Pennsylvania and personally reassert his family's authority.[29] When in May 1732 Lord Baltimore finally affixed his signature and seal to a boundary agreement, all bars to such a visit seemed to have disappeared.

During the 1720s, the tenor of intercolonial relations between Pennsylvania and Maryland had been firmly established. Harassments, assaults, and jailings typified dealings at the local level; procrastination, intrigue, and intransigence characterized activities in Philadelphia, Annapolis, and London.[30] The compromise of 1732, which established the boundary line roughly fifteen miles south of Philadelphia, resolved nothing. When Lord Baltimore arrived in Maryland shortly after concluding the pact, he was quickly convinced that he had given away far too much,[31] and his commissioners, who were to cooperate with Pennsylvania counterparts in surveying the line, scuttled negotiations with their wild interpretation of the agreement text.[32] By August 1734 Baltimore was back in London, making more trouble for the Penns by petitioning the King to transfer control of Delaware, or the three Lower Counties as it was then known, from the Penns to himself. The Lords Committee of the Privy Council dodged the issue by ruling that either party might begin a suit in chancery to determine title to the lower Counties and the exact location of the Pennsylvania-Maryland boundary. Accordingly, on June 21, 1735, the Penns filed suit in equity—a suit that was not to be settled for fifteen years.[33]

While news of Baltimore's unwillingness to honor the 1732 agreement and of his subsequent activities brought gloom to Philadelphia, it brought new hope to Annapolis. The Marylanders, who had everything to gain and nothing to lose, busied themselves furthering a strategy they had already devised. East of the Susquehanna River, where Pennsylvania's authority over the Nottingham lots and the existence of the old Octorara boundary line gave the Penns strong claims, Maryland's gains could be no more than marginal. West of the Susquehanna, however, prospects were much better; there Pennsylvania had made no land purchases from the Indians. Consequently, her claim to land south of the fortieth parallel rested on the slim right of possession established by two Pennsylvanians, James and John Hendricks, who, in 1729, had occupied land on the west side of the Susquehanna directly across from the Pennsylvania settlement of Hempfield. Marylanders contested even that claim, arguing that the

Hendrickses had never enjoyed quiet possession; by April 1731 eight families were settled on the disputed land under Maryland patent, and agents were circulating through western Pennsylvania recruiting German immigrants to do likewise. This sudden wave of Maryland activity apparently influenced public opinion on the frontier, for a Lancaster justice of the peace, John Wright, immediately reported to James Logan that "most of the people" on the eastern side of the river believed that the "hominy" presence on the western shore nullified any right the Penns might have had.[34]

Such black days were not to last. Shortly after Thomas Penn arrived in Philadelphia in the late summer of 1732, he began to encourage the establishment of rival settlements under Pennsylvanian aegis. In 1734 Penn asked local leader Samuel Blunston to distribute special land licenses for plantations in the west. These licenses did not confer title because Penn had not yet made the necessary Indian purchase, but they required no money payment, authorized settlement and surveys anywhere west of the Susquehanna, and carried an implicit guarantee that once Penn had extinguished the Indian claims they could be converted into regular titles.[35] By issuing these special warrants, the proprietor formally served notice of what he had privately stated since his arrival from England: Pennsylvania had a right to the disputed land and he was determined to protect that claim. His forthright action restored confidence in the Penn claim, and settlers with and without licenses moved westward to settle nominally under the jurisdiction of the Quaker colony.

From 1730 through 1738 the rival activities of the Pennsylvanians and Marylanders centered mainly on the land lying directly across the Susquehanna from Hempfield Township. It was there that the Hendricks claim had first been laid out and occupied in 1729, and it was there that the most resourceful Maryland leader, Thomas Cresap, chose to reside. Cresap was one of those first half-dozen Marylanders who had settled there in early 1731, and he was a forceful presence from the moment of his arrival. Before the year ended he was accused of encouraging Pennsylvania Germans to settle nearby under Maryland survey, of stealing an indentured servant from a Hempfield resident, of harassing the local Indians, and of attempting to arrest a Pennsylvania freeman. In return Cresap charged Pennsylvania authorities with denying him justice and attempting his murder. This exchange set the tone for what followed. Over the next four and a half years, reports from the frontier were filled with news of the destruction of livestock, the harassment of residents, and assaults in the name of arrests.[36]

It was not until the latter half of 1736, however, that events took a critical turn. During the summer of that year, Maryland surveyors had been busy setting out a series of new tracts, and in doing so they ran roughshod over a number of old property lines that purportedly carried with them a valid Maryland title. To the German settlers who had bought the plantations and who had abandoned their allegiance to Pennsylvania in order to acquire secure land titles, this was the last straw. They felt that the Maryland magistrates had mistreated them and now their property was in danger. In late August, after consulting with Samuel Blunston, they sent a letter to Annapolis renouncing their Maryland overlords and petitioned the Provincial Council in Philadelphia to accept their allegiance. Shortly after the council had agreed to their request, three hundred Maryland militiamen appeared on the banks of the Susquehanna opposite Hempfield. Thanks to the resourcefulness of the Lancaster County sheriff, Samuel Smith, who quickly managed to assemble a force of one hundred fifty volunteers, and to the disagreements that arose between Maryand's militia leaders and Thomas Cresap, the invading force did not mount an attack. After plundering a few of the German homesteads and making a few half-hearted attempts to squeeze promises of continued loyalty to Lord Baltimore from their occupants, the militiamen straggled back into Maryland.[37]

It was this appeal to force and the exposure of a Maryland-inspired plot to forcefully dispossess the turncoat Germans in the dead of winter that finally stirred the Pennsylvanians to action. Since January 1735 the Lancaster magistrates had possessed a warrant for Cresap's arrest for murder; the time had come to serve it. Unfortunately, Cresap had ample warning of Sheriff Smith's approach, and the Lancaster posse found him barricaded in his cabin. But the Pennsylvanians were not to be deterred by the niceties of due process; they fired the cabin and collared Cresap when he burst through the door.[38]

After this event both sides settled down in preparation for continued hostilities. Blunston and Smith organized a voluntary militia to guard the eastern shore of the Susquehanna and to garrison the fortified cabin on the Hendricks land; the Marylanders established their own stronghold and mounted periodic raiding parties—to terrorize the Germans, to arrest several Pennsylvanians, to assault others, and to raid the Lancaster jail. For a time in the spring of 1737 when the Lancaster residents felt the full effects of Maryland's marauding militia, the morale of the Pennsylvanians dipped low. But time was on their side.[39]

In early 1737 the boundary dispute again came before royal eyes—more Maryland petitions were presented, this time charging the Pennsylvanians with murder, assault, and inhuman cruelty. After reviewing the evidence, the crown issued a quieting order on August 18. Dissatisfied with this directive, which forbade further settlement in the disputed areas, Baltimore and John Penn finally agreed to a temporary settlement of their own making, and on May 25, 1738, an order-in-council approved it. According to the agreement, a temporary line was to run fifteen and one-quarter miles south of Philadelphia east of the Susequehanna and fourteen and three-quarter miles south of Philadelphia west of that river. The actual surveying of that boundary in 1738–39 ended the long reign of the Maryland boundary dispute as the foremost issue in Pennsylvania's public affairs.[40]

During the eight years in which the Marylanders had most vigorously pursued their claims, many Pennsylvania residents shared a common preoccupation with the threat from the south. The Baltimore family claims and the actions of their agents clouded the hopes and expectations of all those who felt that they had a stake in the province's future. Those who treasured their religious freedoms feared Catholic oppression; those who valued Pennsylvania's peculiar constitution decried the Maryland alternative; those who held land in lower Chester and in Lancaster believed they were in danger of losing that possession; those who lived in Philadelphia feared that, if Baltimore gained control of the rich lands of southeastern Pennsylvania and of the Lower Counties, he would direct their trade away from the Delaware River.[41] Because the Maryland threat was a commonly shared, external threat, Pennsylvanians met it with determined unanimity. Members of the proprietary family defended their claims in London, Governor Patrick Gordon and his Council did so in the provincial capitals, and the Assembly identified itself with the common cause on all occasions.[42] What was at stake was the security of many provincial residents, a security that depended directly on the validity of the proprietary charter. Thus, it was the proprietary family that events thrust to the fore, and colonial agents, Quaker interest groups, provincial spokesmen, and local authorities all looked to the Penns for leadership.

Under these circumstances, Thomas Penn's stay in Pennsylvania presented him with a substantial opportunity to build up good will and influence in his province. Throughout the colony there were men who had already committed themselves irrevocably to his cause—not merely the political heavyweights such as Provincial Councillor James Logan, merchant Isaac Norris, Sr., and Assemblymen Jeremiah Langhorne and Andrew Hamilton, but also local residents in Nottingham and western Pennsylvania who had chosen to settle under the questionable right of the Penn family. What they asked for in return for their support was leadership. It was precisely this demand, however, that Thomas Penn could not meet. Handicapped by his account-book mentality and acutely aware of his own claim to social preeminence, Penn was not the man to make dramatic and encouraging appearances on the frontier, to deal with local leaders as partners in a common enterprise, or to actively build up a personal following of any sort. Immediately after his arrival Penn started out on the right foot when he underwrote all expenses incurred in the boundary dispute. But by 1737, as Lancaster politician Samuel Blunston reported with bitterness, the proprietor's behavior in past months had left no doubt about his feelings; he believed that "all his pains and expense" had been "chiefly taken for the benefit of the inhabitants" and they had done little to help themselves.[43] As long as the dispute with Maryland continued, Blunston and others kept their anger under control; county officials strove to keep squatters off the proprietary manors, defending the Penn property just as they hoped the Penns were protecting their titles and claims. But by wasting the initial enthusiasm that Pennsylvanians had for one of their long-absent proprietors, and by failing to convert the cooperation of necessity into mutual trust and friendship, Thomas Penn squandered an important opportunity to guard the proprietary against the day when the boundary crisis would end and the self-interested harmony that accompanied it would no longer survive.

When Thomas Penn sailed for Pennsylvania in the summer of 1732, he believed that his foremost duty was to bring system and order to the Land Office and thereby gain for the family the income to which they were entitled. Back rents and uncollected purchase money were to be called in, and from 1732 new conditions were to apply to the purchase of all Pennsylvania land; quitrents were to rise from two shillings per hundred acres to one-half penny per acre sterling and the common price of land from ten pounds per hundred acres to fifteen pounds ten shillings Pennsylvania currency.[44] But while making alterations in the conditions of land purchase was a simple procedure, thorough implementation was not. Provincial residents continued the practices they had followed in the preceding decade: some took out warrants—at the new price, of course—but then neglected to have their tracts surveyed and patented; others took the first two steps but, failing to make the final payment on their land, were denied formal title; still others simply came and sat down as they had in the past, professing as always that, when properly asked, they would pay for their land.[45]

Despite his intentions, Penn had no alternative but to sanction many of these arrangements. It was impossible to demand full payment in the issuance of a warrant, for seldom did the purchaser have that kind of ready money. Consequently, many made a first payment of one-third the value of the land and agreed to pay the balance in six months, only to default after obtaining the warrant and marking out or having surveyed the limits of their new plantations.[46] In the disputed territory in Lancaster, and even on the east side of the Susquehanna, Penn allowed deputy surveyors Samuel Blunston and Zachariah Butcher to set out lots on verbal or written application alone, and with no money payment other than surveyor's fees, in order to bind the interests of settlers more tightly to the Pennsylvania cause.[47] Of course, on the west side of the Susquehanna River the Blunston licenses established another type of property right, without any consideration money or application for the usual legal instruments.

Expediency dictated these policies, and it was to expediency that Penn bowed. His real sentiments were never in doubt; he pointed out to his agents that the only way to force provincial residents to pay for the land they worked was to stop the sale of improvements. If this could be done, land would have to be paid for and titled before a property transaction could be completed. In practice, however, this was no solution. The locally elected officials, over whom Penn had no effective control, would not lift a finger to implement such instructions.[48]

Although the obstacles were too great to allow Penn to bring about the kind of ordered situation he had envisaged, not all of the proprietor's efforts were lost. The Land Office did begin to issue patents in large enough numbers to bring in some revenue, and the large number of warrants that were taken out signified that many were, at least, asking permission to settle. Two natural inducements helped Penn persuade settlers that they should take out warrants, surveys, and patents: (1) that established improvement rights could be challenged by a new warrantee, an action that could lead to an expensive lawsuit, and (2) that no man was eligible for aid from the Provincial Loan Office unless he had established a secure title or was using the loan to finance that purchase. But, given the great backlog of improvements that had built up, the continuing, rapid rate of immigration in the 1730s, and the difficulties created by the Maryland boundary dispute, systematic regulation and distribution of land titles was dishearteningly slow.[49]

What was eventually to bring the proprietors the greatest amount of trouble was not the demand that new grants of land be subject to a higher purchase price, but that old improvement rights, settled or acquired before 1732, should be subject to the new prices. After William Penn's death, Logan had, indeed, told settlers that he could "neither make nor propose any terms to them," but there was widespread belief that ten pounds per hundred acres, which was the consideration most commonly asked, would be the eventual price.[50] The very indefiniteness of the arrangement, coupled with the fact that the Land Office did on occasion grant land at an even lower price, created a misleading set of expectations among the settlers. In fact, the 1732 increase in the price of land did no more than allow for the depreciation of Pennsylvania currency, so that in pounds sterling the Penns asked no more than they had received prior to the emission of Pennsylvania currency in the 1720s. Such reasoning, however, evoked no sympathy among the tight-fisted immigrants. To them ten pounds had come to mean ten pounds in Pennsylvania currency, and Thomas Penn's appearance in the colony meant the land would now cost five pounds more.

The situation in Donegal, Lancaster County, illustrates both the kind of mistakes Thomas Penn made and the kind of hostility he encountered. In 1719 James Logan had settled a group of Scotch-Irish families in Donegal, hoping that if need should arise they would serve as the nucleus of a frontier militia. In settling them there Logan made no concession beyond the usual ten pounds per hundred-acre land price.[51] Those who did not take out warrants undoubtedly expected the same terms,[52] but in the winter of 1733-34, after turning down their petition for these terms, Thomas Penn gave them a choice of three alternatives, all of which constituted a heavier payment than the old prices and quitrents had been.[53] After two years of negotiations Penn had given some ground, but it was still not enough to satisfy the intractable Donegalians.[54] In the meantime, Penn had accepted Samuel Blunston's advice and ordered him to go ahead and survey the inhabitants' improvements, reasoning that once this had been done warrants could be filled out detailing both plantation size and cost.[55] By the end of 1737, when Blunston had finished up most of the surveying, Penn was beginning to see the folly he had committed. In paying Blunston's surveying fees and allowing him to proceed, the inhabitants had obtained the strongest possible improvement right they could get—a survey—and this without paying any consideration money. Dealing from this new position of strength, the spokesmen for the Donegal residents renewed their requests for the old rates and liberal credit terms.[56]

Faced with this evidence of bad faith, absolutely convinced of his own rectitude and humiliated by his own naïveté, Penn's patience crumbled. In December 1738 he ordered Blunston not to survey any more plantations unless the applicant had taken out a warrant on one of the three sets of terms he had offered in 1733-34;[57] then, nine months later, when news of the Penn-Baltimore agreement reached Philadelphia, Penn acted with swiftness.[58] On November 23, 1738, the proprietaries issued a proclamation condemning all of those who now possessed warrants, surveys, or bare improvement rights and had not paid the necessary consideration money. According to the proclamation they had to pay this money by March 1, 1739, or be "proceeded against according to the law, in order to be removed from their possessions."[59] Proprietary negotiations had accomplished nothing; the time had come for confrontation.

Much the same sort of evolution in proprietary affairs occurred over the question of quitrent payments. The old yearly rates that the Penns had most often reserved on grants of land before 1732 had been either one or two shillings per hundred acres. Throughout the 1720s, however, many refused to pay it because of the confusion over the proprietary title. This excuse remained valid for some of the Chester and Lancaster County residents until 1738. But most of the old settlers in Philadelphia, Bucks, and northern Chester recognized their obligation to pay. The important question, for them, was not whether to pay, but how much to pay. According to their land grants the quitrents were payable in sterling, but after the adoption of a paper currency in 1723 the common standard exchange in the colony had become the Pennsylvania shilling. Moreover, the paper money acts that authorized the printing and distribution of the provincial currency stipulated that it be accepted as legal tender for all outstanding debts. Since the value of twelve English pence, or one shilling, fluctuated between eighteen and twenty pence Pennsylvania currency, local residents were tempted to pay their quitrents in the devalued provincial money.[60]

When Thomas Penn arrived in Pennsylvania, some residents professed their willingness to compromise and pay a four pence premium on the shilling in accordance with an English statute of 1707 that pegged colonial currency at sixteen pence on the shilling.[61] Despite the pressing needs of the family, however, Penn refused to allow his receivers to accept anything but the full amount according to the current exchange rate.[62] Both he and brother John hoped they could persuade the Assembly to exempt quitrents from the legal tender clause of the paper money acts. Predictably, the assemblymen were cold to Penn's initial suggestions, but they were aware that the proprietor possessed the means to force the issue.[63] In October 1737, the Reemitting Act, which had kept Pennsylvania's currency in circulation, was to expire, and the approximately £69,000 bills of credit would thereafter gradually disappear from circulation.[64] Because local opinion was virtually unanimous that Pennsylvania's prosperity depended on the availability of this currency, the proprietary power to withhold executive consent from a new currency act became a powerful bargaining point. Fully aware of this, the Penns instructed Governor George Thomas, when he was commissioned in 1737, to refuse assent to any currency bill that did not expressly state that all proprietary quitrents were to be paid according to the current rate of exchange.[65]

As soon as Governor Thomas reached Phildelphia in the summer of 1738, the Assembly presented him with a bill to reemit and increase the amount of provincial currency. Thomas managed to postpone consideration of the bill by arguing that insufficient time remained in the summer session for him to master such a complex affair, but, when a new Assembly had convened for its January session in 1739, that excuse was no longer acceptable. In the first exchange between the governor and the Assembly, Thomas put the proprietary arguments: the quitrents ought to be paid in the equivalent of sterling because they had been contracted as sterling debts; to "honest men," the "justice" of this proprietary instruction was plain enough.[66] The Assembly's replies stressed a different point: if an exception were made in the case of the quitrents, the value of the currency would be adversely affected and the exchange rates would fall even lower. If this happened, the proprietaries would lose far more from outstanding debts for land than they could ever recoup in the quitrent arrears.[67] Thomas Penn eventually admitted the validity of this reasoning, and in May 1739 the two parties reached a compromise.[68] The proprietors would accept sixteen pence on the shilling; the Assembly would pay the proprietors £1,200 immediate compensation and an annual stipend of £130 during the life of the new paper money act.[69]

On May 19 the relevant legislation passed, and Thomas Penn had no need to bide his time any longer. In August 1738 he had written to John that as soon as a settlement had been reached he would "lose no time to seize on the tenants and use all methods the laws allow to make a speedy collection of the whole."[70] On June 28, 1789, only five and a half weeks after the governor had passed the two acts, Richard Peters, the new secretary of the Land Office, placed a notice in the *Gazette* commanding all who had been in arrears to appear in October and November to discharge their debts; default would result in legal action.[71] In the cases of quitrent arrears, as in all Land Office affairs, the Penns' determination to collect what was theirs, and the settlers' predisposition to avoid payment, produced a growing estrangement between proprietor and people.

§

The politics of the early 1720s in Pennsylvania are well known for their factional quality. William Keith, the gentleman whom William Penn had appointed governor in 1717, had capitalized both on the confusion over the proprietary title and on an economic recession to promote his own interests. Gambling that the crown would expropriate both Pennsylvania and the Lower Counties in the not-too-distant future, and hoping to ease his way to a royal governorship by building up "popular" support in the colonies, Keith courted the electorate as no other Pennsylvania governor had done. Allied with the renowned old champion of Assembly rights, Speaker of the House David Lloyd, Keith took the popular position that Pennsylvania should meet her economic problems by printing paper currency. When those who supported the proprietary interests from their appointive positions on the Provincial Council opposed this inflationary policy, Keith and Lloyd again joined together to argue vehemently that the Council had no place in Pennsylvania's constitution. The provincial government consisted of an executive with full discretionary powers and an elected Assembly; the Council was merely a body that existed on the sufferance of the governor to tender advice if, and when, asked.[72]

The political furor Keith aroused was not to last long into the second quarter of the eighteenth century. Wearied of Keith's insubordination and worried about its effects, Hannah and Springett Penn agreed to appoint Patrick Gordon in Keith's stead, and the new governor assumed office on June 22, 1726, three months before the annual October election. Still, Keith had a breath or two left. Determined to keep his political career alive, the former governor set his eyes on what was the only suitable elected post for an ex-governor to take—the Speakership of the Assembly. Keith's announcement of his political intentions only made public and irrevocable what had already taken place. Ever the realist, and knowing from his own experience that no man was more dead than yesterday's governor, David Lloyd had immediately accommodated himself to the new chief executive and joined in a reconciliation with James Logan. Despite Keith's success in winning the ten Philadelphia City and County seats, the sixteen Bucks and Chester County representatives firmly supported Lloyd in his bid for reelection as Speaker, and once he had secured that position he continued to cooperate with the governor and proprietary allies.

For the next year Keith remained in Pennsylvania, nursing his ambition and his public support in the hopes that fate might intervene on his behalf. After he failed to pick up more seats in the 1727 election, however, he realized that further efforts in Pennsylvania would reap no results and set sail for London hoping that there he could convince the powerful to secure him another governorship.

Following Keith's departure in February 1728, his confederates in the Assembly became increasingly hostile towards their Lloydian counterparts, and in May of that year they attempted to bring the legislative process to a halt by refusing to attend house sessions. After the October election, however, the two groups worked out a compromise, and, when Patrick Gordon agreed to accept a new paper money emission, the Keithians were robbed of popular grounds on which to resume their quarrel. The paper money advocates who threatened to do violence in Philadelphia faded away into silence, and the Keithians again became simply Pennsylvanians.[73]

By the end of the 1720s Pennsylvania's political leaders were tired of the needless contentions that had recently disturbed the province. Once the Penns had discharged Keith from office, he lost the legitimacy he had derived from his position as governor and stood condemned by the universally recognized values of concord and amity.[74] This genuine predilection for peace that Pennsylvania residents shared was reinforced by the growing seriousness of the Maryland boundary dispute—an external threat that drove politicians to subordinate their differences to their common concern for security. When the Penn family dispute was finally settled in 1731, Pennsylvania brightened to the prospect of a new future in which the proprietor could unite with the local gentlemen and freemen in clearing the provincial title and in solving the many public and private problems that the preceding decade of neglect had produced.

By the time Thomas Penn arrived in Pennsylvania in 1732, changes in the political scene already reflected the new provincial circumstances. With William Keith gone and his followers bereft of leaders, with James Logan incapacitated by a broken hip, with former trustee Isaac Norris, Sr., retired to his country estate, and with David Lloyd dead, Andrew Hamilton quickly established himself as the most influential politician in the colony. Hamilton had been educated at the Inns of Court, and about 1715 he finally settled in Pennsylvania, where he became a close associate of David Lloyd's. Like Lloyd, Hamilton cooperated with Keith, accepting the post of attorney general in 1717 and later filling a seat in the Provincial Council.

Despite his public prominence, Hamilton managed to stay clear of the bitter debates that divided Philadelphia in the early 1720s, and in the summer of 1724 he resigned his posts and left the overheated city atmosphere for England. After receiving the Penns' assurance of good will, he returned to Philadelphia in the summer of 1726 and immediately made his weight felt in local politics. He took charge of the proprietary election campaign in the Lower Counties, intervening with such skill that William Keith, who had expended great effort to build up a personal following there, was defeated as an Assembly candidate. Such spectacular success solidly cemented Hamilton's political alliances with James Logan and Bucks County notable Jeremiah Langhorne. In 1727 he was elected as a Bucks County representative to the Pennsylvania Assembly. Two years later he succeeded David Lloyd to the Speakership, and by 1730 he held the posts of recorder of the Philadelphia Municipal Corporation, prothonotary in Philadelphia County, and acting trustee of the Loan Office.[75]

When Thomas Penn arrived in Pennsylvania in 1732, Andrew Hamilton was prepared to use his network of power and influence to support the proprietary interest, and in future years he did perform important services. He served as a provincial representative on the 1732 boundary commission, acted as emissary to Annapolis in 1734, constantly advised Penn on legal procedures, fought for the release of those Pennsylvanians who were jailed at various times by the Marylanders, encouraged applicants to the Loan Office to pay the purchase price of their land to the proprietors, and worked for a quitrent arrears settlement that would compensate the Penns for their losses.[76]

The reasons Hamilton was able to do all of this and still retain the confidence of most Pennsylvanians were several. Of central importance was the belief—widespread among provincial inhabitants—that as long as the Maryland boundary dispute was unsettled they should avoid being at odds with the proprietor. Unquestionably, this worked to prevent the surfacing of animosities that might have produced contention among Pennsylvania politicians, but that is no reason to take anything away from Andrew Hamilton. Despite his occasional unwillingness to "brook a slight from those from whom he expected a better treatment," Hamilton was a consumate politician—a master at generating compromise, perspicacious in his choice of allies, and attentive to his friends.[77] Only once in ten years did he slip. In 1733, after he had become involved in a brief but sharp dispute with Governor Gordon, his friends "dropped" him and he failed election as a candidate for Bucks County. Defeat, however, was momentary. Almost before the returns had come in Hamilton bounced to his feet and began to paste together a new political world. He resigned as prothonotary of Philadelphia County on the condition that the office go to his son James; patched up his quarrel with Governor Gordon; and with the help of Jeremiah Langhorne, who was the most respected political leader in Bucks County, reentered the Assembly in a by-election. In October 1734 he was again chosen by his peers to be Speaker of the House.[78]

Important, too, in explaining Hamilton's predominent role in the politics of the 1730s was his well-deserved reputation as a spokesman for popular rights. As a matter of tactics alone, Hamilton had to assume leadership in popular causes simply to keep control of them, but this was not the only reason that he did so. Despite his concern for proprietary privileges, Hamilton shared the same whiggish sentiments that other popular politicians professed, and in 1735 he displayed them for all to see. In that year his magnificent success in defending printer John Peter Zenger of New York against charges of libel brought him popular acclaim as America's spokesman for liberty of the press.[79]

Thereafter, public esteem for Hamilton continued to grow. Almost as soon as he returned from New York, he emerged as a leading advocate of the rights of Pennsylvania freeholders in their protests against the province's equity court. Since 1720 equity jurisdiction in

Pennsylvania had been administered by a chancery court voted into existence by an Assembly resolve and presided over by the governor and a number of provincial councillors. Although the court sat but seldom, the presence of a vigorous and determined proprietary landlord led to speculation that Penn might use the court to prosecute delinquent debtors.[80] Such suspicions were not entirely ill founded, for the Penns did indeed want a court that was free of elected sheriffs and of juries, one that was composed of "knowing and experienced men," with the governor to "preside therein."[81] Fortunately for those who were worried about possible abuses of the equity court, the best possible grounds were found for revoking the Assembly resolution that had brought it into existence. Article 6 of the 1701 Charter of Privileges specifically stated that no person should "be obliged to answer any complaint, matter, or thing whatsoever, relating to property, before the Governor and council . . ."[82] Along with other legislative spokesmen, Hamilton praised William Penn's foresight in including this provision, which allowed them to repudiate the Assembly resolution and thus forward what in the founder's words was "the great end of all government—to support power in reverence with the people, and to secure the people from the abuse of government."[83]

Throughout the 1730s, then, Andrew Hamilton was the most important political leader in Pennsylvania, and Hamiltonian politics were peaceful politics. There were no major disruptions, no cases of serious contention, and no conflicts among politicians sufficiently quarrelsome, public, and prolonged to warrant being called factional outbursts. That is not to say, however, that there were no significant alterations in power relationships. Even during periods of peaceful politics, rarely, if ever, do the distribution of political power and the reputation of politicians remain static. There is usually a great variety of changes, often subtle and partially disguised, and very often those changes, when exposed, reveal a noticeable drift in public affairs.

In Pennsylvania during the 1730s, public affairs drifted in such a way as to leave the proprietary interests stranded by the decade's end. Despite the good will that greeted Thomas Penn when he first reached Pennsylvania and that brother John continuously encountered during his brief visit in 1934-35, the proprietary was to fail miserably at the task of protecting and expanding the family influence.

At the root of the Penns' difficulties were their land policies. As Thomas reorganized proprietary affairs, collecting past debts, demanding new terms of land purchase, and requesting equitable quitrent payments, "grumblers and malcontents" appeared everywhere.[84] By 1738-39, when Penn could move against those who owed him money for land, these sentiments had spread, and the very circumstances that allowed him at that point to prosecute debtors vigorously—the settlement of the Maryland boundary dispute—removed the outside threat that encouraged men to work with the proprietor and to hold in check what ill feelings they harbored. The proclamation of November 1738, which demanded compliance with Land Office procedure, was followed less than a year later by the quitrent settlement and the June 1739 proclamation demanding immediate payment of all arrears.

In December 1739 Thomas reported on the results of his new tough policies to elder brother John: James Steel, the proprietary's receiver general had "for eighteen months past gone through more business than ever he did for two or three years past."[85] The effects of such officiousness were predictable. When in September 1739 Reverend Samuel Thomson of Pennsborough was examined before the Donegal Presbytery for writing a letter "containing some things which were very offensive to the humble proprietors," his defense was short and pointed: these were "not his own thoughts but the thoughts of the people."[86]

Political changes, too, worked to weaken the proprietary position. Throughout the 1720s James Logan had kept the western reaches of Chester County firmly in the proprietary interest, but by the early 1730s Logan's power had faded badly. A small group of Quakers, the most prominent of whom was Samuel Blunston, moved into the vacuum; and, although they cooperated with Penn throughout the confrontation with Maryland, they simultaneously and somewhat surreptitiously cast themselves as champions of local rights against a grasping proprietor. By the time the fight with Maryland had ended, the foundation for an antiproprietary, Quaker-led alliance between the Scotch-Irish and the German- and English-speaking residents of Lancaster County was well laid.[87]

In the east there were similar changes. Although Andrew Hamilton's popularity with most Pennsylvanians remained high as long as he remained active in politics, his connections with Philadelphia and Chester County politicians clearly deteriorated during the late 1730s. When he and his old crony Jeremiah Langhorne retired at the end of the decade, they left behind two legacies: a political interest network that was in poor repair and the leadership of proproprietary forces in the hands of William Allen, a man who despite his long apprenticeship was soon to prove to all Pennsylvania that he had not matured as a politician.

Thomas Penn, too, contributed to the growing isolation of the proprietary with his selection of administrative personnel. His replacement of Receiver General James Steel, an old and respected country resident who was chiefly responsible for preserving much of the good will the proprietor did neet outside Philadelphia, with the newly arrived sycophant, Lynford Lardner, clearly hurt the proprietary cause. Both Lardner and the man who was to become Penn's chief agent in the colony, Secretary of the Land Office Richard Peters, were Anglican outsiders who lacked friends and contacts in the Pennsylvania country-side. Moreover, Penn himself refused to cultivate the friendship of local politicians. He felt that those whom the family once had trusted had abused that trust—and others would do likewise. In any event, the proprietary claims as landlord and as governor were "just" claims that Pennsylvanians had no right to deny or resent. Because of the rightness of his cause, fair-minded men would, of their own accord, offer political support.[88]

Despite Thomas Penn's unpopular policies and his unwilling-ness to act the politician, at the end of the decade there still existed two roughly defined sources of proprietary support. In Philadelphia, Andrew Hamilton's city friends composed a loose opinion group that was somewhat sympathetic to the Penns and to the executive branch of government. A second current of good will toward the proprietary began to flow in 1734-35, when John Penn, who because of his birth in the colony was known as "the American," visited Pennsylvania. His visit evoked a nostalgic response from some of the old-country Quak-ers, and, when he returned to England to defend the family title against renewed attacks of Lord Baltimore, the good wishes of many Pennsyl-vanians went with him. In London, Pennsylvania agent John Paris and the London Quakers had kept the land-hungry Baltimores at bay until the elder Penn's return, and from that moment the London Meeting of Sufferings and the senior proprietor worked together to protect the Penn title. News of this cooperation between the London Quakers and John Penn reached Pennsylvania Friends and nourished that sense of fondness for the senior proprietor which his brief visit had sparked. Through this vicarious relationship, provincial Quakers came to know an amiable, whiggish John Penn, and their estimate of his character, as such, played an important part in determining Quaker political strategy during later years.[89]

The formation of these two loose centers of proprietary support notwithstanding, the Penn family's influence had declined signifi-cantly in the second half of the decade. Proprietary land policies had generated hostility, and such feelings were certain to find expression in politics, especially if, as Thomas Penn avowed, he was going to try to redress the balance of power between the magistracy and the people.[90] Any attempt to offset the power of sheriffs, juries, and constables by establishing a proper chancery court and a regular militia, or to curb the power of the legislature by ending the Assembly's claim to unilateral appropriation to the Loan Office revenues, would certainly bring on serious political contention. Because the executive and proprietary were so weak, as Penn tacitly acknowledged when he mentioned such reforms, the executive could never hope to control the course of conflict between the two branches of government without support from the electorate and from leading politicians. Not that Penn could have gained widespread support for such extreme measures; surely, he could not. It is conceivable, however, that had he taken full advantage of his opportunities he could have impeded the Assembly's further accumulation of powers; certainly, had he developed closer contacts with local leaders, he would have become much more aware of the possible limits of successful political action. But the proprietor did not seriously try to establish such relationships. By standing on his rights and by refusing to participate in the active management of provincial politics, Penn left himself without the means to effect the kind of policies he was determined to pursue.

CHAPTER 2

A ROUND OF CONTENTION AND MUCH GOOD HARMONY, 1739–1754[1]

§

The political peace that had lasted throughout the 1730s in Pennsylvania was not to continue long into the new decade. Between 1740 and 1743 a group of proprietary-executive politicians challenged a broad, Quaker-led political alliance for the allegiance of Pennsylvania's voters. In the ensuing conflict, the Quakers emerged as the dominant political force and their opponents were badly discredited. Then, with no sizeable proprietary-executive interest to spark further contention in provincial politics, Pennsylvania quickly settled down to another decade of political peace.

§

There were no obvious changes in popular politics that reflected the increased hostility to the proprietary that infected the Pennsylvania countryside in the late 1730s. During these years, Andrew Hamilton's personal popularity, coupled with his predisposition to work with the proprietors, prevented the surfacing of hostile currents. But the quit-rent arrears settlement that Hamilton pushed through the Assembly in 1739 was his last effective political act. Bowing to his physical infirmities and reckoning (wrongly) that the opposition from Chester County assemblymen on that occasion sprang solely from the arrears question, the Speaker of the Assembly retired from politics. Convinced, like Hamilton, that all of the knotty problems in Pennsylvania politics had been untangled, William Allen, James Hamilton, and four of their Quaker confederates announced in the summer of 1739 that they, too, would not seek reelection.[2] Never had they been so right—and never so wrong. True, the Maryland boundary dispute and the quitrent arrears questions had been resolved; but Allen and the others failed to remember that in politics a new, disruptive issue might surface at any time, and they failed to see that antiproprietary sentiment would seep into the vacuum they would leave. Both happened, immediately.[3]

In late August word reached Philadelphia that war with Spain was imminent. Because of the personal pacificism of Quakers and their reluctance as legislators to provide for the military defense of the colony, war had always been a disruptive issue in Pennsylvania; this time was to be no exception. Immediately William Allen and Andrew Hamilton reconsidered their position, but, having publicly announced their retirement, they felt that at such a late date they could not reverse their decision.[4] Consequently, the management of the Philadelphia County slate of candidates fell to men who, with the exception of John Kinsey, were "stiff" Quakers who had never worked very closely with Hamilton or the proprietor.[5] When the election returns actually came in, eight of the seventeen assemblymen who had voted for the proprietary quitrent compromise were no longer members. The retirement of Andrew Hamilton and his gang from the Assembly left the proprietary weak and exposed even before the colony's role in King George's War had become a divisive issue.

Once the election occurred, the war quickly came to the front. By the time the new Assembly convened in mid-October, orders from the English government to issue letters of marque, and a request from John Penn that he try to establish a provincial militia, had landed on Governor Thomas's desk. Thomas, an old military officer, needed no further encouragement; he asked the legislature to put the province into a state of defense, by providing a militia law and passing a bill to pay for arming the militia and financing fortifications. As he might have expected, the assemblymen demurred. The majority of the legislators were Quakers; and consequently they could neither bear arms nor frame a law compelling others to do so. They argued that if some residents felt threatened the governor could always invoke his authority as captain-general and form a voluntary militia. To the assemblymen, however, it appeared that the province was in no serious danger, and the possibility that a military organization might be used for corrupt and oppressive purposes far outweighed any benefits it might conceivably provide. Lastly, they mentioned that their 1711 wartime appropriation of £2,000 "to the Queen's use" to "express their duty, loyalty, and faithful obedience" formed a precedent that could be "no great encouragement for future Assemblies to follow," because on that occasion the governor had appropriated the grant "to his own particular use."[6]

From October 1739 through April 1740, the disagreement between governor and representatives continued. But before the May session of the Assembly began and the old arguments were trotted out again, a chain of events occurred that was to change the nature of the dispute. On April 10 Governor Thomas received further orders from the English secretary of state, the Duke of Newcastle, asking him to invite enlistments for an invasion of the West Indies. Four days later the governor issued a proclamation to that effect. Immediately, a number of indentured servants applied directly to the governor for permission to volunteer, and Thomas encouraged them, allegedly replying that from that moment they had no master but the king. By the time the Assembly convened on May 5 for a ten-day session, the assemblymen knew that a number of influential men had disagreed with the governor's action and that Attorney General John Kinsey had submitted to Thomas, on his request, a legal opinion that denied the king's right to solicit servant enlistments. Hoping that the governor's subsequent silence on the servant question indicated intended compliance with that opinion, the assemblymen did not interject this matter into their exchanges with the chief executive. Rather, in replying to Philadelphia and Chester county petitioners who requested the cessation of servant enlistments and the return of those whose names had been entered as volunteers, they simply stated their position: the king's instructions to enlist "ought not" to have been understood as a power to accept bound servants.[7]

Having made this point, the representatives adjourned, and for approximately seven weeks there were no further developments. Then, on June 25, king's officers, commissions, and further instructions arrived in Philadelphia. Thomas immediately convened the Assembly and presented the latest royal instructions ordering the Assembly to provide food, lodging, transport, and other necessities for the Pennsylvania troops. In addition, the governor demanded an enlistment bounty for all freemen if servants were to be exempt. After some momentary quibbling on July 7, the Assembly went on the following day to resolve that a vote of money be given "for the use of the Crown."[8] Despite this resolution the assemblymen were seriously divided, and John Kinsey, the Speaker of the House, had to cast the deciding vote. The reason for the disagreement was apparent to all: the officers who had recently arrived were enlisting servants as well as freemen. Although a bill was framed voting £2,000 to the king's use and £2,000 to reimburse the owners of servants, it became increasingly obvious that the agreed-upon appropriation would not cover the value of the missing servants. Among some assemblymen there was a marked reluctance to give even a penny to the king, as long as the governor sanctioned the continuing enlistment of servants. Unable to form a consensus on policy beyond resolving to reimburse masters for the loss of their servants, the assemblymen closed debate and adjourned until mid-August.[9]

Governor Thomas was not to be so easily put off. Two weeks after their adjournment he again called the members of the legislature into session, informing them that he now had seven companies of volunteers whose needs lay at the Assembly's door. In the exchange that followed the assemblymen elaborated their views: the enlistment of servants had been an inexcusable infringement by the executive on the freeman's property rights; when the approximately three hundred servants who had been accepted into the provincial forces were discharged and returned to their owners, the Assembly would grant money to the king's use. The Assembly also pointed out that such an action would not jeopardize the governor's good reputation in English court circles. Pennsylvania had only been sent four commissions, and even after the servants had been discharged there would still be four hundred men—enough to form four companies—who, as free-men, had volunteered for the West Indian expedition. Throughout August the Assembly refused to retreat from this position, and the equally intransigent Governor Thomas was forced to finance his seven companies with loans from Philadelphia gentlemen.[10]

The early events in this growing dispute were particularly important because they revealed how a predominantly Quaker Assembly reacted to wartime demands and because the meaning of the dispute, in terms of a long-range political realignment, began to appear. First, it is clear that the Quaker Assembly did not deeply question the consistency of their giving money to the king's use when they were actually faced with the monarch's order to contribute to the cost of a military campaign.[11] Their failure to pass such a bill resulted from an almost equal split in their ranks, between those who would give money to the crown, in addition to reimbursing masters of enlisted servants, and those who would make such a vote conditional on the servants' release. During the last two weeks of July, when the assemblymen were in the country supervising their harvests, the members of the former group realized how strong provincial opinion was against the servant enlistments, and decided to support their colleagues. These, not promptings of conscience, were the circumstances that resulted in the Assembly's apparently intransigent stand not to vote money for the king's use.[12]

Second, with regard to the meaning of the dispute, certain features had become particularly prominent by the fall of 1740. Despite their immediate concern with the Cartagena expedition, Governor

Thomas and his Philadelphia supporters saw the real issue as wartime defense. They believed that coastal inhabitants and Delaware River shipping were in immediate danger and that no reasonable man could conclude otherwise. The fact that most "ignorant countrymen" did not feel threatened and placed the onus for Philadelphia's defense on the residents of that city merely underlined the need for strong and independent Assembly representation.[13] In the eyes of the governor's supporters, the members of the legislature assumed an obligation to put the country in a state of defense during wartime the moment they accepted office. That the Quaker members of the Assembly admitted no contradiction between their religious beliefs and their duties as legislators was a measure of their duplicity. Some of the governor's allies certainly believed that Quaker principles were real enough, for the servant enlistment crisis indicated the extremes to which they would go in order to find an issue that would mask such principles. Others believed that the vague pleas of liberty of conscience were an extremely flexible and useful political tool. In either case, the conclusion was the same: Quaker spokesmen were double-dealing, insincere opportunists who should not be allowed to sit in the Assembly.[14]

To the Quaker assemblymen and their supporters the issue was an entirely different one. The resolution giving money to the crown proved that they could contribute in their own way to a military venture. If at some time extreme danger threatened Pennsylvania, it was not at all clear that some similar measure might not be passed even in the absence of royal orders. For most Quaker representatives, this was enough to erase what public self-doubts they shared about their ability to hold seats in the legislature. Similarly, the charges against their legislative suitability that followed from their refusal to frame a militia law were nicely, if only theoretically, o'erleapt by a provision of Pennsylvania's charter that enabled the governor to raise a volunteer militia force under his authority as captain-general. While many Pennsylvanians were willing to accept these reasonings, Governor Thomas was not, and by his refusal he flatly challenged a major part of the rationale that had allowed Quakers to participate fully in Pennsylvania government over the past six decades. Moreover, he did so at a time when, in Quaker eyes, there could be no honest intention, for despite the state of war it was obvious to them that Pennsylvania was in no serious danger. To the Quakers, then, it was the governor who was insincere. His desire for a permanent militia, his flagrant disregard for personal property rights, his determined effort to expose apparent Quaker inconsistencies, and his slippery defense of his own public actions convinced the members of the legislature that he was spearheading an attack on the rights of freeholder and legislator alike.[15]

That the governor was a man of independent means, outwardly impervious to the Assembly's refusal of support and that Thomas Penn publicly and energetically associated the proprietary with all of the governor's actions reinforced the widespread belief in an executive-proprietary conspiracy against popular privileges.[16]

As the summer session of the Pennsylvania Assembly drew to a close, supporters both of the executive and of the legislature began to prepare for the annual provincial election. Proprietary-executive supporters meticulously lined up tickets for each county, and Quaker assemblymen countered by substituting solid popular-rights men for those who had most favored conciliation. When the votes were finally counted, the old Assembly found that its stand against executive tyranny, its reimbursement of masters for the loss of their servants, and its refusal to pay Governor Thomas's salary had been vindicated. The only changes in House membership were the replacement of one proprietary man and two moderate representatives by three popular Quaker nominees.[17] In the Philadelphia County election, Andrew Hamilton and the defense-minded merchants of the city mobilized support for William Allen, but that ticket failed by some two hundred votes; in Bucks, where the Jeremiah Langhorne-Lawrence Growdon-Joseph Kirkbride interest supported the executive, the defense lobbyists failed to elect a single active advocate of their cause; in Chester, defense candidates polled only 15 percent of the vote, while in Lancaster they attracted a bare 10 percent.[18] Such an unqualified electoral victory attested to the popular acceptance of the assemblymen's construction of recent events: the enlistment of servants had been an unquestionable attack on the freeman's property rights, and the defense crisis was no more than a deliberate smokescreen, designed to cover up an assault by the chief executive on the provincial constitution.[19]

Success in Pennsylvania, however, did not mean that the assemblymen's point of view would meet with equal sympathy in England. After their electoral failure in October, the governor and many of his Philadelphia supporters determined to seize the initiative and press their case in London. On October 20 Thomas sent a scathing report to the Board of Trade in which he defended his actions in the enlistment crisis, arguing implicitly that Quaker principles rendered those who held them unfit for legislative duty; charged that Quakers had acted in collusion with, and deliberately misled, German voters in order to frustrate the real popular will in the last election; and vigorously denounced two customary rights of the Assembly, (1) the appropriation of money by a resolution of the legislature, rather than jointly by

Assembly and governor, and (2) the adjournment of the legislature on the sole authority of the sitting representatives, rather than with the concurrence of the chief executive.

At the same time plans were set afoot for Philadelphia City residents to petition the crown. Although opinion was divided on the wisdom of directly requesting the disqualification of all Quakers from sitting in the legislature, unanimity prevailed about the necessity of asking the king to order that the province be placed in a state of defense. Thomas Penn counseled the necessity of both steps, but he felt the former measure might best be secured by discrete lobbying rather than by formal request. When, in August 1741, Penn finally left for England after nine years in Pennsylvania, he carried with him a firm resolve to unseat the Quakers and a representation, signed by many of Philadelphia's leading citizens, petitioning the crown for an order-in-council demanding defense preparations.[20]

When Penn arrived in London, however, he found his brother John of another mind. Early in 1741 a warning from Thomas Penn that such a representation would be forthcoming, and that the Quakers were considering their own counterpetition urging the crown to expropriate the proprietary title, had reached John. The senior proprietor reacted with alarm; in order to refute the rumor that the Penns were authorizing an attack on the Pennsylvania charter, he forwarded to Speaker of the Assembly John Kinsey a copy of the proprietary instructions to Governor Thomas. Later he cautioned Thomas that all activities that might push Parliament toward "examining into and altering the Constitution of any of the Colonys or Islands" should, at all cost, be avoided.[21]

In Pennsylvania, too, the proprietary-executive supporters found themselves weaker. When they heard of John Penn's cautions, they began to fall out. Some, led by William Allen, argued that their petition should be presented no matter what the chief proprietor decided to do, for the desirability of defense and possible disqualification of the Quakers more than balanced the risk of a potential royal takeover; others were prepared to back off on the proprietor's advice. And, as they became more divided among themselves, they were confronted with growing public hostility. Richard Partridge, the Assembly's London agent, had obtained a copy of Governor Thomas's outspoken letter to the Board of Trade, and by May 1741 Assembly supporters had published excerpts from it in Pennsylvania. This letter, and Thomas Penn's close association with the governor until he left in mid-1741, convinced many freemen—John Penn's assurances notwithstanding—that a proprietary and executive plot was well on its way to overturning the constitution.[22]

The 1741 election supplied abundant evidence of both the disorganization and the unpopularity of the defense advocates. While William Allen, James Logan, and a few of their fellows were determined to get together an effective opposition ticket, at least for Philadelphia, others refused, arguing that nothing should be done until the king had answered their petition.[23] As a result, no alternative candidates were put forward for any of the three old counties. Out in Lancaster, the one county in which there was an organized effort to unseat the Quaker incumbents, results were disheartening. Despite the cooperation of Lancaster notables Thomas Cookson and Conrad Weiser with James Logan, and the organization of a campaign in which Weiser made a strong pamphlet appeal for the support of his fellow Germans, proprietary supporters were soundly defeated. Of the 1,150 votes cast in Lancaster, barely 200 went to the defense candidates.[24]

The lack of opposition in the 1741 election confirmed the assemblymen's fears: the greatest danger to their position lay not in opposition activities in Pennsylvania but in executive and proprietary lobbying in London. With the election over, the assemblymen turned their attention to the difficulties of countering the Philadelphia petition, asking the crown to put the colony in a state of defense, that was about to surface, in Thomas Penn's hands, in England. Early in the summer, when Governor Thomas's letter to the Board of Trade appeared in print and when rumors of the impending petition may well have first leaked out, the more radical Quaker leaders suggested that they ask the crown to take over the colony.[25] In October 1741 the Assembly members considered this solution but quickly rejected it.[26] Instead they determined to send a petition to the proprietors blaming Governor Thomas for the state of contention and asking for a replacement.[27] In taking this action, the Quakers gambled that John Penn was in sympathy with their cause and that as chief proprietor he could override the objections that brother Thomas would certainly raise. What encouraged them in this course was the trust the Quakers had developed in John Penn during the Baltimore negotiations; a knowledge of his whiggish principles; an awareness that he had dealt squarely with Kinsey by forwarding a copy of the proprietary instructions; warm, nostalgic memories many had of Penn's visit in 1734–35; and a naïve predisposition to rely on the man who was both their chief proprietor and an American.[28]

With both the Quakers and their opponents having referred their respective cases for English adjudication, an easing of tension might have been expected in Pennsylvania. But rather than lessen, the spitefulness that had come to characterize dealings between the parties to the dispute increased. Governor Thomas was determined to avenge himself on John Kinsey, the man who had "publically vilified" him "for two years past."[29] With that end in mind he soundly upbraided Kinsey when the Quaker spokesman was presented as Speaker by the 1741–42 Assembly and then proceeded to strip him of the office of attorney general.[30] After the same election the governor further alienated the assemblymen by refusing to confirm the Quaker candidate, Mordecai Lloyd, as Philadelphia County sheriff even though he had polled the greatest number of votes.[31] Finally, the governor started a rumor that he held in his possession an attorney general's opinion which supported his authority to prorogue or dissolve the Assembly without the legislature's consent.[32] These tactics provided new fuel for the Quaker assemblymen, who were already burning with anger on account of Thomas's letter to the Board of Trade and the Philadelphia petition for defense. They were determined to dump Governor Thomas, if not by proprietary order then by rendering his position intolerable, and through the winter and spring of 1741–42 they used their position in the legislature to constantly harass him.[33]

Thus, despite the two pending petitions, the one to John Penn and the other to the crown, political affairs in Pennsylvania had a peculiar momentum of their own. Because local political adversaries were preoccupied one with another, and because these men were already determined to vent their resentment and bitterness through the 1742 election, the proprietaries' answer to the assemblymen's representation and the Board of Trade's recommendations to the crown on the Philadelphia petition did not seriously alter the existing pattern of political events. When in mid-May the assemblymen received a reply that completely vindicated Governor Thomas and associated the proprietary with all his activities, the one course of action all could agree on was to hold onto their legislative power until a new long-range plan could be settled on. The Board of Trade report to the Lords Committee of the Privy Council, which was the first indication of what the crown's response might be, reached Philadelphia in August. In the face of its recommendations that the crown order the province put into a state of defense, the assemblymen were, if anything, more determined to maintain control of the legislature.[34]

Among executive supporters, the proprietary statement and the Board of Trade report also served to rouse interest in the forthcoming election. Early in 1742 there had been some evidence of differences among Quaker supporters as to what tactics their assemblymen should follow. The proprietor's reply to the Assembly's representation boosted morale and encouraged them to try to exploit those differences. At the same time, many had begun to doubt the wisdom of petitioning the crown. None of the petitioners could suggest a realistic method by which an order-in-council to put the province in a statement of defense could be implemented, and they feared that even if the crown issued such an order nothing would happen. Alternatively, if the English politicians were seriously stirred up by the Pennsylvanians' petition, Parliament might intervene; along with legislation ensuring the colony's defense might come other measures adversely affecting personal and provincial rights.

Another possibility was that Thomas Penn might refuse to support the petition before the upcoming hearing of the Lords Committee of the Privy Council and there would be no action, at all, on it. This seemed possible, for by early 1742 brother John had convinced Thomas that the petition might precipitate royal or parliamentary intervention in Pennsylvania prejudicial to their charter rights. The best response the proprietary-executive supporters could hope for, then, was a positive but ineffective order from the crown to put the province in a state of defense. And there they would be still, standing on the banks of an undefended Delaware River, without help from England and locked out of the legislature in Pennsylvania. Thus, they were determined to help themselves by gaining some voice in the Provincial Assembly. For the proprietary men as well as their Quaker-led opponents, October 1, 1742, was to be an extremely important day.[35]

Preparations for the 1742 election began early. In June the popular Quaker leaders were already gathering opinions on who should be seated in the new Assembly. By August executive supporters were puzzling out their own tickets. The Assembly spokesmen, determined to fight the election on the record of their past activities, did not drop a single representative from their slate. As for the proprietary men, they tried to exploit Quaker weaknesses in each county. In Bucks, influential leaders Joseph Kirkbride, Jr., and Lawrence Growdon were to head a coalition ticket with their Presbyterian, Anglican, and Reformed allies; in Lancaster, James Hamilton was to attempt to revive his old interest and at least to split, if not sweep, the Scotch-Irish Presbyterian vote; in Chester, disaffected Quakers Jacob Howell and Jane Hoskins were to select appropriate candidates; in Philadelphia, strongman William Allen was to join with merchant Jonathan Robeson and others in directing election efforts. By September the optimism of the defense advocates seemed warranted. Their opponents appeared to be divided and they themselves were organized as never before. One month later, however, the hopes of the executive supporters had been dashed and the influence of that group as a political alliance had been almost totally destroyed. What had gone wrong?[36]

One of the reasons why the proprietary-executive failure seemed so great was that much of the optimism that infused their ranks had been based on false hopes. Prior to the election, they had seen evidence of substantial support among Pennsylvania's freemen because they had wanted to see it, not because it had actually existed. Nothing had occurred to alter the voter's opinion that the proprietary and the governor, rather than the Spanish, posed the greatest threat to individual rights, liberty, and property. In Lancaster, James Hamilton and his fellow candidates were sweepingly repudiated, while in Bucks the defense advocates did not cut into the margin by which they had been defeated in 1740. In Chester and Philadelphia counties, the threatened division between moderate and popular Quakers never developed. Despite their assurances, those who had not approved of the contentious conduct of the present assemblymen failed to put together an alternative ticket. In Philadelphia, however, the real disaster occurred; there the proprietary disgrace was due not only to lack of popular support but also to the election riot on October 1.[37]

In preparing for the 1742 election, proprietary supporters in Philadelphia remembered well their experiences of two years past. They knew that if they were to win the contest they would need a group of men to help direct and control the crowd of voters that would assemble on election day in Philadelphia's market square. The reasons were twofold. Early in the day the freeholders would decide, by gathering around their favorite candidates, who the election inspectors would be. These officers determined who was qualified to cast a ballot, a crucial question when political interest was high enough to draw to the polls large numbers of freeholders who ordinarily did not vote.[38] Later in the morning when voting actually began, the outcome could be affected by one other well-known means. At the court house a crowd could surround the base of the staircase which a voter had to ascend in order to cast his ballot, thereby intimidating any freeholder whose choice of candidates was not favorable to its interests.[39] What the proprietary supporters needed, then, was a group of men who could surreptitiously swell the ranks of voters for the right inspectors and, later, muscle out the opposition at the stairs. For men who were merchants the problem of recruiting manpower was not a difficult one; on their ships were sailors ready to do their bidding.[40]

Although the idea of using seamen must have sounded feasible enough to those gentlemen who privately discussed it in Philadelphia's taverns, in practice it was a disaster. The subtle act of mingling with and influencing a crowd of Philadelphia freemen required an adeptness that no unpracticed group of sailors could perform. Sea hands were part of an alien world outside Philadelphia; they felt themselves such, they were recognized as such, and from seven o'clock on election day morning they acted as such. At that time forty to fifty sailors "armed with clubs" assembled "on Andrew Hamilton's wharf."[41] From their actions it would appear that they had only been given the most tentative instructions about what they should do in the early morning. After roaming about haphazardly, visiting at least one tavern and facing the complaints of several magistrates, the sailors charged at the assembled freemen just as the sheriff opened the election for inspectors. A short time later, after regrouping, they attacked a second time only to be beaten back to their ships. When the election resumed later that day, the executive supporters were resoundingly defeated.[42]

Immediately after the election riot it appeared that the violence had driven assemblymen and their antagonists even further apart. Blood had been spilled, bruises counted, bitterness voiced. Quakers trumpeted that the election events revealed the true depths of proprietary depravity, and the Assembly's investigation into the riot confirmed and publicized the Friends' judgment. On the other hand, the maligned executive supporters saw themselves as victims of an elaborate political frameup.[43] But despite the riot and the hostility it engendered, peace was clearly on the way. In January 1743 Governor Thomas struck a bargain with the Assembly spokesmen: the chief executive was to receive a payment of £500 on his arrears and the customary £1,000 annual support for the current year in return for passing certain Assembly bills. Five months later it was generally conceded that an apparently impossible reconciliation had somehow been effected.[44]

In retrospect, the working out of a compromise peace between governor and Assembly immediately after the 1742 riot was not so surprising. Shortly after the election, Provincial Councillor Thomas Lawrence approached Richard Peters and the governor, hinting that John Kinsey and some of his assemblymen friends wanted to settle their differences. As evidence of his receptivity to accommodation, Governor Thomas determined to avoid penning angry messages to the Assembly and to pass some legislation.[45] There were two reasons why Thomas was predisposed to accept any face-saving accommodation the Assembly might offer: he both desired to collect the £2,500 in support the Assembly owed him, and he recognized the weakness of his own political position. On the latter count he knew that both John and Thomas Penn favored an accommodation, and, in a proprietary colony, what the proprietors wanted their chief executive had best try to procure—if he wanted to keep his post.[46]

Of course, Governor Thomas could not have made peace on his own; he needed and received the cooperation of the assemblymen. One common ground on which they could unite was their sense of responsibility—a recognition that Pennsylvania could not afford many more months of legislative inactivity. The £5 Act, the Inspectors Act, the Excise Act, and the Loan Office trustee appointments were due to lapse before the summer of 1744, and there were other bills that needed attention. Public obligation and self-interest demanded that the disputants attend to those needs.[47]

Reasons other than the obvious, however, predisposed some Quaker assemblymen to move toward a peaceful settlement. The truth was that by the summer of 1742 the Quakers were suffering from divisions that would require time to heal. Difficulties had begun in 1741 when Governor Thomas's letter to the Board of Trade and the impending Philadelphia defense petition caused great anxiety about what Assembly policy should be.[48] A number of radical city Quakers wanted to petition the crown for a royal takeover, but fear of what the king might exact in return deterred them from this course. The one plausible alternative, an alternative that was particularly favored by Friends who rather naïvely remembered a kind and affable John Penn, was a representation to the proprietors to remove Governor Thomas. Even when the assemblymen agreed to the latter course of action, however, the differences between Quakers continued, this time based on tactics and the degree of personal involvement in the existing dispute. Of those who had pressed for the representation, many were content to await quietly what they thought would be good news from John Penn.[49] This was particularly true of men from the outlying areas; distance insulated them from the extreme heat of partisan politics. Others, mainly from the city of Philadelphia and nearby areas who were fully caught up in the circle of personal acrimony with nearby proprietary supporters, were not so patient. They believed that the proprietary might pay heed only if the public outcry against Thomas continued. In the polemical battle that ensued, the Assembly, pushed by the legislative radicals, was as much the aggressor as the chief executive.[50] By March 1742 the more moderate Quakers, some of whom were powerful religious leaders in the counties and closely attuned to Quaker ideals, had become outspokenly critical. They "openly" described the Assembly radicals as "a set of people who act from a spirit of resentment more than the public good."[51] The disaffected Quakers—Jane Hoskins, Jacob Howell, Thomas Fletcher, Henry Reynolds, and Samuel Morris—were moderates in that they wanted to tone down the acrimonious debates with the governor, but they were no more moderate than the Assembly radicals whom they criticized on the issue of defense preparations.

In May a vindication of Governor Thomas, written by the proprietaries in response to the Assembly representation against him, burst the bubble within which this controversy had developed.[52] The

Quakers again considered the old question of whether they should petition the crown for a royal takeover, but, if anything, this alternative looked less attractive in 1742 than it had a year earlier. The only sensible solution was to maintain control of the Assembly and, bargaining from strength, to work out some sort of accommodation with the governor. The Assembly radicals continued to be over-wrought, but they had no acceptable alternatives to suggest, and cooler heads could safely begin to assert themselves.

In the 1742 election one important split in Quaker ranks did occur, but this division took place for reasons other than those mentioned above. In Bucks County, Joseph Kirkbride, Jr., and Law-rence Growdon, the two leading candidates on the opposition ticket, were moderate Quakers, not only in that they wished to end the present state of contention but also in that they, like James Logan, sanctioned defense preparations. Despite the prominence of these politicians and the attention that historians have paid to Logan's 1741 statement on behalf of defense preparations, there is no evidence to indicate that those who openly agreed with him constituted more than a small number of Philadelphia Quaker merchants, their old political confed-erates in Bucks County, and a sprinkling of residents in other outlying areas.[53] But no matter how fragmentary a splinter group such men might have been, this example of dissent, like that of the threatened disaffection of the other, much larger group of Quaker moderates, was a danger signal to consensus-oriented Friends. The mere existence of these divisions was sufficient to send Quakers searching for an amica-ble settlement.

Before the election a second important development predisposed the most influential Assembly leaders to seek an accommodation with Governor Thomas. News of the Board of Trade's recommendation to the Privy Council that Pennsylvania be put into a state of defense reached Philadelphia sometime in August and clearly frightened Quaker spokesmen. Because there was no way for colonial administra-tors to force a recalcitrant Assembly to appropriate money for defense, it was conceivable that Parliament might intervene. This specter and all that it suggested in the way of abridged rights and privileges convinced some assemblymen of the absolute necessity of peace.[54] Their reaction was reinforced by the advice of English Friends, who counseled them to bury their differences, strive to keep control of the Assembly in 1742, moderate their strident tones, and unite with them and agent Richard Partridge to present the legislature's case in the best possible light in private and public hearings with British officials.[55]

Prior to the 1742 election, then, numerous Quakers were predis-posed toward a reconciliation. The events of that election pushed them even further in this direction. With the benefit of five months' hindsight, Richard Peters put his finger on a generally unrecognized but major result of the election riot. After remarking on how the "storm" of contest had subsided with remarkable speed, he went on to observe that "the Governor's friends, by the detestable riot, have put the people so absolutely into the power of their adversaries that they could never hope to become instruments to bring about peace and therefore there was a necessity of it being done some other way."[56] Until October 1742, defense advocates believed that they had the political strength to gain entrance to the legislature and, once this had been accomplished, the influence to direct the course of Assembly policy. Any accurate measurement of their popularity from 1740–42 would, undoubtedly, have discredited these pretensions, but that was irrelevant. The point was that these men thought and acted as though they had the power, and in the limited Philadelphia environment they did have enough weight to lend some plausibility to their pretensions and enough bravado to cause some apprehension among their opponents. The election, however, revealed their true strength by exposing their weakness and stripping them of whatever vestiges of popular support they once had. The election events crushed their hopes and pretensions just as they crushed the Quakers' fears.

Carried along by the events of 1742, the popular politicians who wanted peace built up a steady momentum. The most active Quaker radicals, led by James Morris, went along with the balance of Quaker opinion when their own strategy of contention failed. But the personal animosities that had developed over two and one-half years of fighting died hard among this radical group. When, in late January 1743, Kinsey finally engineered the trade with Governor Thomas of partial arrears and current support for the passage of a number of bills, eight radical Quaker members from Philadelphia and Bucks counties refused to accept it. When the deal was made public, opinion in Philadelphia turned strongly against Kinsey, his city moderates, and country allies. Once both the executive and the assemblymen had committed themselves to a reconciliation, however, the accumulated anger and bitterness gradually began to wear away.[57]

The two and one-half years of serious contention from 1740 through 1743 were of considerable importance in the political development of Pennsylvania, for during this period changes in the configurations of politics that had begun to take place in the 1730s were logically extended and then hardened into durable form. Forged in the heat of political conflict, the new patterns of alliances, associations, and ideas formed the basis for the political configurations that would characterize Pennsylvania for the next fourteen years.

One basic change that the crisis brought about was the almost total loss of proprietary influence in the counties and a serious weakening of that influence in the city of Philadelphia. The executive's demands for defense measures and Governor Thomas's disregard for the owners of servants, coming, as they did, on top of Thomas Penn's tough land policies, convinced many that the proprietor and his governor were potential tyrants.[58] With the single exception of Bucks County, where a tradition of proprietary support kept members of the Kirkbride, Growdon, and a few other families loyal, public sympathy for the executive was thereafter almost totally confined to Philadelphia County and City. It would take the bloodying of the frontier during the French and Indian War before that pattern would be much altered. Even in the city of Philadelphia, where the proprietor and chief executive had their greatest following, the defense crisis and the 1742 election riot shattered support for them. By 1743 members of the old city interest lay prostrate, splintered, and weak; during the next twelve years the best they could do was occasionally to offer—unsuccessfully—a candidate for one of Philadelphia's two Assembly seats.

The other major effect of the 1740-42 crisis was the complete identification of Quakerism with popular rights and legislative privilege. As early as 1740, Governor Thomas and his Philadelphia supporters saw the opposition as a "Quaker opposition" and condemned it as such. Supporters of the legislature made the same connection, seeing the cause they backed as the Quaker cause; it was the Quakers, the freeholders concluded, who were best equipped to protect their rights, and anyone of that religious affiliation who joined with the executive's Anglican and Presbyterian supporters was no longer a real Quaker but an "unsteady person."[59] This association of freeholder rights and Assembly privileges with Quakerism led to a new kind of polarization in Pennsylvania politics. The old term "proprietary-Quaker" had lost its relevance; henceforth political dynamics would involve interplay between a strong "Quaker" coalition of popular politicians and a diffuse, often divided "proprietary-executive" political interest.

§

Once the governor and the Assembly had convinced each other of their good faith, the overheated Pennsylvania atmosphere began to cool down. Of course, there were still some sources of tension: a few of the governor's supporters were angered by the appointment of John Kinsey to the chief justice's post and a few of the Quaker radicals considered his acceptance as a betrayal; in June 1743 the city radicals incited the Philadelphia shallop men to challenge the regulatory authority of the Philadelphia Corporation; in September 1743 this same group mounted enough pressure to have the Assembly order the publication of the affidavits taken by the legislature during their investigation of the 1742 riot; and, during the winter months, rumors circulated that the Assembly might refuse to trade the excise and Loan Office bills for the rest of the governor's arrears. Despite these minor disturbances, however, relations between Assembly and governor continued to improve.

While John Kinsey managed to keep his fellow legislators under control, Governor Thomas gave ample demonstration of his determination to keep the peace. Thomas asked for his arrears quietly and accepted his loss of one thousand pounds in back pay with equanimity. When, during the spring of 1744, French military activities gave renewed importance to the defense question, he stated his conception of the province's needs in restrained tones and listened to the Assembly's demurs with resignation. With France in the war, Pennsylvania's situation was more dangerous, but the governor knew that no unequivocal demands on his part could possibly induce the Assembly to provide for the colony's defense.[60]

Aside from his personal predilection for peace, what motivated Governor Thomas to be so conciliatory toward the legislature was his acute awareness of his personal isolation. The 1742 election had driven executive supporters into disarray, and, with William Allen's failure to assume Andrew Hamilton's mantle, men who were potential proprietary followers were left leaderless and without direction. Another difficulty was that many of the Philadelphia merchants who had been advocates of defense felt betrayed by the proprietary in the aftermath of the election riot. In his statement to the Assembly when it was investigating the affair, Richard Hockley, son of Thomas Penn's old London business partner and a favorite of Penn's, implied that responsibility for the riot lay with prominent proprietary supporters. While accepting at face value the denials of complicity that followed this charge, Penn still defended Hockley, declaring that he was obliged to recount what he knew to be true.[61] Nor was this the only reason the Philadelphia gentlemen felt betrayed. Reports filtered back to Pennsylvania that when the Lords Committee of the Privy Council held their June 1743 hearing on the Board of Trade's recommendation that Pennsylvania be put into a state of defense, the Penns had deliberately mismanaged their presentation of the Philadelphia petitioners' cause. According to the local merchants, the younger proprietor had played "cat-in-the-Penn" and "left them in the lurch."[62]

In addition to being so divided among themselves throughout the ensuing decade that they could in no way be conceived of as a "party," the proprietary-executive supporters in Pennsylvania were left with only the barest shreds of political popularity. The charges of conspiracy and potential tyranny that adversaries leveled against proprietary and governor appeared to be well founded, documented as they were by the chancery court rumors, the enlistment of servants, Governor Thomas's letter to the Board of Trade, the Philadelphia defense petition, and the 1742 election conspiracy. Proprietary spokesmen such as Richard Peters failed to recognize, immediately, how drastically their position had changed, in fact for much of the next decade reputations continued to suffer from these events. The stigma of attacking the constitution was all but impossible to shake when, as in this case, it was generally believed.

Throughout the 1740s then, the proprietary had few friends and attracted little support. Despite the fear produced by the entry of France into King George's War and the successful operation of enemy privateers in the Delaware Bay in the fall and spring of 1747–48, public support for the executive did not visibly increase. Even though the Assembly refused to provide leadership in organizing the defense of the province, the old representatives were "re-elected without opposition, it appearing manifest that had there been a contest there could be no hope of success . . ."[63] While proprietary supporters had been fatalistic about their loss of influence during the early 1740s, they were not prepared to spend a prolonged period of time as unpopular placemen rather than respected politicians. With their failure to gain noticeable support in the 1747–48 crisis, however, they began to see this possibility as a real one.

Not until the late 1740s and early 1750s did proprietary spokesmen fully recognize the extent of their beleaguerment; and, when they did, they began to take notice of the conditions and events that accounted for their isolation. While they had failed to remark on the continued reelection of the radical Quaker legislators[64] who had refused to vote for the 1743 settlement with the governor, they did point with despair to the infusion of new blood that this "stiff and unyielding" strain of Quakerism received in 1750.[65] In that year James Fox, William Clymer, Israel Pemberton, Jr., and John Smith were elected to the Assembly and the more moderate voices of Israel Pemberton, Sr., Thomas Leech, and John Kinsey ceased to be heard.[66] Kinsey's death was recognized for what it was—a disastrous blow. In the middle and late 1740s, the proprietary-executive men had enjoyed some inside knowledge of legislative affairs and possibly a small amount of influence in the Assembly through Richard Peters's friendship with the former Speaker of the House.[67] In 1750, however, none of the proprietary allies enjoyed a close contact with Kinsey's successor, Isaac Norris, Jr.

Even before Kinsey's death and the aforementioned changes in Assembly personnel had taken place, executive supporters had begun to notice other indications of their weakness. The most important of these were the attempts of legislators to upset the existing distribution of power. Despite his helpfulness, Kinsey, for example, had used his power as chief justice on the Supreme Court to subvert the constitution. By allowing original suits and appeals that rightly belonged in the county courts, Kinsey used his powers to enhance his own reputation and to increase his influence over members of the electorate.[68] The most serious challenges to the established powers of the magistracy, however, came from the legislature. No sooner had the new governor, James Hamilton, arrived, in 1748, than the Assembly presented him with a bill for the emission of £40,000, in which there was no clause requiring quitrents to be paid at the rate of sterling exchange;[69] in 1749 Hamilton disagreed with the assemblymen over the terms and wording of the act appointing Loan Office trustees and over the clauses of a poor-relief bill that encroached on the authority of the Philadelphia magistrates.[70] In 1750 the governor eventually agreed to the Philadelphia night watch bill, even though he felt it surrendered some of the magistracy's prerogatives to elected officials,[71] but the register general's bill, in which the Assembly intended to restructure the whole administrative procedure in the probate of wills, never did gain Hamilton's assent.[72]

In the broader field of Indian relations, quiet disagreement also typified relations between executive and popular politicians. During the late 1740s, the Assembly pressed Governor Hamilton to ask the Penns to share the cost of Indian gifts and of related expenditures. When Thomas Penn refused, through his governor, the legislature petitioned him directly, only to meet refusal again. On the other hand, when Penn did offer £400 toward the construction of a fort on the Ohio and £1,000 per annum maintenance, the Assembly refused to have any of the scheme. Later in the spring of 1754, when the French had occupied the Ohio country, the Assembly procrastinated for some time before the representatives finally agreed to the executive's request for money to meet the threat.[73]

These new instances of the assemblymen's hostility to proprietary claims and policies, coupled with the failure of proprietary supporters to gain back any of the popularity they had lost during the early 1740s, prompted Hamilton, Peters, and their few friends to see excessive dangers in circumstances they had previously accepted as normal. Earlier, they had noted the political disadvantages that association with proprietary land policies brought, but by the late 1740s the political isolation of proprietary supporters made that liability seem much greater than ever before.[74] After Thomas Penn left the colony, the governor became chief landlord as well as chief executive, and Governors Thomas and Hamilton were robbed of whatever protection that

distinction had afforded their predecessors. For those who were actively engaged in the management of proprietary land, difficulties
seemed to increase as the frontier advanced. Out in Cumberland and
Northampton squatters sat down with impunity despite warnings.
Having done so they ignored ejectments, actively resisted proprietary surveys, and, when they eventually agreed to take out warrants,
refused to pay interest from the time of settlement.[75] Penn's agents
were kept busy distraining for rent, prosecuting for trespass, intro-
ducing suits for debt, commencing ejectment actions, and trying to
bring settlers into long-term leases. By 1752 the only hope that Richard
Peters could voice was that the proprietor's return to Pennsylvania
might inspire men to "avow (his) just rights" and unite together
to restore the reputation and authority of the proprietor's
friends.[76]

The executive supporters remarked, with even more frequency in
the early 1750s, on the proprietary's heavy reliance on Quaker officials.
Key appointments such as deputy surveyors and justices of the peace
often went to Quakers.[77] Because these country Friends were intimate
members of their local communities and meetings, more closely tied to
the Quaker-led political opposition than to the men who had appointed them, they symbolized the proprietary beleaguerment. Nor was
there an easy solution to this dilemma. The Quakers constituted a
legitimate interest in the province, and thus they did have a valid claim
to office. More importantly, they were often the only men of sufficient
stature and ability in a given area to merit appointment. When Richard
Peters set out to find a replacement for the deceased deputy surveyor
Benjamin Lightfoot, he could not find a qualified non-Quaker to fill
the post. When the Assembly created the new counties of Berks and
Northampton, the proprietary men could not find a loyal supporter
who was a local resident and who was capable of filling the various
court offices of prothonotary, deputy register, and clerk. Consequently,
they had to dispatch William Parsons and Charles Read from Philadelphia to occupy those posts and to try to organize local proprietary-
executive political support.[78] Earlier, at the birth of Cumberland
County, Richard Peters simply threw up his hands and left it to John
Kinsey to recommend "a good man" to occupy "the several posts in
that county."[79] If their dependence on the services and advice of some
Quakers was not bothering the proprietary-executive men, the refusal
of other Quakers to accept office was. When two prominent Quakers
refused to accept magistrates' commissions, a practice that had been
common enough in the past, James Hamilton raved about the "inveteracy . . . in these people against the magistracy."[80] Either way,
acceptance or refusal, the decision reminded the proprietary men of
their own isolation.

Other events seemed somehow to symbolize the proprietary beleaguerment. The arrival of great numbers of German immigrants in 1749–50 aggravated their sense of insecurity; the attempt of provincial councillor Abraham Taylor to blackmail Thomas Penn and the momentary disaffection of Attorney General Tench Francis in 1753 reminded them of how thin and unreliable their ranks were;[81] the neglect of Quaker leaders to come from outlying areas to Philadelphia on the arrival of Thomas Penn's nephew, John, in 1753 appeared to demonstrate the low esteem local residents paid to the proprietary and his supporters.[82] Such was their frame of mind during the early 1750s.

Throughout these years the defenders of proprietary right and executive prerogative felt so weak—and, in fact, were so weak—that they did not at any time try to challenge the Quaker-led political opposition. Despite the dangers of war, the failure of the Assembly to prepare for an enemy attack against the colony, and the efforts of the legislators to continue their encroachments on executive privilege, dealings among executive and Assembly, proprietary spokesman and popular politicians were peaceful. As Richard Peters summed up the situation in 1752, "all the while, as nobody speaks there are outward appearances of peace, liberty, and law and just decisions."[83]

By June 1752, however, Thomas Penn had decided that it was time for the executive to speak out. His intentions were clear in his 1748 instructions to Governor Hamilton, in which he required his new chief executive to work for the establishment of a regular militia and a proper chancery court. Yet Penn approved Hamilton's avoidance of these issues and he also made it possible for Hamilton to forestall an immediate confrontation with the Assembly over the reservation of proprietary quitrents from payment in Pennsylvania shillings.[84] As the 1750s moved on, however, Peters's and Hamilton's letters encouraged Penn to follow up these intentions, for they constantly told of their weakness and of Assembly attacks that had "so plucked" the executive that scarcely a feather remained.[85] Knowing that the institutional weakness of the executive had begot much of the practical political weakness of the proprietary, Penn and his confidants were determined to reclaim one of the most basic executive prerogatives that had been lost to the Assembly some years before—executive participation in the appropriation of all public money. A decade earlier, Governor Thomas put his finger on this power as the one the executive must have, and Peters, Hamilton, and Penn agreed with their old colleague. In July 1751 Penn sent informal instructions to Hamilton that he should not sign legislation increasing Pennsylvania's currency supply without stipulating that the executive participate in the appropriation of all interest money that would come from the new emission.[86] The stage was about to be set for a new round of contention.

CHAPTER 3

THE POLITICIAN'S WORLD

§

The eye-catching public issues of any period always reveal something of the politician's experiences, but often in a way that colors rather than clarifies. The Maryland boundary dispute, proprietary land policies, and the 1740-42 defense crisis—to name only the most obvious—were important parts of the Pennsylvania political experience, but no analysis of these issues can convey an accurate impression of the conformation of Pennsylvania politics at mid-century. Too much is left out, too much goes unnoticed. Only by broadening our scope, by focusing on the commonplace as well as the unique, on the quiescent as well as the turbulent, can we gain the perspective necessary to understand the politician's world.

§

Between 1726 and 1755 the world of the Pennsylvania politician was a relatively quiet one. During the long periods of peace in the thirties and forties, the politicians clearly preferred to promote harmonious relationships among themselves, and they succeeded, overall, in doing so. Issues that were potentially disruptive surfaced regularly, but officeholding politicians treated them carefully.

The most explosive political problem that appeared in the 1730s was the quitrent arrears question. Thomas Penn was determined to gain compensation for the depreciation of Pennsylvania currency if he was to accept it in lieu of sterling for old quitrent debts. But Andrew Hamilton and others worked hard to prevent a split on this issue—advising Penn what type of settlement was possible and reminding recalcitrant assemblymen of the contractual obligations that lay at the root of Penn's claims. So, too, in the conduct of Indian affairs, in the question of extending Assembly representation to the backcountry, and, with the exception of 1740-42, over the problem of defense preparations—all of them difficult and to some extent ongoing issues-—politicians worked to compromise their opinions rather than break over them.

The political body that most clearly exemplified the conciliatory tone of Pennsylvania politics was the Legislative Assembly. Within its doors representatives carefully and most often quietly worked out a common stance they could defend in public. Rather than intensify policy differences, intra-Assembly debate tended to blunt them; rather than overheat tempers, it tended to cool them. Because of the established traditions of legislative behavior, and because of the intimate nature of Assembly politics, the legislative environment was a relaxed one, conducive to reflection and dispassionate dialogue.

This is not to suggest, however, that the assemblymen invariably avoided sharp language in their fraternal dealings or in their interchanges with persons out of doors. Occasionally, elected representatives did clash over some issue; occasionally, they spoke bluntly to proprietary and governor; occasionally, they became involved in a heated exchange of pamphlets or newspaper articles. Yet, to a remarkable extent, the political environment out of doors in mid-eighteenth-century Pennsylvania was peaceful and calm. With the exception of the Keithian disturbances of the late 1720s and the Philadelphia election riot of 1742, there was a marked absence of the kind of orderly mob activities that commonly expressed dissatisfaction with eighteenth-century colonial government. Moreover, and again with the exception of the twenties, there were few pamphlet wars of any description. In Pennsylvania the politician was relatively free of the various forms of extrainstitutional popular pressure that could make the public world an unsettled and uncomfortable one.

The critical juncture between politics indoors and those outside was the annual provincial election. There, too, the predominant mood was one of conciliation, restraint, and at times even boredom. During the many years of peaceful politics, when policy differences among popular politicians were imprecisely defined if not purposely blurred, there were no instances in which competing sets of Assembly candidates vied for electoral support. Insofar as there was outright competition for the legislature, it was of an unstructured kind in which individual candidates declared themselves and competed as individuals for a lesser number of seats. But even this type of conflict was more often avoided than not. Electoral competition was usually forestalled by influential politicians and community leaders who, in preelection meetings, decided who should sit in the Assembly for the ensuing year. Thus, during the thirties, there were only one or two instances of contested elections, and in the forties and early fifties Isaac Norris, Jr., regularly reported to Robert Charles that ". . . we have no parties powerful enough to make any considerable opposition."[1] In fact, so quiet were political affairs that from time to time the independently minded would feel free to deviate from the normal patterns of electoral behavior and cast ballots for the undeclared. In October 1747 Philadelphia Quaker John Smith confided to his diary that "for my part, I thought the last six [of the eight agreed-upon and acknowledged Philadelphia County candidates] had been in long enough and therefore voted for . . . [six alternatives]."[2] This kind of relaxed idiosyncratic behavior was indicative of the low-keyed style of politics that predominated in Pennsylvania.

From the perspective of the active politician, there was much that was certain about the road to office. The informed web of interests that controlled access to office was recognized as a legitimate aspect of community relationships, a network through which political ambition ought to be channeled. Because of the prospective politicians' need for widespread community support, the process of building up a political interest was a gradual one. There were, of course, frustrations and failures, and political advancement was not inexorable. But the process was an accepted one, its underpinnings were known, and the gradual unfolding of new political careers demonstrated its effectiveness. Moreover, once an individual had gained a seat in the Assembly he had relative security of tenure. Most incumbents left office permanently because they chose to, not because they were defeated by an opponent. The respect and influence they gained in order to achieve office was not the kind that eroded away in a hour. Electorally, this was not a capricious world.

While most of the politicians' years were peaceful, there were times when compromise failed and contention occurred. The most obvious type of overt conflict that appeared in Pennsylvania was that between executive and legislature. In all such battles an air of unsettled expectancy was introduced into political affairs. In the 1740–42 confrontation over servant enlistments and defense, relationships among politicians did change, and the relative strength of contending groups was not entirely known until 1742. Moreover, no one knew with certainty tactics competing Pennsylvania politicians would adopt, or what those of proprietaries, English Quakers, and Board of Trade would be. But to speak only of uncertainty is to leave too much unsaid, for Pennsylvania politicians did not, for two and a half years, live on a razor's edge. By the fall of 1740 the basic political realignment had

taken place and the issues were clear. Thereafter, as time and experience hardened the new divisions, the politics of contention became
familiar and in numerous ways, predictable.

The few incidents of political contention that did take place stood
out in bold relief because they ran counter to the prevailing mood of
Pennsylvania politics. Contemporaries thoroughly believed that politics ought to be harmonious, and they were willing to work to that end,
both by actively promoting political compromise and by avoiding
issues that involved irreconcilable differences. This produced what can
only be described as a relaxed political atmosphere. Take, for example,
the question of political "faction." Like most American colonists,
Pennsylvanians recognized that one of the greatest dangers to the well-
being of a state was the formation among personal acquaintances of
informal political alliances. By definition such alliances came together
to pursue their private interests at the expense of liberty and the
constitution. But, despite universal recognition of the subversive
nature of factional behavior, there was a notable absence of the kind of
political posturing against such behavior that in a brittle environment
could actually encourage it. Not that Pennsylvanians failed to use the
term "faction"—of course they used it, but in a remarkably offhand and
imprecise way. Faction was something that out of principle all could
condemn; faction was something one determined not to be a party to;
faction was a term applied indiscriminately to anything from vague
circles of casual friends to identifiable politicians who supported one
another on a given issue. At times—during periods of contention
between executive and legislative supports, for example—the word
exuded animus; more often it expressed pique or traditional dislike;
often, too, it was used with detachment simply to describe some well-
known and accepted situation.

One of the best indications of the relative benignity of Pennsylvania politics was the occurrence of a whole series of potentially
"factional" situations that never became that. The Norris-Hamilton
disputes of the 1720s and 1730s were never given full-blown political
expression; the group of Chester County assemblymen who were
opposed to any quitrent arrears settlement in the thirties never openly
broke with those who disagreed; the differences between those Quaker
politicians who believed it their duty to provide the means of fighting a
defensive war and those who did not never came to a head—not, at
least, until 1755; finally, in Bucks County, where between 1740 and
1743 two groups of politicians fought three elections over the defense
issue, there was a total absence of the kind of inflamatory rhetoric of
factionalism that might have produced irreparable division. Pennsylvania was simply not the kind of fragile society that constantly

produced a factious state of mind. Even in the late twenties, when the Keithians were widely recognized as a factional political group and generated some of the furor usually associated with factional politics, most Pennsylvania politicians viewed the disturbances as a serious but short-run irritation; at the same time that factionalism indicated present political weaknesses and dangers, it also offered assurances of future political peace.

To the Pennsylvania politician who was active during the second quarter of the eighteenth century, political relationships seemed orderly and regular. There were definite patterns of political behavior and assumptions, and it was in reference to these that politicians saw themselves and the roles they played. There was, for example, a peculiar strain of contentious Quakerism that existed throughout the decade. William Keith's Quaker allies were replaced by the anti-quitrent-settlement Quakers, who in turn gave way to the radicals of the 1740–42 crisis, who were replaced and reinforced by the stiff and unyielding Quakers of the late forties and early fifties. The personnel changed, the issues changed, but the tradition of political behavior remained the same. Politicians located themselves within, without, or marginal to the tradition; by reference to it they knew what to expect from others and felt what their own stance should be. So, too, was there a continuous triangular relationship among proprietary and chief proprietary agents, the few resident politicians who were, in varying degrees, prepared to work with the proprietary and governor, and the other provincial politicians. The shape of that triangle and the distance and tension between any of its three points varied considerably over time, but it nonetheless existed as a fundamental feature of Pennsylvania politics. Structural continuities such as these provided a durable political context—one that made the politician's world finite and familiar.

This is not to say that change and crisis played no part in the politician's life. Of course they did. There was an important shift in the alignment of politicians in the late 1720s as the Keithians were absorbed; the contentious days of 1740–42 did bring change and harden political divisions; so, too, would there be a further reorganization in 1755–56. While in one sense these moments of political restructuring were unsettling, in another they were essential features of an orderly world. Simply put, they imparted a rhythmic quality to political life as contention gave way to peace, peace to contention, and contention again to peace. That was something most politicians felt; they sensed the cyclical pattern of political affairs as contention appeared "again" and as incidents of conflict "again" dissolved into peace. Clearly attuned to the rhythmic character of life in a preindustrial society, they perceived politics, with its own peculiar regularities and seasonal swings, as part of that world.

To emphasize the importance of these deeper levels of political awareness is not, of course, to suggest that Pennsylvania politics was without its occasional hysterical figures. James Logan's conspiratorial frame of mind and his extreme sensibility to slights belied his position as one of Pennsylvania's most secure and cultured men; Provincial Secretary and chief proprietary agent Richard Peters saw lurking devils where others did not; Quakers Israel Pemberton, Jr., and James Morris were exceptionally shrill in their politics—as were Anglicans William Keith and William Smith.

Perhaps the best example of how overwrought some politicians could become was the reaction of a small number of proprietary-executive supporters to the increasing rate of German immigration in the late forties and early fifties. Governor James Hamilton, Provincial Secretary Richard Peters, Chief Justice William Allen, and educator William Smith were the chief spokesmen for a group of men who deeply feared that German enclaves were swamping the hinterland, thus threatening the integrity of Pennsylvania's English colonial culture. To these men, politically beleaguered and incapable of analyzing their weakness objectively, the Germans became a scapegoat for their many political failures. They blamed German voters for their past defeats at the polls, disparaged the German culture, and laid plans befitting a mad alchemist's mind—to convert the German voters' antipathy to admiration by providing charity schools for their children.[3]

To single out the attitudes and actions of a handful of Philadelphia politicians and leave it at that would be as misleading as to ignore entirely such evidence of the anxiety-ridden mind. Most revealing about the whole episode involving the Germans was not, however, the random ravings of three or four impotent politicians but the reaction of the predominantly Quaker assemblymen. City Quakers, who apparently shared some of their political opponents' apprehensions about a growing German hinterland, uttered not a word of their fears. Rather they quietly worked out with their country colleagues two classic pieces of gerrymandering legislation. In it the assemblymen created two new counties that included much of the German-occupied area in northwestern Philadelphia and Bucks counties and gave these new areas only limited Assembly representation. Thus, they bestowed on backcountry residents the institutions of local government that those residents had always wanted; they kept the support of the German voters; and they completely defused what might have become a contentious political issue.[4]

This penchant for avoiding contentious politics was something most Pennsylvania politicians shared. They preferred to keep political relationships low keyed and controlled, in a subsidiary relationship to many of their other concerns. Excepting a very few individuals, the chief interests of politicians were not politics per se: they were business deals of one sort or another; they were the planting, harvesting, and general management of the plantation; they were the administration of justice in township and county; they were a whole series of social, religious, and familial concerns. Politics was interwoven with all of these other strands, and the best politics were those that tore no rents in the fabric. There were enough uncertainties in life without adding avoidable political ones; and the difficulties of business or social life were disruptive enough without adding a political dimension to them.

Consistently true to their intent, Pennsylvania politicians were largely successful in molding a stable political world. When there was contention, it quickly gave way to peace; when uncertainties did appear, rarely did they generate extreme and continuing anxiety. The politicians regularly went before their constituents for sanction and regularly attended the State House in Philadelphia, there to discuss the problems that regularly cropped up. What kept excitement in everyday politics were the adventitious events that continually occurred; from the frontier came reports of the Marylanders' depredations; from the countryside came news of conflict over fish dams; from the coffee-houses came speculation about who should replace the retired Andrew Hamilton or the deceased John Kinsey. Here were the kinds of issues that could challenge and entertain a man, yet not threaten the fundamental stability he craved. Here were the politician's daydreams—varied enough to keep interest alive, but bound within a world of comfortable routine.

PART TWO

THE BASES OF POLITICAL STABILITY

§

It was no accident that the politics of mid-eighteenth-century Pennsylvania were predominently peaceful and the world of the politicians usually a harmonious one: the politicians worked to achieve these ends. As events unfolded they reacted in what they thought were logical ways, and their words and their actions pointed out obvious reasons why the factionalism of the 1720s died out, why proprietors and Pennsylvanians cooperated during the thirties, why the political differences of the early forties were resolved, and why the proprietary failed to mount any overt attacks against Assembly powers in the forties and early fifties. But explanations on this level cannot entirely account for the prevalence of peace in provincial politics, and certainly not for the quiet mood of the politicians' world; they simply do not go deep enough. Only by going deeper—by analyzing the social and economic organization of Pennsylvania, the structural details of politics, and the social and political values that most Pennsylvanians shared—is it possible to expose the various sources of colonial political behavior. Many of these underlying features of colonial society are well known—some might even say commonplace—but together and in proper proportion they explain, as much as anything can, the political world that was Pennsylvania's.

CHAPTER 4

THE SOCIAL AND ECONOMIC CONTEXT

§

One of the important underpinnings of political stability in mid-eighteenth-century Pennsylvania was that society's social and economic structure. Because of the dynamic character of Pennsylvania society, observers have often mistakenly described the social organization of the colony as fragmentary and weak. In fact, Pennsylvania possessed a strong, flexible, and coherent community structure—one that could, without shattering, absorb the kinds of impact potentially disruptive social issues generated, and hence one that was particularly well adapted to the needs of a rapidly changing society. So, too, did the prosperity that Pennsylvanians enjoyed tend to produce political stability. Widespread economic opportunity, a commonly shared belief in the possibility of upward mobility, and a broad consensus on both the worthiness and the most suitable expressions of acquisitive values worked to prevent the accumulation of deep dissatisfactions and to promote the cause of social unity.

§

If, in 1755, some hypothetical, middle-aged Pennsylvanian returned to the place of his birth after thirty years' absence, he would have been quick to conclude that provincial society had undergone great change. Perhaps nostalgia would have had to bear some responsibility for this conclusion, but not entirely, for the earlier Pennsylvania had been dramatically transformed. The transformation was partly a demographic and geographic one. Only the sixth largest colony in 1726, by 1755 Pennsylvania ranked ahead of all the thirteen colonies save Virginia and Massachusetts. Population had increased from about

40,000 to 150,000; Philadelphia had grown from a respectable town of 9,000 to a city of 16,000; five new counties had been formed to the west of the original three; new centers of economic, political, and social activity had popped up inland at Lancaster, Reading, Easton, and York.[1] But it was the changes that were inextricably combined with Pennsylvania's demographic and geographic development, rather than this development itself, that underlined the transformation of provincial society. It was the large-scale immigration of Germans and Scotch-Irish that so radically changed the weave of Pennsylvania's social fabric, creating, by 1755, a pluralistic colonial society that had been unknown thirty years before.

Of course, even by 1726 Pennsylvania was a culturally diverse society.[2] At that time only about 60 percent of the population was composed of English or Welsh settlers. Of the remaining 40 percent, approximately 23 percent was German and about 12 percent Scotch-Irish. Interspersed with these dominant groups were the miscellaneous—a few French; a sprinkling of old Dutch, Finnish, and Swedish families who had occupied the area before the colony was organized in 1681; and a number of Irish Quakers, who had arrived in the 1690s and the early decades of the 1700s. As might be expected, religious differences matched up, to a degree, with categories of national groups. Most of the English and Welsh settlers worshiped as Quakers, Anglicans, or Baptists; the Germans were largely Mennonites, although a significant proportion belonged either to some small sectarian group or to the German Reformed or German Lutheran churches; the Scotch-Irish were almost exclusively Presbyterian.

The cultural diversity of mid-eighteenth-century Pennsylvania was thus foreshadowed in the pluralism of the 1720s, but at that time no one imagined the magnitude of the changes that were to take place in the next thirty years. While the old streams of English and Welsh immigrants dried up, Germans and Scotch-Irish newcomers poured into Philadelphia during the summer shipping months. Between 1726 and 1755, 40,000 Germans arrived in Philadelphia and 30,000 Scotch-Irish settled on Pennsylvania soil. What had been an English and Welsh majority became a minority, comprising some 25 to 30 percent of the provincial population. The Scotch-Irish, numbering about 40,000 people, made up an equal proportion, while the 60,000 German residents who constituted 40 to 45 percent of the population had become the largest minority group in the province. Related changes, of course, took place in the relative strength of the different religious denominations. The Quakers were still among the largest and best organized of all the groups, but as a proportion of population they had dropped from one-third to about half that. The largest church was the

Presbyterian with 20 to 25 percent of Pennsylvania's residents owing at least nominal allegiance, followed by the German Reformed and German Lutheran churches, which shared, in roughly equal proportions, about 35 to 40 percent of the population. Bringing up the rear were the Mennonites, the Anglicans, the Baptists, and a whole array of fragments—English and Swedish Lutherans, Scottish and Dutch Reformed, Moravians, Arminians, Socinians, Schwenkfelders, Old Dunkers, New Dunkers, Ephrathites, Sabbatarians, hermits, and independents.[3]

The province's geographical profile also reflected these changes in the cultural composition of Pennsylvania society. By 1726 the English and Welsh had established themselves in the eastern sections of the three original counties of Bucks, Philadelphia, and Chester—the English well represented in all three counties; and the Welsh mainly situated in Chester and Philadelphia counties, in areas north and northwest of the city of Philadelphia. Although there were numerous centers of German concentration, the largest and best known were the old settlement of Quakers and Mennonites eight miles north of Philadelphia at Germantown, the large agglomeration of German-Swiss Mennonites who had settled sixty miles west of Philadelphia on the Lancaster plain between 1710 and 1718, and the cluster of Reformed and Lutheran church people who had moved from New York into the unoccupied frontier land of the Lebanon Valley in 1723. The Scotch-Irish, who had arrived in a wave in 1717 and 1718 and in trickles thereafter, located in a variety of places: some chose land in south-central and southwestern Chester County, others settled in the south-eastern and frontier areas of what would become Lancaster County, and still others formed small pockets of settlement in Philadelphia and Bucks counties.[4]

Thirty years later the scene had changed dramatically. There were more areas of overlap between the major cultural groups in 1755 than in 1726, but there were also larger areas where one nationality tended to dominate, in some places virtually to the exclusion of all outsiders. The English, of course, continued to predominate in the old areas of the eastern counties, but even here there were changes. The Scotch-Irish extended their old concentrations in Chester, Lancaster, and Bucks and created new settlements in Northampton County; Germans also settled in the older areas, forming recognizable concentrations, but at the same time intermingling with members of other national groups in Philadelphia, Bucks, and northwestern Chester counties. In the main, sheer weight of numbers drove immigrants from both Ulster and the Rhineland beyond the fringes of existing communities. The majority of the Scotch-Irish drifted west of the Susquehanna River and

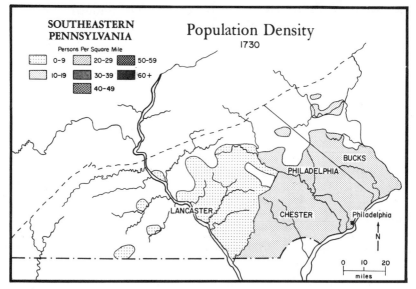

FIGURE 1
SOURCE: James T. Lemon, *The Best Poor Man's Country* (Baltimore: The Johns Hopkins University Press, 1972), p. 45.

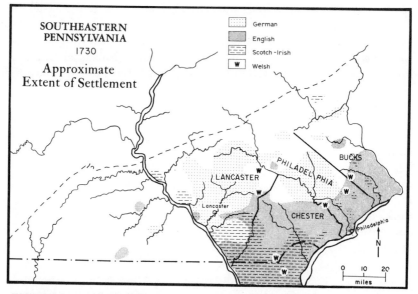

FIGURE 2
SOURCE: Lemon, *Best Poor Man's Country*, p. 49.

settled in York and Cumberland counties; the bulk of the Germans gravitated northwest out of Philadelphia into northwestern Bucks and Philadelphia counties (what was to become Berks and Northampton counties) or in a more westerly direction into north-central Lancaster and central York counties. Here, on the periphery of settlement, unclaimed frontier land awaited the newcomer no matter his nationality.[5]

Perhaps the most remarked-upon feature of European settlement in Pennsylvania was the apparently haphazard manner in which immigrants dispersed themselves throughout the land. Beset by a myriad personal and political problems, William Penn had lost effective control of settlement in the first two decades of the colonies' existence. Then, after Penn's death in 1718, a family quarrel tied up his estate for the next fourteen years. This circumstance—along with the Baltimore family's claim that much of southeastern Pennsylvania was really part of Maryland, the rapid rate of immigration to Pennsylvania, and the predilection of eighteenth-century immigrants to settle on large, consolidated farm lots rather than in organized villages—put an end to all planned settlements. Newcomers clustered here and there, and artisans' shops, mills, churches, and taverns popped up irregularly in or near these settlement concentrations. The large size of counties, a high degree of geographical mobility among residents, the continuous flow of newcomers into and through settled areas, and the diverse religious and cultural composition of provincial society only served to intensify the impression of apparent disorganization.[6]

But appearances notwithstanding—and perhaps more resolutely because of those appearances—Pennsylvanians worked to establish ordered relationships among themselves. When a sufficient number of settlers to bear the costs of local government had gathered in areas beyond the effective administrative boundaries of older counties, they invariably petitioned the Assembly to be incorporated as a new county.[7] Such status would bring them greater influence over local administrative and legal procedures, as well as a full complement of local officers whose chief duties were to provide the public services necessary to facilitate economic exchange, protect property rights, and control social deviants.

The institutions and offices of government certainly made the most obvious contribution to order, but they were not alone. Possibly, the most powerful agencies of order and stability were private rather than public, economic rather than political. In a society where economic growth meant widespread opportunity and a generally shared, rising standard of living, regular business relationships between

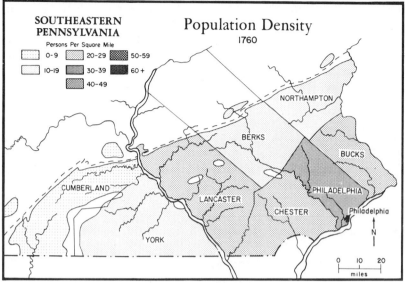

FIGURE 3
SOURCE: Lemon, *Best Poor Man's Country*, p. 46.

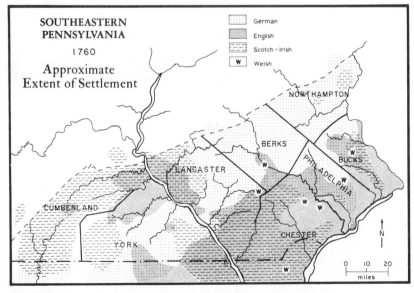

FIGURE 4
SOURCE: Lemon, *Best Poor Man's Country*, p. 50.

yeoman and miller, freeman and shopkeeper, farmer and blacksmith were conceived of as reciprocally beneficial. The growth of a vital market economy in Pennsylvania was convincing evidence of how readily men shouldered the burden of customary commercial relationships in the pursuit of the prosperity that stable business conditions promised. Thus, market, mill, and shop symbolized a self-imposed discipline built on the foundation stones of regularity and responsibility.

Despite the multiplicity of Pennsylvania's religious organizations, the congregation or comparable sectarian unit also played an important role in community organization. There were variations, of course, in the degree of group dominance: the Quakers, Mennonites, Baptists, Reformed Presbyterians, Moravians, and Schwenkfelders produced a more closely knit membership than the Anglicans, Presbyterians, German Reformed, or German Lutherans, for the latter denominations were neither so dedicated to mutual aid nor so demanding of interested participation by their members. Unlike the sectarian groups, some of which rejected the notion of a learned clergy, and all of which were composed of relatively small, tightly unified congregations, Pennsylvania's four major churches were hampered in their efforts to organize by a dearth of ministers. By 1750, however, 60 to 65 percent of Pennsylvania's three hundred fifty congregations were affiliated with church rather than sectarian groups.[8]

Membership in a religious organization implied a willingness on the part of the individual to accept church discipline. Here, again, there were variations from group to group both in standards and enforcement. Because of their relatively tight membership, the sectarian organizations were best able to discipline deviant members of their society, but church organizations were also able to exercise some control over their members. Presbyterian elders, in conjunction with the minister, could deny a member access to the church sacraments because of his feud with a neighbor, involvement with a woman of ill repute, or some other questionable action.[9] The presbytery made regular rounds of the congregations, one purpose of their visit being to encourage elders to maintain good discipline.[10] Responsibility for discipline in similar situations among the German Reformed and Lutheran congregations was not so clearly recognized. A few congregations showed evidences of maintaining discipline in the 1730s and early 1740s, and certainly the efforts of German Reformed minister Michael Schlatter and Lutheran leader Henry Melchior Muhlenberg on behalf of their respective churches tightened up the standards of behavior in the late 1740s and early 1750s.[11] Overall, however, the formal disciplinary activity in the congregations of the two established German churches was comparatively weak.[12] Yet, even among such groups, informal means of control did operate: peer group pressure and the subtle influence that went with recognized ability and positions of leadership operated within congregations to bring about conformity and ostracize troublesome deviants.

These three forms of organization—political, economic, and religious—constituted the most readily recognizable basis of community structure. Viewed together, they point out the most important feature of that community structure: the relative absence of membership congruence between political, economic, and religious groups. Residents of a given area acted first as members of one group of neighbors, then as members of another to pursue a variety of political, economic, and religious goals and to fulfill the basic social needs they shared as individuals. Because the county encompassed several townships, because the members of several denominations lived in the township, and because economic relationships were individual and selective in nature, the social world of eighteenth-century Pennsylvanians consisted of participation in a whole series of overlapping social groups.

This type of social network was duplicated on the most basic levels of interpersonal relationships. Among first-generation settlers it is clear that neighborhood relations, defined in the ordinary geographic sense, were of primary importance. Settlers often traveled in groups, and they congregated in clusters. In helping each other raise cabins, clear land, coil hay, and harvest grain, they were bound together by self-interest; in attending fairs, horse races, and shooting matches together, or in hunting, fishing, and sleighing together, they fulfilled each other's need for camaraderie; so, too, in attending to one another's personal needs, in sharing their celebrations and hours of mourning, they formed familylike attachments.[13]

As time passed, however, family members grew to maturity and often moved to different townships or new counties. Because of the propensity to associate with and rely upon those relatives whom an individual found agreeable, family ties tended to draw men and women beyond the boundaries of the narrow geographic neighborhood.[14] Improvements in roads and the new economic relationships men were able to forge once transportation facilities were improved also gave to the individual a wider range of choices in forming personal contacts. In one sense, personal attachments may also have narrowed slightly; as provincial society became more stratified, it is probable that throughout the social scale individuals tended to associate intimately with others of a similar status level.[15] But this should not be too heavily emphasized, for the offspring of old families maintained relationships despite differences in status; nonrelatives often kept their old friendships alive despite the development of a status differential in the course of their careers; and informal social activities, religious obligations, public service, and private enterprise kept men in touch with many of their neighbors.[16] The important point is that, by the time an area had been settled for a generation, the network of social relationships that most residents had forged not only included local tavern, church, and blacksmith shop, but also extended far beyond.

In discussions of community structure in situations where the associational groups to which the individual belongs have no town to give them concrete expression, individual relationships are sometimes treated as purely functional and the "community" given no more meaning than the sum of its parts. It is clear from any examination of social interchange among eighteenth-century Pennsylvanians that this kind of definition will not do for Pennsylvania society. Despite dispersed settlement, individuals and families wove together associations that, on the whole, created a unity qualitatively different from the strands of which it was composed. Individual, family, and group relationships came together to form organic communities that in turn gave order, context, purpose, and—at the risk of being trite—meaning to the men and women who were members. Because different individuals identified with, and felt they belonged to, the local community as they perceived it, Pennsylvania society had a cohesiveness that appearances belied.

The other major characteristic of Pennsylvania's community structure, its flexibility, is best illustrated by a direct comparison with that well-known entity, the New England town. In New England the importance of the town as the basic unit of settlement dated back to the days of seventeenth-century colonization, when each Puritan town was intended to be a utopian community. Residents of a given town covenanted together to secure the conformity that the Puritan conception of the godly society required, and those not fit to participate in such an enterprise were systematically excluded. With their control over town government the covenanted members of the community were able to enforce, to a considerable degree, the conformity and exclusion deemed necessary to achieve their religious ends.[17]

The eighteenth-century town, as swarms of New England historians have assured us, was simply not that of the seventeenth century writ large. Nonetheless, to the outside observer the most striking feature is not change but the persistence of certain characteristics. Beneath the clash of individual interests that signified the deterioration of the old corporate spirit, there still lurked in the community a very vital sense of moral purpose and a conformist tradition. Supported by a consensus

that there ought to be such a moral purpose, town authorities were able
to mobilize strong support to strengthen and protect prescribed forms
of social behavior. The sense of corporate identity, evident still in the
townsmen's tribalism and their concern for solidarity, appeared as well
in the continued identification of men as townsmen or outsiders. And,
despite the breakup of the nuclear village, the appearance of two or
more Congregationalist churches within a town, or even the establishment of an Anglican congregation, enough of the old congruence
remained to allow civic and religious authorities to work together to
defend what they deemed to be in the town's best interests.[18]

Compared to mid-eighteenth century New England, Pennsylvania's community structure was much more flexible. Whereas the New
Englander's utopian experiment had equated religious liberty with
conformity, the Quaker "Holy Experiment" had begun with a commitment to the principle of religious toleration. Rather than a settlement
composed of exclusionist towns, Pennsylvania was a society dedicated
to inclusiveness. The same squatters and tenants who were somehow
other than townsmen in parts of New England were welcomed into
Pennsylvania society. The Quakers, much more churchlike than
sectlike by 1726, were outward looking in their relationships with
members of other religious groups and extended the rights and
privileges of Pennsylvanians to all newcomers, regardless of nationality or religion. Whereas New Englanders possessed the means, through
the congruence of town government and parish unit, to ensure conformity, Pennsylvanians as a rule did not. In the few cases where a high
congruency of governmental and Quaker meeting boundaries still
existed, the easy infiltration of non-Quakers into these areas, and the
continuing impotence of township officials symbolized the virtual
absence of the "closed corporate utopian" spirit in Pennsylvania.[19]

What made Pennsylvania a comparatively flexible society, then,
was its traditional openness. From early in the eighteenth century it
had been consciously pluralistic because Quakers accepted the diversity
that tolerance implied, and immigrants arrived knowing that the price
of the religious freedom they expected to enjoy was the death of
uniformity. So, too, was it an individualistic society. Compared to New
England, the possible roles individuals could play and how those roles
should mesh was much less rigorously prescribed. Amid the loose lines
of community organization there was much more opportunity for the
individual simply to opt out of specific roles, and to establish a pattern
of relationships that, although incomplete and irregular by New
England standards, was a legitimate expression of acceptable community involvement in Pennsylvania. In their conscious pluralism and
in their individualism, Pennsylvanians were prototype Yankees long
before the Puritans had completed their transition.

Once the character of Pennsylvania's community structure is clear, it is more readily apparent why the large influx of German settlers into the colony was not highly disruptive. When German nationals arrived in Pennsylvania, they were free to move in groups to unoccupied land and to settle informally, in clusters, as English and Welsh, Scotch-Irish and fellow Germans, had done before. In areas where they found themselves interspersed with established residents of other nationalities the newcomers could reach out and in varying degrees link themselves to established patterns of social intercourse. The tendency for associational patterns to cut across cultural cleavages was most obvious in newly settled areas of mixed nationality, for there men were more dependent on their neighbors. But even where cross-cultural ties were strongest, there was still a natural tendency for individuals to form their most intimate relationships among fellow nationals. What sanctioned this behavior and prevented it from being the source of serious polarization was the easy informality of community formation. Most contemporaries accepted the premise that individuals and families should have the widest possible choice in building up personal associations and should be able to choose whether, or in what degree, they would participate in larger community activities. Widespread acceptance of this principle of voluntary association, the absence of any countervailing tradition of ostracism, and the sense of security that cohesive community relationships fostered, meant that neighborhood contact between national groups was relatively relaxed and free of hostilities.[20]

In those sections of the colony where Germans predominated, community formation was simplified because community members were free to work out among themselves the kinds of interpersonal contacts that best suited their needs. Moreover, in the absence of strong township government and tightly knit communities, there was no easily recognizable entity to draw attention to the German preponderance in given areas and, hence, to crystalize whatever nascent Germanophobic sentiment occasionally swirled through other rural communities. In county and provincial politics, German spokesmen counseled their countrymen to continue their low profile and not jeopardize the good relationships that normal community activities fostered. Whereas the Scotch-Irish shared provincial political office with the Quakers, enjoyed a portion of the Assembly's patronage positions, and were heavily represented in the important local offices of county commissioner, sheriff, and justice of the peace, German voters made no election-time bids for a comparable role.[21]

Following Germantown newspaper publisher Christopher Saur's advice to put good men in office but avoid the worldly pursuits and strong vanities that a political career entailed, influential Germans simply linked themselves in subordinate fashion to the existing networks of political influence that honeycombed the countryside. There is no indication that any German ever stood for election to the Assembly; further, those who served in county offices—such as Emmanuel Carpenter, Simon Adam Kuhn, Conrad Weiser, Edward Smout, and Martin Mylin—either showed evidence of the acculturation that long residence in the province had brought or possessed a reputation that to English-speaking residents conferred a special claim to office.[22] Along with such obvious factors, then, as the late arrival of the Germans, the economic prosperity of the times, the sheer size of the colony, and its ability to absorb a large minority group without crowding the newcomers on top of others, it was the nature of Pennsylvania's community structure, coupled with the reluctance of the Germans to draw attention to themselves as a special-interest group, that prevented the appearance of serious and sustained tensions between the Germans and English-speaking colonists prior to 1755.[23]

In addition to the long-term influence of Pennsylvania's community structure on relationships between members of different national groups, there was one occasion in particular when the cohesiveness and flexibility of local society helped prevent dramatic social and political disruption. In the early 1740s, when the religious revivalism of the Great Awakening swept through the British colonies, social and political patterns in Pennsylvania were only minimally disrupted. The relative immunity of Quakers and Anglicans to Awakening enthusiasm, the paucity of New Light Presbyterian clergymen, and the ecumenical attitudes of the Moravian missionaries were partially responsible. Beyond that, the peculiar, pluralistic structure of community relationships reinforced this result. In the short run, of course, the burning intensity of new-found religious concern drove many men and women to question, and in some cases reject, parts of their existing patterns of social behavior. But because those established associational patterns were expressions of a vital community life, they had a compelling logic of their own. As soon as the religious enthusiasm that inspired the new patterns of behavior waned, many individuals felt the pull of their traditional associations. Either they slipped back into their customary roles in the network of community relationships or, in deference to their recent experiences, they modified the old framework by substituting new but equivalent kinds of associational patterns for some of the old. In either case there was little difference in outcome; the basic structure of society remained unchanged.[24]

As for those who participated in the public debates the Awakening occasioned, they shared a similar fate. In societies where there was religious uniformity or a pretense of uniformity, open, religiously inspired contention could easily destroy political peace and undermine stability; in societies where religious diversity was accepted and where denominational attitudes were widespread, it could not. Since Pennsylvania had been a consciously pluralistic society since the early eighteenth century, the noisy wrangling of Presbyterians and German churchmen generated no social and political changes of more than marginal significance.

The point, then, is clear: while on the one hand individuals and families were able to create the kind of cohesive associational networks that signified a vital community life, on the other there was sufficient flexibility in those relationships to accommodate the province's social dynamism. Communities existed as islands of stable social relationships in the estuary that was Pennsylvania. As immigrants floated along with the current, some attached themselves to and became part of existing islands, while others joined together to form new ones; always there was the effect of the changing winds and current, for families that had long been part of one set of community relationships drifted off to join a different network, while individuals who had never established any firm set of attachments clung to one island momentarily, then swirled away to the next. There was movement, there was change, but there was also the stability that community ties secured.

The fact that Pennsylvania's open, resilient community structure was an important requisite of political stability does not mean, however, that the province was somehow free of social conflict. On the contrary, in a pluralistic society conflict will occur often, and in innumerable ways. One day in 1743, for example, a group of men gathered at a neighbor's farm in Londonderry township in southeastern Chester County to help him raise a new house. As often happened at "bees," a few men paired off to notch the logs. David Allen and William Armstrong were two who had done so. On the first log Armstrong finished ahead of Allen, and with a smug face he sauntered down to Allen's end. "I have beat you."

Allen's response was right to the point. "You have stinking breath."

"Stinking or not, I have beat you."

"You are a liar."

"Don't call me a liar or I will pull you down by the nose."

Then the hair pulling, gouging, kneeing, and grabbing began.[25]

Because the house or barn raising has always been symbolic of "community" on the American frontier, this episode has its point: in an open society like Pennsylvania the very same activities that were expressions of community relationships could often occasion conflict. Where interpersonal relationships were multifaceted and constantly shifting, they were also constantly conflicting. But despite the incidence of low-level individual and group contention, the chances of one of these minor disagreements developing into a major confrontation were small. Whereas in eighteenth-century New England the concentration of community relationships within the town meant that a religious dispute, for example, could very easily affect a whole range of political, economic, and social relationships, in Pennsylvania this was not so. Here, the broad structure of overlapping associations inhibited the extension of comparable disputes into other types of group relationships. Paradoxically, while the structure of community in Pennsylvania did little to restrain the occurrence of minor social conflict, it did much to prevent those minor contentions from developing into major social and political dislocations.

§

Between 1726 and 1755 Pennsylvanians enjoyed sustained economic development and marked prosperity. A variety of indices—such as the growth in the colony's population from 40,000 to 150,000, the organization of five new counties, the founding of twenty new towns (compared to none in the preceding twenty years), and the doubling of the ship tonnage clearing Philadelphia between 1725 and 1739—point this out.[26] Perhaps the most important indicator, however, is the record of trade between England and Pennsylvania. Over the three decades, 1726 to 1755, exports almost quadrupled and imports from England rose from approximately £38,000 to £200,000 per annum.[27] These statistics are worth a good deal of attention because the magnitude of their change underlines the fundamental importance of the export trade to the provincial economy.

The development of overseas and coastal markets had begun early in Pennsylvania's history. In comparison with the period from 1720 through 1755, when most of the immigrants who came to Pennsylvania were relatively poor men,[28] those who arrived in the late seventeenth or very early eighteenth centuries were somewhat better off, and used their capital both to establish productive economic enterprises and to seek out export markets for locally produced goods.[29] Because of their efforts and resources, Pennsylvanians quickly overcame the early economic difficulties that every new colony faced, and by the second quarter of the eighteenth century a solid foundation for further economic growth had been laid in Philadelphia.[30] A powerful merchant community —largely made up of Quakers—had come into existence, and among members of this group both opportunity and motivation for the expansion of business were ever present: their firm religious and kinship ties gave them reliable business contacts in commercial centers across the Atlantic and in North America, their need to repay their overseas suppliers for the increasing number of imported goods Pennsylvanians were purchasing forced them to carry on a never-ending search for lucrative markets for provincial produce, and the promptings of the profit motive were reinforced by their acknowledgment of a Quaker obligation to serve God by diligently following their vocation or "calling."[31]

In response to these opportunities and motives, Philadelphia's merchants entered into competition with New England, New York, and South Carolina and managed to gain and hold a substantial share of the West Indian and coastal trades. In the former, merchants supplied sugar planters in the Caribbean with "country produce," while in the latter they distributed goods up and down the mainland coast. When these traditional markets became restricted or failed to expand with Pennsylvania's ability to produce, the merchants cooperated with their overseas connections to exploit new areas. In response to these pressures in the early 1730s, Pennsylvania quickly developed a trade with Ireland and with the distant but lucrative southern European market. Between 1724 and 1739 ship clearances from Philadelphia to Ireland and southern Europe grew from 800 tons to 5,030 tons, while the coastal West Indian trade increased from 2,950 tons to 5,010 tons. Certainly the resourcefulness of the Philadelphia merchants in exploiting export markets played a fundamental part in creating and continuing conditions of prosperity.[32]

If one of the determinants of Pennsylvania's prosperity was the availability of markets for agricultural produce, an equally important and closely related condition was the ability to produce such goods. The province contained an abundance of rich agricultural land, which in conjunction with a long growing season promised high levels of productivity,[33] and it was word of this good land as well as the Quaker colony's reputation for peace and liberal government that attracted many settlers to Pennsylvania.[34]

The mere existence of this land was not enough, of course. More important was the fact that it was relatively easy to acquire. New settlers were not forced to rent or sharecrop land if they could not afford immediate purchase, for the Penn family did not have the necessary administrative machinery to enforce an outright purchase policy. In the 1720s and early 1730s it was enough for a man of initiative to mark out the limits of his intended plantation on unoccupied, proprietary-owned land and begin to cultivate the soil. Courts and county officials early recognized such "improvement" claims, viewing them as a form of personal property. By the time proprietary representatives pressed for payment of principal, interest on the purchase price, and back quitrents, the land in question had often produced enough to make the payment far less onerous than it would have been had it been collected at an earlier date.

Even after Thomas Penn reorganized Pennsylvania's land administration in the 1730s, the practice of occupying land for some time before tendering payment was common, and, for those who wanted to secure a regular patent as soon as possible, the financial strain imposed by what was, in comparison with Maryland, a high price for land could be eased by applying to the Pennsylvania Loan Office.[35] Loans, ranging in size from £12.10.0 to £100 in provincial currency, could be taken out, provided the borrower could offer as collateral twice the value of his loan in "messuages, lands, tenements, and rents."[36] The terms on which currency might be borrowed were specifically designed to make credit available to "the poor, industrious sort of people."[37] Theoretically, the mortgagor had to own the land before he could borrow on it, but in fact the loans usually financed the original purchase. In 1755 Assembly spokesmen estimated that one-half of the outstanding loans had been taken out to buy proprietary land; a good portion of the remainder probably financed private transactions.[38] When John Swift, a young Philadelphia merchant who managed a large tract of land for his English uncle, sold the tract to a number of settlers, he joined with them to convey title after one payment had been made.[39] The new landowners could then use the money they borrowed to expand their operations and hasten the liquidation of their debts. With the exception of the nine years (1730–38) during which Speaker of the Assembly Andrew Hamilton used his influence as acting trustee to curtail the number of loans, Pennsylvania's paper currency constantly circulated through land loans, for the number of applicants who wanted to purchase their own plantations expanded constantly.[40]

Even with her ready markets and abundant supply of rich agricultural land, Pennsylvania's economic development, like that of most American colonies, suffered a shortage of liquid investment capital. Yet circumstances in the Pennsylvania colony were not as straitened as they might have been. The Provincial Loan Office, in effect, created capital for borrowers; the money was used not only to buy land but also to purchase labor and to make other investments that raised productivity.[41] Although generally poor, immigrants did bring some accumulated savings with them, and this money was not merely for consumption when the new arrivals first reached Pennsylvania but for purchasing capital goods that enabled them to begin productive activities.[42] Those who had little, and were motivated, recognized the opportunities to accumulate capital that expanding economic conditions provided. Some made good wages as laborers or tradesmen; others sharecropped or rented a plantation until they had gained enough experience and money to strike out on their own as landowners.[43] Once an individual acquired land, appreciation could be counted on to increase the value of his original investment.[44] In short, available markets, rich land, a high rate of immigration, and provincial institutions such as the Loan Office helped Pennsylvania to generate its own capital.

The substantial increase in immigration between 1726 and 1755 also contributed to Pennsylvania's prosperity. The approximately 70,000 people who came from Europe to settle in Pennsylvania during these three decades stimulated the economy in a variety of ways. They provided a growing market not only for European imports but also for locally produced goods. Recent arrivals bought necessities from neighbors until they could begin to supply their own needs. Thereafter, those intent upon becoming farmers purchased their seed grain and the nucleus of their livestock herds from established residents; those who joined the growing body of rural tradesmen[45] continued to rely on their farming friends for whatever their garden and few acres did not supply; those who became town dwellers in Philadelphia and the lesser centers consumed great quantities of agricultural produce that farmers from the surrounding areas were quick to supply.

At the same time as they stimulated demand, the new immigrants helped the province provide for those markets by hiring out their labor. Many joined the free labor pool, while others, possibly as many as one-half of those who settled in the province, served some time as indentured servants. An indentured servant was an individual who entered into a contract in which, for a lump sum payment and a few fringe benefits, he or she sold his or her labor to some other person for a given period of time—usually four to five years. Once this contract had been concluded the master could put the servant to work, hire him out to someone else, barter him for some product such as half a ton of bar iron, or simply assign him to some other individual either to pay a debt or to establish a credit. On a continent in which chronic labor shortages hampered production, Pennsylvanians enjoyed a labor supply entirely adequate to the province's needs.[46]

In her expanding markets, rich land, growing pool of capital, and rapidly growing population, Pennsylvania possessed the physical resources that could produce a flourishing colony; in the acquisitve values of her residents and the liberating experience of immigration lay the sources of personal motivation that activated the provincial economy. The much-heralded "Puritan ethic" was most visibly internalized among the Quaker merchants in Philadelphia and among the rural

Quakers and Mennonites who had established prosperous plantations and businesses in Chester and Lancaster counties. Aside from these peculiar religious fraternities, however, manifestations of belief in a secular calling and in the intrinsic value of work appeared in the behavior of adherents to a wide variety of religious denominations. Scotch-Irish Presbyterians and Covenanters, German Lutherans and Calvinists, all drew on this common reservoir of motivation for economic achievement.[47]

The marked allegiance of Pennsylvania residents to the values of nascent capitalism arose, in part, from a selective immigration process.[48] Many immigrants were competent, ambitious men who had fused their yearning for economic success with their image of the New World. They were prepared to risk all they had to pursue the promise of that vision. But what intensified their strivings and often lit the fires of ambition where there had been no flame was the liberating effect of the immigrant experience. Despite former frustrations, failures, and fears, the immigrant found conditions in Pennsylvania conducive to personal optimism and effort. Here land was available even for the man of very limited means; whereas in Europe he would likely sink to the level of a laborer or landless mechanic, in Pennsylvania he could still become a landowner; whereas in Europe he felt victimized, dependent, and insecure, in Pennsylvania he could enjoy freedom, independence, and security.[49] Economic opportunity in Pennsylvania abounded: available jobs, expanding markets for agricultural goods, a growing demand for locally manufactured goods, advancing specialization, and appreciating land values all met the immigrant's eye.

Nor was personal economic endeavor confined by a maze of local or regional strictures and customs, for the rules of the marketplace in Pennsylvania were relatively simple. What magnified the liberating effect of those innumerable personal confrontations with economic opportunity was the relatively unsophisticated social structure of Pennsylvania, which in comparison with European societies was open and devoid of rigid subtleties and extremes. The accumulated customs of European society—built haphazardly on various traditions of place and degree, restraint and order—no longer pressed down directly on the settlers' shoulders. By crossing the Atlantic they had stepped out from under this weight of custom to a province where rapidly accumulated wealth could bring both respect and the prospect of participation in the social life of the provincial elite. For the great mass of immigrants who came to Pennsylvania, the fruits of diligence were visible as never before.[50]

And many learned to their pleasure that with diligence they could enjoy a modest prosperity, that they could as they had hoped "make an inheritance for [them]selves and [their] children."[51] During the second quarter of the eighteenth century, all but the poorest and most unfortunate Pennsylvanians succeeded in continuously amassing more wealth, whether in the form of clothes, livestock, tools, household furnishings, notes and bonds, or real estate. Here, what the individual predominently experienced was not the frustration of economic expectations but the opportunity for fulfillment.[52]

Of course there were instances of economic failure, but such individual misfortunes were to be expected. More important was Pennsylvania's avoidance of any of the kinds of serious disruptions that often occur along with economic development. Recessions, when they hit, were only short pauses in a rising secular trend. Specialization increased, but there occurred no major alteration in the techniques of production or organization of trade that caused serious dislocation.[53] Moreover, in a new, rapidly growing and changing settler society, increased production and consumption did not mean, as it did in traditional societies, that established patterns of behavior were being wrenched apart by the developing market economy. Rather, it indicated that the immigrants had established, and were continuing to establish, the kind of ordered relationships by which they could both contribute to, and enjoy, Pennsylvania's economic abundance.

Just as many settlers shared in Pennsylvania's prosperity, so, too, did they share in the apparent upward mobility that accompanied it. For many Pennsylvanians, income began to exceed consumption soon after their arrival, and with their savings they were able to buy more land (that would appreciate over time), take steps to increase the production of their plantations, or expand their businesses. What exaggerated the results of this process was the context in which it occurred: as population grew, as the proportion of servants and laborers, poor artisans and tenants increased—mainly as a result of immigration—so did the wealth of the established freeman relative to the average of all, including newcomers, in the local community.[54]

The vertical mobility that many Pennsylvanians saw in the relative bettering of their economic positions was, in turn, interpreted as an extension of the upward social mobility that was intrinsic in the move from Europe. By leaving a more rigidly structured society where concentration of wealth and minute social differentiation formed a comparatively weighty and elongated social framework, craftsmen, freemen, tenants, merchants, and laborers experienced a social relocation equivalent in some respects to a movement up the social scale. Merchants and country entrepreneurs were no longer "middling"—and probably poor middling—folk, but were the economic, political, and social elite in Pennsylvania; freemen, craftsmen, and laborers were not so far submerged in this telescoped society that they could fail to see both evidence and promise of significant economic advancement. In Pennsylvania, where distinctions of wealth and rank were not so great, economic and social movement that might have been very limited in the context of old European societies was more readily discernible and because of the truncated social order appeared to represent a much greater advance.

The peculiar nature of upward social mobility in rural Pennsylvania—depending as it did not solely on individual and family efforts to attain success within a closed community but also on relative changes in economic position due to large-scale immigration—points out one important trend in the development of local society: prosperity created a growing disparity between rich and poor. Although tax lists suggest a pause in the trend toward wealth concentration, there is reason to doubt that such an interlude took place.[55] Assessors, chosen from the ranks of the more well-to-do, undervalued the estates of the rich, a procedure that was perfectly legitimate in circumstances where the officials were allowed to consider not just the estate but "the necessary expenses" of each man before assigning him an assessment ratio.[56] Even if the movement toward concentration of wealth was gradual, however, between 1730 and 1750 the gap between the top 20 percent and the lowest 20 percent of property owners increased significantly. Although the percentage of wealth held by each group remained roughly the same, the increase in the province's wealth meant that those in the upper economic strata had benefited much more. And this growing economic disparity did have important practical consequences; not only did the lesser merchant or tradesman have a longer route to travel if he aimed to enter the ranks of the most successful businessmen, but also the country freeholder had to branch out into milling, land speculation, tanning, or some other commercial business if he were to join the company of the richest rural residents.

But despite the increasing distance between rich and poor, no signs of severe social strain appeared. As society became more specialized and population continued to increase, opportunities for the rapid accumulation of wealth were certainly no less noticeable and could, conceivably, have increased. The number of poor actually supported by the townships was never very large even in the older settled areas,[57] and the growth in numbers of lesser property holders on tax lists reflects the impact of immigration on the society rather than the polarization of second- and third-generation residents into antagonistic groups of prosperous and deprived. The expanding economy, the existence of unoccupied land on the frontier, the growth of new urban centers in the backcountry, and the appearance of new faces at centers of economic or political power (even if they had previously accumulated a substantial stake in Europe or another colony),[58] reinforced the notion that Pennsylvania was an open society. Finally, in provincial Pennsylvania, where economic means were judged to be directly related to differing personal capacities, a growing economic disparity was to be expected—in all, a perfectly natural phenomenon.[59]

The desire to attain wealth certainly existed in Pennsylvania, as did the opportunity to acquire it. Financial means meant leisure time, ease, comfort, and security. It meant the ability to free oneself from the strictures others imposed and to participate fully and independently in provincial society. But despite the heavy rhetorical emphasis of contemporaries on the desirability of economic success as a guarantor of independence, clearly Pennsylvanians quietly accepted a correlated implication. As an individual's economic resources increased, so did his capacity for effective social action—whatever that action might be. On the one hand, the man of wealth, whether he be farmer, miller, builder, or merchant, found that the gates that led to the centers of political and social activities, and that were firmly latched in the face of the poorer man, opened to his touch; on the other, he found that he had considerable leverage over the men who worked his fields, operated his mills, framed his houses, unloaded his ships, or retailed his goods. Wealth conferred power, and as such it commanded respect.

Regard for wealth arose, too, out of the symbolic relationship that existed between affluence and the capitalist ethic. Despite the unwillingness of Quaker spokesmen to view poverty as divine punishment and hence as evidence of moral failure, they widely acknowledged worldly success as a fitting reward for diligence, self-discipline, frugality, sobriety, and honesty.[60] In a society so thoroughly permeated with these values, and so thoroughly acquisitive in its tone, the achievement of wealth could only be interpreted as evidence of ability and virtue, unless in some individual cases there was undeniable evidence to the contrary.[61] Deference to affluence, which very often followed the unreserved acceptance of these values, served to reinforce the legitimacy of those very values. By doffing their caps to wealth, Pennsylvanians were providing for one another the kind of open approbation they sought to sanction the "Puritan ethic" they embraced.

More important, however, than the respect men gained simply as economic successes was the opportunity riches afforded them of assuming new social roles and thereby gaining additional status. With wealth, an ambitious man could surround himself with expensive possessions, gain an acquaintance with the popular books of the day, socialize with the prominent, and acquire a country estate. In short, it allowed the economically successful to adopt a life style that accorded with the most preferred forms of behavior sanctioned by the provincial value system.

Because the merchants of Philadelphia were the most successful businessmen in the colony, and because their presence in the provincial capital allowed them to occupy many of the seats of power, they quickly became the recognized social leaders of the province. The norms that they followed and the values they expressed took observable form in a peculiar local style of subdued extravagance, controlled ostentation, and obvious comfort. The house of a merchant was commodious enough by eighteenth-century standards and was furnished with care: mahogany chests, black walnut desks, finely carved chairs, silver plate, and handsome clocks adorned the interior. Books, both borrowed and bought, stood near a quiet, comfortable corner. In the bed chamber, extensive personal wardrobes were sumptuous and colorful, if not foppish and gaudy. In the dining room epicurean proclivities were fully indulged, while outside landscape gardening and other plantation projects provided suitable outlets for the practical, creative urge and for aesthetic tastes. Tea parties, coffeehouse talk, and other forms of social intercourse filled the increasing leisure hours.

Nor did religious or political differences gain expression in significant deviations from common forms of behavior. Architecturally, and in their furnishings, the houses of rich Anglicans and Quakers duplicated each other far more than they differed. At a time when "public friend" Thomas Story could send to James Logan's family "crystal sleeve buttons set in gold cut brilliant fashion" and "bright red Cornelian buttons set in silver" the differences in personal apparel between a "plain" Quaker and a stylish Anglican were minimal.[62] In general, Philadelphia Anglicans and Presbyterians, many of whom were lapsed Quakers, the offspring of former Quakers, or close associates of Friends, shared the same social tastes as the leading Quaker families.[63]

From the very early years of settlement, Pennsylvania trading magnates had not been content with a narrow, city-oriented merchant life style; they had followed William Penn's example of establishing county seats on private plantations. As Frederick Tolles observed, "Every Quaker [and he might have added non-Quaker] merchant, as soon as he was able to afford it, built a country house outside the city. . . ."[64] Some, like James Logan, Edward Horne, and Anthony Palmer, established full-fledged, working country estates, while others were content to build small retreats where they could spend a day or a weekend. No matter the scale; the gesture was the important thing. By expanding the orbit of their activities to include country life, the city merchants were neither merely emulating William Penn nor creating the means to escape Philadelphia's summer heat. Rather, they were expressing allegiance to the customary English pattern of social mobility—a pattern that, over the course of several generations, saw commercial wealth converted into land and a country seat—and, above all, they were trying to reconcile the realities of their dependence on commercial life with the prevailing value system that reserved for the independent country gentleman the highest esteem.

In Pennsylvania, as in other colonies, the English "country ideology" dominated political thought.[65] According to this particular set of postulates, the chief threat to the provincial constitution was the executive branch of government; independent country gentlemen were the best able to withstand the corrupting influence of the executive's power. Independence, the chief attribute of the idealized gentry, implied both the ability to withstand external pressures and a highly developed internal sense of moral incorruptibility. According to common belief, the ownership of land—in Pennsylvania productive or potentially productive land—ensured the former condition and in some rather mystical way contributed to the latter. Thus, in the Pennsylvania colony the provincial variants of a country ideology and a country life style mutually supported one another, creating at the apex of Pennsylvania society a clearly recognizable social pattern. Heavily impregnated, as it was, with orthodox value judgments, the uppermost "set" of provincial society commanded admiration, respect, and emulation among members of the lower social strata, thereby lending a fundamental coherence to the whole society.

Of course, the Philadelphia gentry was not a group that could be precisely defined, for no clear-cut criterion such as honorific titles set it apart.[66] In fact, the nature of the gentry's business relationships and the general life style they evinced tended to link them very closely with numerous non-Philadelphia County leaders. The land dealings of Philadelphia speculators William Allen, James Hamilton, and Isaac Norris brought them into personal contact with local leaders in outlying areas;[67] business arrangements of Philadelphia importers and retailers with Chester and Lancaster County shopkeepers such as Peter Dicks, Job Ruston, and John Carnahan drew the participants into various forms of social intercourse.[68] Businessmen Thomas Potts, Thomas Rutter, Samuel Flower, and William Branson were as much a part of the outlying communities that centered on their ironworks as they were members of a city elite.[69]

Similarly, individuals whose roots were firmly planted outside the provincial capital could, because of personal, political, and business ties, conceive of themselves, and be accepted, as a part of Phila-

delphia society. The legal practices of Abraham Chapman and John
Mather brought them out of Bucks and Chester counties into a
provincial orbit;[70] the appointment of lawyer Caleb Cowpland of
Chester as Supreme Court judge in 1750 merely confirmed his already
full-fledged provincial social standing.[71] Just as John Owen's public
service as Chester County sheriff and assemblyman made him a man of
both country and city, so did John Wharton's business interests in
Philadelphia and Chester counties.[72] The same may be said of Jeremiah
Langhorne, Joseph Kirkbride, William Moore, John Taylor, and
Joseph Parker, all of whom were prominent Bucks and Chester County
businessmen who were active in provincial politics or administration.
By the second quarter of the eighteenth century, city had joined with
country to produce a readily recognizable group of social leaders—a
genuinely province-wide elite.

Not surprisingly, county-based members of Pennsylvania's social
elite adopted a life style similar to, if less ostentatious than, their city
counterparts. Like their Philadelphia friends, they supported their
country life style with diverse business enterprises. By investing in
retailing activities, tanneries, flour mills, saw mills, fulling mills, malt
houses, ironworks, and land and bonds, county leaders were able to
generate the income necessary to purchase goods that symbolized social
success.

Naturally enough, a typical working plantation of a member of
the country elite did not differ much in external appearance from one
maintained by his Philadelphia counterpart. Instead of being flanked by
fish ponds and a small formal garden, the solid stone plantation house
stood in naturalistic surroundings with orchards and a garden close by.
The well-kept appearance of several outbuildings and the substantial
acreage of cleared and meadow land indicated that large-scale farming,
in itself, could be a profitable venture. Inside the house, books, silver
plate—supplemented by pewter and brass—a clock and case, and a few
pieces of expensive furniture graced the lower floor. Upstairs could be
found stylish bedroom furniture, and the owner's selection of clothes,
suitably set off with such items as gold buttons or a silver watch,
accompanied at least one mirror in which a man might inspect his
"presence." Behind the house was stabled the valuable riding horse that
bore the owner wherever he traveled; occasionally a chaise, drawn by a
single pacer, was a preferred means of transportation.[73]

Of course the county leaders could never match the scale of
ostentation indulged in by a Philadelphia merchant such as Isaac
Norris or Israel Pemberton, but they could, and did, match the
economic success of other, lesser representatives of urban society. No

doubt envy of the city lurked in the countryside, and clearly differences of environment and outlook could never be completely bridged. Moreover, country residents could invoke a reverse snobbery against their urban counterparts, for the former were obviously the real "countrymen." But such presumed divisions are easier to hypothesize than to document, and on balance it is clear that the concrete interests of business, politics, and pleasure and an acute awareness that they shared a common value system created a strong underpinning for mutual respect and a cooperation between leading men in city and country.

By the second quarter of the eighteenth century, those who composed Pennsylvania's provincial elite were a well-entrenched, if loosely defined, group. Lesser members of the community deeply respected their position and power because elite models of behavior expressed widely shared beliefs: in a society that acclaimed both the utility and intrinsic merit of the capitalist ethic, social and political leaders paid service to that ethic; in a society that believed in the moral superiority of the country gentleman, those who would be leaders established claims to that role. Thus, legitimacy and coherence flowed from the self-fulfilling nature of value orientation and behavior: acquisitive, hard-driving men produced an elite in whom they could see their reflection; farmers, sharecroppers, renters, and country artisans supported an elite purified by the soil, for they, too, shared that purification.

Nor did Pennsylvanians generate any widely recognized alternatives to the dominant norms of provincial life. Certainly, a few businessmen poured all their earnings back into their commercial enterprises and refused to enter into a more expansive way of life, but such a pattern bespoke a worship of mammon singularly unattractive to most men. At the opposite extreme, the unworldly communitarian experiments of the Ephrathites and Moravians, were to most Pennsylvanians the object of idle speculation rather than serious investigation. Other German sectarians who had not withdrawn so far from the world simply provided grist for the established mill: in rejecting secularization they affirmed the capitalist values of diligence, order, and simplicity; in berating ostentation they uncompromisingly coupled virtue with land ownership.

Despite the rapid demographic growth, swiftly moving economic relationships, and cultural diversity that characterized Pennsylvania society, physical appearances and modes of behavior that were accepted as statements of success varied little. Local wealth and selected aspects of an imported English political culture came together in the early years of colonial settlement to form the general outlines of a recognizable provincial life style. Once the peculiar mold of provincial society had hardened, purpose and coherence infused the whole social process. The existing symbols of power and status determined how ambitious men channeled their resources and efforts; in turn, their support of the familiar gave new strength to the ideal values that society's leaders claimed as their own.

CHAPTER 5

THE STRUCTURE
OF PROVINCIAL POLITICS

§

In the social world of mid-eighteenth-century Pennsylvania, deference was relatively high, and access to provincial office was restricted to appropriate members of the colony's elite. The social requisites of Assembly officeholding point out what kinds of criteria narrowed the field of potential officeholders, while the informal means of choosing candidates, the usual nonparty form of electoral competition, the unquestioning acceptance of established means of expressing political differences, and the customary apathy of the eligible voters underline the fundamental orderliness of provincial politics. Inside Pennsylvania's small Assembly, most legislative power was concentrated in a few hands. Contests for a share of that power occurred, of course, but the Assembly was so well insulated, changes in the locus of power so infrequent, and the sense of corporate identity among members so strong, that such contests did not develop into sustained public disputes. Despite the apparently closed character of Assembly affairs, legislators were attentive to the opinions and expressed needs of their constituents. Thus, they defused the potential for instability always inherent in extreme political insularity.

§

Between 1726 and 1755, deferential attitudes in Pennsylvania were more in evidence than at any other time in the eighteenth century. The colony had an established provincial elite, which by virtue of its members' social pretensions and the willingness of "lesser" men to recognize the legitimacy of those claims, formed a recognizable, if roughly defined, group of "natural" superiors; the basic allocations of

political power, which had been the source of much intraelite conflict
in Pennsylvania's early years, had been worked out and those compromises sanctioned by time. Provincial society had gained sufficient
time to "set," yet the colony had not become so large, dispersed,
complex, or specialized that power had become diffused among a great
range of individuals, associations or institutions. In fact, an extremely
high incidence of overlapping membership characterized the colony's
political, religious, and economic elites. Leading provincials commanded deference, not simply because they enjoyed one form of
deference entitlement, but because they possessed several. They
controlled large fortunes, shared a common life style, exercised political power, spoke with weighty voices in religious affairs, and were
educated men. Of course, perfect congruence between the memberships
of specific elites did not occur, but kinship connections and associational patterns among occupants of the upper social strata reinforced
the concentration of deference entitling properties among a relatively
small segment of the population.[1]

Despite the limited size of Pennsylvania's social elite, those who
stood at the apex of provincial society are divided into two loose but
recognizable groups. One group was composed largely of Quakers who
intermarried with their coreligionists; participated in group social
activities, mainly with other Friends; dominated elective offices in the
county and province; and espoused a rather piecemeal, whiggish
political philosophy. The second group is somewhat more difficult to
describe. On the political level, it was composed of a very loose
confederacy of individuals and families who gained definition by
membership in the Provincial Council and the Philadelphia Corporation, as well as by the occupancy of a number of appointive offices,
such as clerk of the Provincial Council, keeper of the Great Seal, judge
of the Vice-Admiralty Court, attorney general, and register general.
With a few exceptions, notably among representatives of the Philadelphia Corporation,[2] membership in these bodies generally implied a
willingness to support the governor in contests with the legislative
branch of the government. The sense of cohesiveness that sprang from
this identification with the chief executive, and from the belief that the
magisterial authority should not be further weakened, was in many
cases reinforced by religious affiliation; most were members of the
Anglican and Presbyterian churches and clearly considered themselves
the true representatives of English culture, for Quaker dissenters, by
definition, could form no part of a legitimate religious establishment.

Kinship ties and common social activities further strengthened
these bonds of political and religious allegiance. In the Philadelphia
Corporation, for example, about 85 percent of those admitted between

1727 and 1750 were related to existing members, and much informal socializing such as dinners and tea parties revolved around the various nuclei of these family relationships.[3] Participation in the activities of such groups as the Saint John's Masonic Lodge, the Philadelphia Dancing Assembly, and the colony on the Schuylkill gave additional social definition to those outside the orbit of strict Quaker society.[4]

Despite the differences between an Isaac Norris and a William Allen, the distinctiveness of Quaker and proprietary-executive supporter should not be overemphasized. Differences of opinion about the responsibilities of legislators and about the balance of Pennsylvania's constitution flared up into high-tempered political division only once between 1726 and 1754.[5] With the exception of the years 1740–43, legislative and executive spokesmen cooperated to a considerable extent: in the 1730s Speaker of the Assembly Andrew Hamilton worked closely with Quaker leaders; in the 1740s Proprietary Secretary Richard Peters cooperated with popular politician John Kinsey; and in the 1750s Governor James Hamilton worked out several compromises with the province's elected representatives. As one might expect, such political dealings paralleled a comparable range of intercourse on the broad social level. In the early 1730s Debby Norris, the sister of Quaker politician Isaac Norris, Jr., included the governor's family and the proprietor, Thomas Penn, among the members of "our mob," and in the 1740s and early 1750s men of differing religious and political connections mingled together at club meetings, dinners, and other social occasions.[6]

A significant qualification also must be added to the general statement that Assembly supporters were Quaker and executive-proprietary men Anglican or Presbyterian. Prominent Anglicans like Thomas Leech, Evan Morgan, and John Kearsley cooperated, in differing degrees, with popular Quaker leaders, while moderate Quakers such as Lawrence Growdon and Jonathan Robeson worked with proprietary men. And as the religious boundaries of Quaker and executive supporters were uneven, so were the kinship groups that underlay them. Although the Quakers were highly endogamous, the dismissal of some and defiance of the meeting by others who married outside their religion created a situation in which kinship ties cut across religious boundaries. For example, Charles Read, a prominent Quaker merchant, became an Anglican and sired a son, Charles, Jr., who remained an Anglican, and two daughters, who married Quaker notables James Logan and Israel Pemberton.[7]

While it is clear that two deference groups did bifurcate Pennsylvania's elite, they were rough divisions at best. Because there were considerable differences in membership among the political, religious, and social institutions that gave them shape, and because political calculations and circumstances, if not issues, were constantly changing, these two groups were oppositional clusters rather than well-defined polarities. The fact that Quaker assemblymen and Anglican placemen were both members of a single, highly visible provincial elite should never be lost from view. The assumptions they held about society, the values they espoused, the manners they displayed, the homes they lived in, the literature they read—all bound them together as common social and political leaders in a unique colonial setting.

Despite the social preeminence of those Philadelphians who gave support to the proprietor and governor, the Provincial Council and City Corporation on which they mainly relied for a sense of political identity were weak political institutions. The council had been defined by the 1701 Charter of Government as a purely advisory body without any role in the legislative process; the Philadelphia Corporation lacked a popular base and suffered from the constant intermeddling of the Assembly in Philadelphia affairs.[8] Clearly, the Provincial Assembly was the most powerful political institution in Pennsylvania. The sole legislative body in the colony, the Assembly was well equipped to hold its own in any altercation with governor or proprietor. By 1726 it had gained both the right to vote its own adjournment and to appropriate, without executive concurrence, the income from the excise tax and Loan Office mortgages.[9] Although compared to modern ideas the legislative goals of eighteenth-century government were limited in scope, the significance of the assemblyman was not proportionately reduced, for he was still responsible for framing the basic provincial laws governing administrative procedure and for regulating economic activities.[10] Equal to, if not more important than, this function was his role as watchdog: like the English House of Commons, the provincial legislature was the guardian of liberty, and consequently the elected members were to be the most able men the province could provide.[11] Because the office of legislator was so important, Assembly politics largely determined the character of provincial politics in mid-eighteenth-century Pennsylvania.

According to the rhetoric that accompanied Pennsylvania's annual Assembly elections, the most important qualifications for political officer were independence, virtue, and capacity.[12] Because of the intangible nature of such attributes, they were as difficult for contemporaries to measure as for later observers. But those who became assemblymen did display a number of characteristics that undoubtedly helped to convince voters that they, rather than others, possessed the necessary qualities. Possession of wealth was, certainly, one of the more important means of demonstrating public worthiness. Economic independence was a prerequisite of political independence, and the possession of solid financial resources indicated that a man was no stranger to diligence, sobriety, and virtue, that he was capable in worldly affairs; and that he could afford, intermittently, to sacrifice his private affairs in order to attend to the public business. Of the forty men who served as Chester County assemblymen between 1729 and 1755, thirty-two were in the top decile of the county's property holders, four were at the 80 to 90 percent level, three at the 70 to 80 percent level, and one at the 60 to 70 percent level.[13] Despite, however, the marked tendency for provincial legislators to be among the richest residents in their respective counties, wealth alone assured no one of political office: only a small percentage of the wealthiest men became office-holders, and a sprinkling of assemblymen were not particularly well off.

Closely related to wealth was life style, and, as in the case of wealth, members of the Assembly tended to be exemplars of the country way of life. In Philadelphia County, Isaac Norris, William Allen, and Israel Pemberton moved in the highest circles of society; in the country men such as Jeremiah Langhorne, Samuel Blunston, William Moore, and Joseph Pennock set the style with their large plantations, impressive stone houses, extensive lists of personal property, and rounds of informal socializing. Believing that independent countrymen were best able to protect the freeman's rights, electors naturally chose men who displayed some correspondence with that ideal pattern.

A third way in which men could demonstrate ability was through prominence in religious affairs. Anglicans and Presbyterians had some opportunity to do so by serving as vestrymen, church wardens, or elders, but it was among Quakers that service within the appropriate religious organizations was of greatest importance as a requisite of political officeholding. Of the thirty-six Quaker legislators who sat for Chester County between 1729 and 1755, twenty-five had represented their monthly meetings at the quarterly level and fifteen had been authorized to attend the Philadelphia Yearly Meeting. Nor was Chester County exceptional in this respect: of twenty-five Quakers who represented Bucks County over the same time span, seventeen attended the Yearly Meeting; and in Philadelphia County and City sixteen of the twenty-five Quaker representatives did the same.[14]

The high level of political participation by Quaker religious leaders was not without reason. Despite being dissenters and advocates of separation of church and state, Friends felt that their sect rightly enjoyed a peculiar prominence in Pennsylvania and that society should be directed by closely cooperating centers of religious and civil authority.[15] Tradition, rooted in the colony's early years when Quaker meetings performed all the functions of local government, and principles of mutual aid, which were institutionalized in the practices of local meetings, meant that men rose to prominence in the Quaker hierarchy not simply because they were pious men but because they were capable administrators who understood the needs of local society. It was solid reputations as good Quakers that provided two of Pennsylvania's most successful politicians, minister John Wright of Hempfield and elder Thomas Cummings of Chester, with the base they needed to launch and maintain their political careers.

Local administrative experience, somewhat akin to what many leading Quakers gained by handling meeting affairs, was another obvious means of judging capability for higher office. If the record of Chester County assemblymen is any indication, virtually all of the provincial legislators had served one or more years as township constable, supervisor of highways, or overseer of the poor. Even in the performance of these low-level jobs, there was opportunity to demonstrate ability and concern. On the county level, other more responsible offices could lead to that of legislator. Of the forty assemblymen who served Philadelphia County and City between 1729 and 1755, five had gained prior experience as city or county assessors and an additional six had served terms both as city or county assessor and as county commissioner. In the outlying areas this pattern was less distinct but still recognizable.

A fifth criterion by which prospective assemblymen were judged was that of education. Despite the ostensible aversion of Quakers to higher learning, they did recognize the value of a sound practical education and a thorough acquaintance with contemporary European political literature. It was doubly incumbent on a prospective legislator to be able to meet reasonable educational standards, for not only did day-to-day tasks of the assemblyman require legal knowledge and literary skill, but a basic tenet of the dominant English political culture was that both freemen and representatives should be well educated. Liberty could only be preserved by educated men, who, with the benefit of reading, study, and contemplation, could uncover the sinister and designing plots of power-hungry politicians. Unfortunately, there exists no readily available way of testing just how well educated Pennsylvania's legislators were, but from scattered evidence in wills, inventories, newspapers, and pamphlets, and with due regard for the geographical distribution of assemblymen, it appears that the provincial politicians were among the better-educated men in the province.[16]

The importance of wealth, life style, religious reputation, experience in local office, and education as prerequisites for office suggests that voters measured prospective assemblymen by their achievements as well as by how they conducted themselves in attaining these goals. Nor did reference to past performance stop with the candidate himself; the "merits of his progenitors" were examined to see if family name warranted a legitimate "claim" to "advancements."[17] Even if a man appeared to fulfill all of the most important qualifications for office, including the advantage of having ancestors who played a significant role in provincial affairs or had been men of "parts" in England, his ability to attain Assembly office was severely limited if he did not have close personal or family relationships with the acknowledged Quaker leaders of his county. The nature of those relationships was important evidence of a man's integrity.

Pennsylvania was popularly conceived of as the Quaker colony, and the peculiar conditions that made Pennsylvania so attractive to immigrants—tolerance, prosperity, and peace—were accepted as evidence of the laudable convictions and genuine ability of Quaker legislators. What strengthened the popular belief in the judiciousness of electing Friends—if not in their right to office—was their English background. Preservation of the good life in Pennsylvania depended not simply on the benevolence of Quaker politicians but also on reverence for the English constitution that had been tailored to fit local conditions in the colony. Among the Germans, in particular, opinion had it that a sensible course of action was to elect those Englishmen who were best schooled in the art of resisting civil and religious tyranny.

The majority of Quakers had always been among the stoutest defenders of popular freedoms, and they continued to follow this tradition in Pennsylvania during the second quarter of the eighteenth century. On the question of property rights, an issue that was constantly in the minds of Pennsylvanians from 1726 through 1755, Quaker leaders gave shape and direction to the freeholders' interests. In the 1730s, when Maryland claims to Pennsylvania property were the greatest threat, Quaker politicians worked closely with Andrew Hamilton and Thomas Penn; thereafter, when proprietary land "rights" became the freeman's chief grievances, Quaker leaders voiced that sentiment. Similarly, it was Quaker legislators who stood united against proprietary demands for a continuation of the chancery court, a provincial militia, and executive participation in the appropriation of government funds.

Throughout the second quarter of the eighteenth century, then, the Quakers "had the ears of the people," and nowhere was that more obvious than in Lancaster County.[18] Despite the fact that by 1755 there could have been no more than one hundred resident Quaker families, the most prominent politicians throughout the first twenty-five years of the county's existence were Friends or nominal Quakers. The three Wrights—John, James, and John, Jr.—Samuel Blunston, Thomas Lindley, Peter Worral, James Webb, Calvin Cooper, and Anthony Shaw formed the nucleus of a county political elite that operated as an integral part of the provincial Quaker establishment. The province as a whole demonstrated Quaker prominence equally well: the one-sixth to one-third of the population that was Quaker supplied 67 percent of Pennsylvania's legislators.[19]

The county was the basic unit of political activity in Pennsylvania. Each county was represented in the Assembly by a given number of seats, and resident freeholders voted for legislators to represent their county. Residents of Bucks, Philadelphia, and Chester each elected eight assemblymen, those of Lancaster four. In addition to voting for the eight Philadelphia County representatives, residents of the city of Philadelphia chose two assemblymen—burgesses, as they were known—of their own. Toward the end of the period, eligible voters in York and Cumberland each sent two assemblymen to Philadephia and those in Northampton and Berks each sent one.

Under normal circumstances, provincial elections were not wide-open affairs where freemen voted haphazardly for any combination of men that caught their fancy; nor were they highly institutionalized contests in which slates of alternative candidates competed. Generally, by the time election day (October 1) arrived, influential county residents who, by common consent, met informally once or possibly several times, had agreed on a group of candidates. The size of this group might vary from the number of seats available to one-half again that number. Before 1740 Quakers and non-Quakers cooperated in this procedure in the four Pennsylvania counties.[20] After that date the polarization of Quaker and proprietary-executive groups precluded any such easy intercourse in Philadelphia County. While in the outlying counties the old pattern of cooperation between all groups resumed after 1742 and continued through 1754, in Philadelphia the proprietary-executive men were so estranged from the established Assembly leaders, and so bereft of popular support, that they no longer participated.[21] Thus, between 1743 and 1754 the informal decisions as to who should be assemblymen for Philadelphia County were left to the popular Quaker leaders and their political allies.[22]

The informal process of choosing candidates was acceptable in a society like Pennsylvania, where deference entitlements were heavily concentrated in the hands of those who were the main participants in such decisions. Men of stature, obliged to use their interest for the public good, rarely found fault with this orderly method of organizing

political affairs.[23] Although it is impossible to gain entrance, histori-
cally, into the taverns, coffeehouses, and dining rooms where candidates were selected, sufficient evidence remains to allow some
comment.

One of the most important characteristics of the preelection
meetings was that old assemblymen and other aspiring candidates
generally participated in local "interest making." Popular politics in
Pennsylvania was not run by a group of backroom Quakers who held
power but avoided office. The context of preelection activities included
cooperative participation by men of the upper and middle social strata
who corresponded and talked about politics, and who winnowed out
from the pool of suggested candidates those who appeared least capable
of serving the province. At well-attended meetings, specific questions
were raised and answered. Who on the basis of past performance
deserved to be continued? Who because of illness or difficulties in his
personal affairs wanted to sit out the year? Who had support among
Germans and Scotch-Irish as well as among English Quakers? Other
considerations were those that the voters were urged to weigh—a
man's capacity, reputation, integrity, and his possession of those
symbols which attracted respect.[24]

Finally, there was one other consideration that played a large part
in the political decisions of all groups but particularly of the Quakers.
Friends were highly endogamous, and both consanguineous and
affinal ties were strong. At election time the "merits" of one's "progenitors" and the reputation of one's relatives provided valuable trading
points. Those who had political ambition as well as notable family had
the advantage.[25] At the same time, it is clear that certain families, such
as the Kirkbrides, Norrises, Pembertons, and Ashbridges, who were
highly visible politically, did not operate in a peculiar, self-contained
world of political influence. At any given time, candidacy for public
office signified only one aspect of a broader pattern of power distribution among kin groups. The relationship between religious and
political influence will never be entirely untangled, but certainly the
reputation family members gained in the monthly meeting could
vitally affect the political interest the family could mobilize. Not that
Quakers committed themselves, hard and fast, to specific individuals
before they met or corresponded with non-Quaker political leaders;
the whole process of candidate selection was too informal for that.
But in working out acceptable political alternatives, and in determining how a man stood in character and reputation, ancestry and
kinship ties constituted very important considerations.

Although most participants accepted the customary method of
settling on candidates, and although all participants argued that they
were looking for men of reputation and capacity, preelection politics

did produce moments of friction. Even when the character of alternative candidates was weighed more diplomatically, to prefer one individual was, in fact, to discount others. Often such comparisons were less than diplomatic; while one man's friends were public-spirited, those who opposed him were self-interested, designing, or, at best, suffering from extreme myopia; while a favorite candidate was a man of probity and intellect, his major competitor might be a mean man of no real merit. Thus, the process of forming a political consensus on the county level was by no means free of conflict. Competitors struggled for whatever advantage they could gain, gushing praises and emphasizing strengths on one hand, pointing out weaknesses and impugning motives on the other. But despite the excesses of enthusiastic campaigners, moments of concentrated and prolonged contention were certainly few. The general process of candidate selection placed a premium on persuasiveness, and the deference customarily accorded the most weighty county residents ensured peace, if these men could work out a compromise. Lastly, should the number of major candidates who were still in the field by October 1 exceed the number of seats available, the ballot box was universally recognized as the legitimate and final arbiter. The electors chose the eight men they preferred as assemblymen from among those nine or more nominated.[26]

As practical politicians who knew the value of a united Assembly and who were strongly oriented toward a consensual mode of decision making, Pennsylvania's Friends were quick to recognize the legitimate claims of non-Quakers to a share of political power. Conversely, spokesmen for other groups were generally ready to cooperate with Quaker leaders, not only so that they might enjoy elective office but also because they perceived their interests to be much the same as their Quaker neighbors'. The best example of this process of mutual cooperation occurred in Philadelphia and Bucks counties between 1730 and 1739. During those years, Andrew Hamilton and other representatives of the growing Anglican-Presbyterian elite worked openly with city and county Quakers; in turn, Quaker politicians were more than willing to have such talented men working with and, in a very real sense, leading them in Philadelphia's dispute with Maryland. Just as Andrew Hamilton's successful career pointed out the validity of these conciliatory tactics, the disastrous failure of his successor, William Allen, sharply illustrated the futility of confrontation politics. When Allen and his Philadelphia friends openly condemned the Quaker assemblymen during King George's War, they were mauled so badly that seventeen years elapsed before Pennsylvania's electors would overlook the scars they bore.

Outside Philadelphia County, contemporaries looked on and learned well. Throughout the remainder of the 1740s and the 1750s, conciliation and cooperation characterized political dealings. As they had in the 1730s, Quakers continued to share political representation with the Presbyterians in Lancaster, the Dutch Reformed and Presbyterians in Bucks, and with an odd Anglican or Presbyterian in Chester and Philadelphia counties. The most important precondition of participation in provincial officeholding by a non-Quaker was to cooperate with Friends or, as Richard Peters bitingly observed, to become "Quakerized."[27]

Of course, there were times in Pennsylvania when the informal consensual mode of selecting candidates was somewhat altered. Abnormal electoral practices occurred when the whole colony or the residents of one particular county were polarized into two competing groups. Between 1728, and 1755 there were three years—1740, 1742, and 1754—when severe political divisions modified normal election procedures throughout the province, and on five occasions—Philadelphia in 1726 through 1728, Lancaster in 1741, and Bucks in 1743—individual counties suffered a similar dissension. Under such circumstances a variety of practices appeared.[28]

Furthest removed from the normal procedure of pluralistic competition within a generally cooperative framework was the practice of selecting two complete alternative tickets. In the 1740 and 1742 elections for Bucks County, Quaker leaders openly split, and two opposing slates of candidates competed for votes.[29] In Philadelphia County in 1740 a similar situation occurred: although no overt split divided Quaker ranks, William Allen headed up a full ticket that included one of his old Quaker cronies, and the independent Thomas Leech, as a respected incumbent, was included in the Assembly ticket as well. Even under these circumstances, however, in which politicians had set up the prototype of "party" competition and public opinion was badly polarized, some electors resisted such organizations. They continued to practice their customary procedure of picking out individuals rather than simply choosing one of two alternative tickets.[30]

In other elections where differences ran high, traces of the traditional election procedures were much more apparent. In the much-noticed 1742 Philadelphia election, proprietary managers reverted to the old practice of trying to place two or three spokesmen in the House, but the results of the election manifested the futility of any tactics not based on cooperation with popular Quaker leaders.[31] In Lancaster and Chester, similar campaigns reaped similar results. Proprietary supports in both counties did not promote a full ticket in 1742 but backed one or two individuals whom they hoped would become persuasive voices in the new Assembly. In each case these men polled no more than a sprinkling of votes.[32] In the 1740 Lancaster election, the advocates of defense preparations had organized a settled

ticket of four main candidates, but voters spurned their efforts. Almost
to a man, freemen supported three of the incumbent assemblymen. The
five candidates who supported the chief executive competed among
themselves and with a new pro-Assembly Quaker candidate for the
fourth position.[33]

The same polarization that produced these abnormal political
practices in the counties continued in concentrated form throughout
the 1740s and early 1750s in the city of Philadelphia. Not surprisingly,
elections for the two city burgesses served several times as the focal
point for direct political confrontation between the proprietary politicians, who in the context of a restricted urban environment felt strong
enough to attempt such tactics, and the city allies of the popular
Quakers. Thus, after 1740 a highly localized type of city politics
developed, characterized by sporadic electoral competition between the
candidates of two self-conscious political and social groups.[34]

Despite the peculiarities of elections in the city of Philadelphia
and the occurrence of several abnormal confrontations on the county
level, the general context of politics in Pennsylvania was one of
cooperation and conciliation. Those who participated in the informal
arrangements governing candidate selection considered themselves
bound by common interests: the defense of Pennsylvania property
claims against Maryland, the circumscription of a potentially tyran-
nous executive, the protection of property rights from an omniverous
landlord. Not that individual and group interests did not conflict—they did, occasionally with bitterness—yet the nature of the
conflict underlined the pluralistic rather than the strict "party" nature
of elections. Out in Lancaster County in 1732, Quaker John Wright
and Presbyterian Andrew Galbraith fought a wild election battle even
though their respective backers substantially agreed on the other
Assembly candidates.[35] Bad feelings undoubtedly emanated from such
confrontations, just as jealousy snapped at the heels of advancing
reputation, but generally, in cases where personal antagonism developed, differences were soon obscured by new exigencies or were submerged beneath more important long-run political considerations.[36]

While the methods of candidate selection illustrate one aspect of
the provincial political structure, the forms of election campaigning
reveal another. Ideally, the disinterested gentleman did not "court"
men's "favor," and in fact there is evidence that candidates refused to
solicit for themselves or even be seen near the polling station on
October 1.[37] On the other hand, most men had to take part in the
preelection "politicking" if they hoped to become candidates, and
when, in the course of a campaign, differences ran high, principals
often did take their case to the voters.[38] In the 1742 election Samuel

Blunston harangued the Lancaster crowds on behalf of himself and the other opponents of the governor; two years earlier, William Moore had canvassed the countryside in Chester, and the leading candidates in Philadelphia County turned out at the Court House to influence whomever they could.[39] In the 1732 Lancaster election, it was not enough that Wright and Galbraith should head their own campaigns; Galbraith's wife, Ann, mounted her mare Nelly and scoured Donegal for freemen who would support her husband with their votes.[40]

In addition to the private deals and public appeals a politician might make during his bid for office, the candidate could use the press to influence opinion. The devices employed by pamphleteers and editorial writers varied widely. Some partisan tracts set out broad statements of political principles; others picked out one or several incumbents and trained the guns of literary malice on these targets; an exceptional one or two solicited votes for a specific candidate. But with the exception of the later 1720s, when penmanship became a popular game of one-upmanship in the politically polarized atmosphere of Philadelphia, recourse to the press during campaigns was relatively infrequent.[41]

As important as the candidates' campaigning style might be in some circumstances, and as persuasive as a razor-sharp polemic might be in others, the majority of voters were swayed by something quite different. At a time when word of mouth was the most effective means of communication, a politican's strength depended on the number and reputation of friends and relatives who would speak out for him. It was the candidate's allies who called in their debts—mentioning a recent extension in personal credit, or the Loan Office's laxity in calling in quotas, and reminding people how valuable the good offices of a justice of the peace, a county sheriff, or some powerful neighbor could be. It was the candidate's allies who praised his integrity, pointed out his accomplishments, measured his reputation, interpreted his feelings about proprietary and executive power, "treated" or bribed as the occasion demanded, and passed out tickets that included his name. A man was known by his friends, and by election day it was clear who those friends were.[42]

The existence of these different forms of influence points out some of the important reasons why Quakers dominated electoral office so completely. Quakers and the local allies of Quakers held sway as the national economic and social elite of the province and could, in addition to mobilizing influence in their private capacities, bring the leverage that the offices of magistrate, sheriff, county commissioner, Loan Office trustee, and deputy surveyor provided. Then, too, Friends could quickly recruit substantial support for political favorites because of the highly organized nature of the meeting structure. In the general context of dispersed settlement that characterized Pennsylvania, Quaker meeting houses stood out as strategic centers of influence. Nor did Quaker politicians ignore the latent possibilities of other denominational gatherings; they cooperated with ministers, elders, and vestrymen who, as spokesmen for other religious groups, could use the opportunity afforded by congregational meetings to promote their version of the political choice.[43] Finally, although in a normal election year it may be assumed that no one individual or small group totally controlled the flow of information on public affairs that might influence the voters' minds, during times of executive-legislative controversy Quaker assemblymen did have a virtual monopoly on political news outside of Philadelphia. There were few proponents of executive-proprietary policy in the country, and when these men spoke out they were immediately classified as defenders of arbitrary authority and special interest and their construction of events thereby discredited.[44]

But no matter how successful various candidates were in lining up influential supporters, it was the voter who finally meted out success and failure.[45] Unfortunately, it is impossible to find out who those voters actually were. What may be estimated, however, is the relative degree of voter participation compared to the number of mature males in the provincial population.

Table 1 summarizes the provincial voting statistics for the years in which total vote counts are available for both winning and losing candidates.[46] The 1740 and 1742 provincial campaigns, as well as the 1741 Lancaster elections, were abnormal because they occurred during times of extreme political ferment. As the *Gazette* reported on October 7, 1742, "there was a greater number of votes in all the counties of this province than have appeared for several years past." This observation was substantiated by John Smith's comment that the 1750 Philadelphia election—which, in number of votes cast, approximated the 1740 and 1742 levels—was remarkably large.[47] The 1742 Lancaster results are suspect not only because they were so far out of line with the others but also because hard-fought campaigns in Lancaster often culminated in ballot-box stuffing.[48]

With these two reservations in mind, it is possible to make some tentative conclusions about voter participation. Between 1730 and 1755, the number of men who took part in provincial elections was unlikely to have exceeded one-third the number of taxables in any county and, given the complaints about voter lethargy that appeared in the press, may often have been no more than one-fifth to one-quarter.[49] But the very steadiness of the Philadelphia figures (1741 compared to

TABLE 1

VOTER PARTICIPATION IN PROVINCIAL ELECTIONS

County	Year	No. of Voters	No. of Taxables	%
Bucks	1740	800	2,500	32
	1742	1,000	2,600	38
Chester	1740	700	2,800	25
	1742	1,000	3,000	33
Lancaster	1740	1,000	2,900	34
	1741	1,150	3,070	38
	1742	1,800	3.240	56
Philadelphia	1740	1,800	4,850	37
	1741	1,500	4,950	30
	1742	1,900	5,050	38
	1750	2,000	6,900	29
	1752	1,500	7,300	21
Philadelphia	1742	600	1,850	32
City	1751	831	2,100	39
	1752	730	2,100	35

SOURCES: Election Statistics—*PMHB* 32 (1908): 180; John Smith's Diary, 1 October 1750, 2 October 1751; Isaac Norris, Jr., to Robert Charles, 11 October 1740, INLB (1719-56); Richard Peters to John Penn, 20 October 1741, RPLB; Isaac Norris Jr.'s Journal in Taylor's *Almanac* (1742), LCP; Minutes, PYM, 1747-79, FHL, p. 55.

Taxables—Evarts B. Greene and Virginia D. Harrington, *American Population Before the Federal Census of 1790* (New York, 1932), p. 117; *Gazette*, 18 May 1749.

1752 and 1740 and 1742 compared to 1750), as well as a comment in the *Gazette* in 1742 implying that in past years there had been comparable voting totals, points out a significant structural change in Pennsylvania politics. The political community, as defined by those who voted in elections and in comparison to the proportions of freeholders who did not vote, was certainly no more than holding its own and, quite possibly, was becoming more narrow.

In the light of the "yeoman tradition" that deemed the widespread participation of incorruptible freemen in the electoral process essential for the preservation of the constitution, the relatively low level of politicization warrants some explanation. Certainly there is no evidence that franchise requirements kept participation low,[50] nor is it likely that the large numbers of Pennsylvania's German population failed to participate in elections and that their absence kept the total percentage of voters low. Not only does literary evidence show that Germans did take active part in elections, but also, in Lancaster County, the voting figures were at least as high as for other areas (Table

1). Conversely, in Chester, where the percentage of Germans was lower than in any other county, the percentage of votes was actually lower than in any of the other counties. Although nonparticipation by certain groups of Germans and the lag period produced by their seven-year wait for naturalization probably did mean that overall the percentage of Germans who exercised the franchise was somewhat lower than among the English and Scotch-Irish, this factor alone could not explain the continually low level of participation in provincial elections.

In the absence of evidence suggesting other reasons, it seems likely that many qualified Pennsylvanians failed to vote simply because they lacked interest. Some had to travel long distances and the trek was too troublesome. Others, closer to the county seat, found excuses in the weather, the uncompleted harvest, the fence that needed repair, or in a sense of moral superiority that condemned the drinking, conviviality, and enjoyment of leisure that election day brought. In any case, those who customarily attended to politics seemed to be managing very well, for Pennsylvanians enjoyed liberty of conscience, peace, prosperity, and low taxes. The indifference of Pennsylvania's freeman was the indifference of the satisfied.

There are any number of inferences one could make about Pennsylvania politics on the basis of these voting statistics, but one is of particular importance for the structure of provincial politics. The relatively constant and low level of political participation prevented the complex web of Quaker political interest from being significantly altered. Because the balance of political power lay in the three old counties, and because the size and nature of the electorate was virtually unchanged, the organization and management of popular politics was virtually the same in the early 1750s as it had been thirty years earlier. While the process of economic and demographic expansion transformed Pennsylvania on a number of levels, it was not accompanied by anything like a similar rate of politicization. In so far as new men participated in politics, they did so through the existing political network. Consequently, established patterns of deference continued, constantly reinforced by the success of the political establishment in providing satisfactory government for local residents.

Although Pennsylvania's House of Representatives shared many characteristics with the other provincial Assemblies, the legislature did have its own distinctive character. Because the Assembly constituted the entire legislative branch of government, and because the governor's claim to magisterial independence was clouded by his relationship with the proprietor, assemblymen and citizens tended to see the House as representing the whole people and not just a part.[51] In addition, the common eighteenth-century notions that the legislature was a delibera- tive, corporate body were given special emphasis in Pennsylvania by the Assembly's closed debates, terse minutes, and refusal to record votes. A painstaking reader might have gleaned hints from the House journals of how different representatives reacted to specific petitions or proposed legislation, but the assemblymen's determination not to record their divisions, save in a sprinkling of cases where the dissen- tients insisted, precluded close public supervision.[52]

What motivated the legislators to insulate themselves from the public was not merely a belief in the corporate nature of government, nor the acceptance of the common political imperative that demanded legislative independence; it was the Quakerism of the representatives. Because so many of the assemblymen had always been Friends, normal legislative proceedings were carried on in a meeting like atmosphere. Silences were common as members waited for the inspiration to speak, and when debate was done the Speaker might simply declare the sense of the House rather than call for a vote.[53] As well as being appropriate, the procedures of the Pennsylvania Assembly were perfectly managea- ble. Assembly membership only grew from twenty-six to thirty-six from 1726 to 1755, and the turnover rate was not high enough to threaten continuity in leadership. The average annual turnover was 23 percent, but a more significant figure was the number of men admitted annually who had never before served in the House. This figure was 14 percent, and the average four new faces in a thirty-member, or five in a thirty-six-member, House could easily be assimilated by their peers.[54]

The small size of the Assembly and the relatively low turnover in that body indicates how insular and closed Assembly membership was. What made it even more so was a bias in geographic representation that heavily overrepresented the city of Philadelphia and its immediate environs. Most Philadelphia County representatives had business interests in the city, and 80 percent of Chester's membership came from townships within a twenty-four-mile radius of Philadelphia.[55] From the point of view of social composition, too, Assembly membership was restricted and inequitable. Political representatives tended to fall into one of two groups: some were first-generation settlers who, supported by uncommon ability, religious reputations, wealth, power- ful connections, or any combination of these, had been openly accepted into the ranks of the governing elite;[56] most, however, were the sons and grandsons of men who had established the family name in politics, business, and religious affairs.[57] In one of his angry moments, Gover- nor Thomas aptly characterized the Assembly as "a conclave" rather than "a body of men who are accountable to their Electors."[58]

Although there were, with the exception of the Speakership, no formal distinctions in rank among legislators, leadership patterns did emerge. In any given year approximately 30 percent of the House membership controlled an average of 70 percent of the major committee appointments and 55 percent of the minor.[59] This small group of legislators included the very prominent politicians who were largely responsible for framing legislation, directing discussion, composing public statements, investigating complaints, and dealing with the chief executive. In their hands lay much of the Assembly's power.

Among legislative leaders the same sorts of geographical bias occurred as were evident in the total Assembly membership; appendix II.5 points out how overrepresented Philadelphia County and City were.[60] Under different Speakers, of course, committee appointments did vary slightly: Andrew Hamilton's were the most equitable geographically (probably because of his alliances with the county leaders who helped to destroy the Keithians); John Kinsey tended to pick Philadelphia Quakers (perhaps because of the legislature's dispute with the governor and the maritime military threats that occurred during his term of office); Isaac Norris did begin to place western representatives on committees, as new counties were formed in the early fifties. But, in all, such tendencies were no more than minor variations in a commonly held bias.

While being elected as a representative of Philadelphia County visibly increased a politician's chances of becoming a recognized legislative leader, the attainment of such stature was by no means guaranteed. Only a city burgess could unfailingly expect to become a major legislative voice, and even in his case prominence owed less to geographical consideration than to the character of the incumbent. That social position and reputation outside the Assembly played an important part in the designation of leaders within was apparent from a number of careers. Andrew Hamilton, William Allen, Joseph Kirkbride, Jr., James Morris, Samuel Blunston, Israel Pemberton, Jr., and others took their place among the House leaders the moment they entered the State House. But others who possessed impeccable social credentials, such as Isaac Norris, Thomas Leech, James Wright, and Mahlon Kirkbride, spent their first two or three years in the Assembly picking up a few odd committee appointments before they blossomed into recognized legislative leaders.

Even among this very small group of legislative leaders political success varied from individual to individual. Some assembly men played a major role in Assembly activities for only a year or two, while others, by their long occupancy of the seats of power, became the dominant politicians of their day.[61] Of the twenty-four men who could legitimately lay claim to such status, sixteen had been brought up in politically active families.[62] Early exposure to the working world of politics, and acknowledgment of an obligation to perpetuate the family reputation in provincial affairs, presented young minds with the opportunity to absorb the subtleties of political management and predisposed them to exploit the benefits they shared.[63] But as important as the advantage of family training was, it was no guarantee of political success. Ability, character, personality, and motivation were the decisive factors in determining who, among the sons of a political family, could succeed as political leaders. The possession and determined use of political talents made the difference between an Isaac Norris and his brother Charles, a James Wright and his brother John, Jr., a James Hamilton and his brother Andrew. Likewise, personal ability and motivation made it possible for Edward Warner, Joseph Trotter, and Evan Morgan to move from the lesser levels of Philadelphia merchant society into the ranks of political leaders and for Andrew Hamilton, John Wright, William Allen, John Kearsley, and Benjamin Franklin to penetrate from outside Pennsylvania "society" into the very centers of political power.

Proficiency in the art of combining high-minded commitment to principle and an appearance of rectitude with concession and conciliation were clearly the most important factors in political success. Andrew Hamilton's public career was witness to this, as was that of master strategist Jeremiah Langhorne and Machiavellian Samuel Blunston. But, in a colony long distinguished by a tradition of political professionalism, none was the peer of John Kinsey.[64]

John Kinsey, Jr., was first elected to the Pennsylvania Assembly in 1730–31, and, after serving nine consecutive years as a representative of Philadelphia County, he was chosen Speaker of the Assembly, a post that he occupied until his death in 1750. It was during his decade-long tenure as Speaker that Kinsey most openly displayed his political talents. Despite the fact that his leadership of the Assembly spanned a time troubled by war and marred by one major period of political contention, there was never a dissenting vote recorded in the Assembly journals. And it was the measure of John Kinsey that one has to resort to the public records in order to write anything about his political opinions. A superb example of the complete opinion broker, his private remarks consisted of promises of good will, while his public utterances were masterpieces of political double-talk.[65] Of course, he shared general whig principles, for all successful assemblymen did, but beyond that it is impossible to go.

Fortunately, the circumstances that brought Kinsey to power and the tools that he used to maintain his position are not as illusive as his opinions. Like so many other provincial politicians, Kinsey had been born into an active political family. He had established a sound reputation in New Jersey politics in the 1720s before moving to Philadelphia at the end of the decade.[66] During the 1730s, he carefully cultivated a close relationship with Andrew Hamilton, and when, in 1739, Hamilton, Allen and several of their close friends decided to retire, they placed Kinsey in Hamilton's old position as acting trustee of the Loan Office and secured his appointment as attorney general.[67] The following year Kinsey was chosen Speaker of the House, and once ensconced in that position he was unshakeable. Inside the Assembly he used his power over committee appointments to rescue a grateful Isaac Norris from three years of relative obscurity under Andrew Hamilton. By judicious distribution of offices of profit—the Loan Office trustees, currency signers, and excise collectors—he built up a powerful network of influence.[68] In the broader setting of executive-legislation dealings, Kinsey used his power as House leader in combination with the more subtle arts of persuasion, flattery, and practiced sincerity to repair the divisions that had marked his first years as Speaker, and to establish a relationship of confidence with executive spokesmen.

Outside the constricted orbit of placemen and provincial politicians, the situation was no different. Kinsey's positions as acting trustee of the Loan Office and as chief justice of the Supreme Court secured for him an unprecedented power over the Pennsylvania electorate. Despite the fact that he was a lawyer in a Quaker colony where prejudices ran high against pettifoggers, he occupied the most prestigious and influential religious office—the clerkship of the Philadelphia Yearly Meeting—that Quakers could confer.[69] Knowledgeable about meeting affairs, and in close contact with the most weighty elders and ministers in the Society, Kinsey was able to fit together the religious and political sides of Quakerism as no other man could.

Pennsylvania's Provincial Assembly displayed all the signs of a well-insulated, relatively closed political body. The informal network of influence that underlay election procedures served to winnow out all but a handful of political aspirants, and these were certain to have been born, or have won their way, into the upper social strata. The very limited number of seats in the House of Representatives and the lower turnover in that body only underlined the exclusiveness of Assembly membership. But that Pennsylvania's legislators came from a rather narrow circle and were well insulated against strict public supervision, did not mean they would fail to provide good government. There is every indication that Pennsylvania's legislators did, in fact, measure up to the expectations of their constituents.

On questions that related to the power of the executive and proprietor, there was no doubt where the legislators stood. Again and again they adopted whiggish stands, which, by protecting or extending legislative power, symbolized their commitment to a whole range of popular privileges. Their destruction of Sir William Keith's chancery court in the mid 1730s, and their subsequent attempt to establish one in which Assembly nominees rather than proprietary appointees presided, their strong stand against the governor's enlistment of servants in 1740, their determination to refuse defense appropriations that might strengthen the chief executive, and their absolute refusal to give the governor a vote in the appropriation of provincial funds during the currency crisis of the mid-1750s, certainly demonstrated to provincial residents that the men they elected to protect their rights were performing this task. Occasionally there were mutterings from some freemen that the legislature had sacrificed their best interests—in 1739, when the Assembly agreed to subsidize the Penns in exchange for acceptance of Pennsylvania's currency in lieu of sterling for quitrents contracted prior to 1732; in 1742, when the Assembly and Governor Thomas were locked in a bitter feud; and in 1747-48, when Spanish and French privateers threatened the safety of eastern provincials— but at no time was the dissent more than mild.

On questions that were not so prominent politically, it is somewhat more difficult to gauge the relationship between assembly-men and constituents, but by referring to the record of petitions that provincial residents sent to the Assembly, it is possible to see what freemen expected their representatives to do and how the politicians responded. Between 1726 and 1754, 545 petitions were presented to the Assembly, 284 of which requested action that would require legislation.[70] How responsive assemblymen were to these pressures is indicated by the fact that the legislature acted on 38 percent of the 180 issues raised in these petitions. In terms of the Assembly's overall legislative record, 54 percent of the hundred acts passed during those years were in answer to petitions.[71] This legislation included acts to raise the wolf bounty, to prevent swine from running free, to streamline litigation procedure for small debts, to bar entailment of estates, to regulate all provincial fees, to create committees, and a variety of others.[72]

These bare statistics and a sampling of the facts that gave them substance cannot in themselves do justice to the case for the popularity and responsiveness of Assembly action. Demands for such legislation as naturalization acts, an increase in the currency supply, and a change in the procedure of oath taking were important requests, and by paying close attention to them legislators established credit with their constituents.[73] Some of the most popular legislation that the assemblymen framed never became law because the chief executive refused to sign it. In the late 1740s and early 1750s, for example, the Assembly tried to increase Pennsylvania's currency supply, as it had in the past when petitions for more money had appeared, only to find that the governor would not assent to its bills.[74] Other popular legislation— to establish a popularly controlled chancery court, to institute a county commission system for Philadelphia City, and to regulate ferry rates— ran up against the same difficulty.[75]

Sometimes, petitions requesting legislation were ignored because the assemblymen felt that the existing laws already covered the situation;[76] whatever failure there had been was administrative rather than legislative. Sometimes, too, when faced with a request by particular interest groups, the Assembly simply resolved that the petitioners might frame their own bill; having been granted this permission, lobbyists failed to agree among themselves on what specific provisions they wanted, and thus the issue died.[77] At times, when their constituents were clearly divided, the assemblymen tried to work out acceptable solutions, but such accomplishments were seldom reflected in the legislative record. For example, when the Philadelphia justices of the peace and county commissioners clashed over their jurisdictional boundaries, the assemblymen resolved the conflict;[78] when some inhabitants of Philadelphia complained against the practices of city tanners, the legislators allowed them to suggest methods of self-regulation by which the chief complaints of the objectors might be met.[79]

However accommodating the Assembly was generally, there were times when legislators bluntly refused the demands of petitioners. This willingness to deny special interests when the public welfare, as they construed it, suffered was as important for good government as were positive, facilitative actions. Local distillers were denied any kind of bounty or protection from competition, iron producers met refusal when they requested that a duty be put on Maryland iron, and Philadelphia shopkeepers and merchants who were adversely affected by public vendues were turned down when they petitioned the Assembly to stop those sales.[80] Throughout this period, too, the Assembly persisted in maintaining strict inspection of flour for export despite the complaints of some millers, farmers, and merchants that the provincial standards were too high.[81]

Just how much resentment interested parties felt against legislators can never be known, but the fact that no literary evidence mentions these issues indicates that few people challenged the Assembly's judgment. Similarly, a whole list of issues, such as a revision of the Pounds Act, regulation of cattle importations from

Virginia, extension of the powers of highway overseers, and passage of a law against small trespasses, that petitioners presented but that were never acted on, appear to be of marginal significance.[82] A few people felt the effort to draw up and circulate a petition was worthwhile, but they failed to convince their representatives that the issue was important enough to warrant legislative action.

Measured by the criterion of responsiveness to petitions, then, the assemblymen's performance was certainly adequate, and as independent legislators their record was equally good. They conscientiously renewed acts when they elapsed, worked out an acceptable stance on Indian affairs, tried to improve various aspects of the provincial administrative system, increased the number of acts that regulated the quality of Pennsylvania's exports, and carefully set out legislation that affected the Loan Office and excise tax.[83] When, as in the case of the 1730 Insolvent Debtors Act, constituents protested against something they had done, the assemblymen listened and made whatever adjustments they thought necessary.[84]

Despite the restricted nature of popular politics at the provincial level, the legislature was quite responsive to public opinion. One reason for this was that committee representation in the Assembly was much more equitable than it appeared. Although the most powerful legislative leaders were Philadelphians, and although the metropolitan area was overrepresented, on issues that had peculiar relevance for outlying areas, or were popular politically, county members did have committee representation and influence.[85] Moreover, members of the provincial political elite, whether they were from Philadelphia or Lancaster, were always in close touch with local society. Economic interests and social ties kept them in close contact with large numbers of men and women who represented a considerable cross-section of Pennsylvania's populace. Agricultural pursuits, whether experimental or purely practical, meant that legislators shared common interests with many of their constituents.[86] As leading Quakers in their local meetings, many legislators occupied religious offices that, because of the obligations they entailed, forced the individual to become acquainted with the needs and interests of the less fortunate Friends.[87]

Finally, for those who had wide experience in Pennsylvania society as well as for the few who had not, the use of legislative power implied certain obligations. To Quakers, the Assembly membership meant the opportunity to promote good harmony among men and to provide the conditions under which the colonists could best develop their talents. Whether Quaker or not, the assemblyman, as gentleman and social leader, was obliged to seek relationships with dependents and neighbors, which if not paternal were at least benevolent.[88] Most important, the representative assumed, with the office of assemblyman, a direct obligation to be responsive to the electorate. The public welfare was not something a small group of legislators could arbitrarily decide; it was to be worked out among representatives who took fully into account the "minds of [their] constituents."[89] The interests of the assemblyman were, ultimately, the interests of the freeman.

CHAPTER 6

LOCAL GOVERNMENT
AND POLITICS

§

The structure of local government and politics was every bit as important as that of provincial politics for preserving the kind of stability that characterized Pennsylvania affairs. In the administrative organization of county, township, and borough was embodied regularized procedure and division of authority; in the case of local officeholders, patterns of selection either dovetailed neatly with those on the provincial level or stood, well established, on their own. Moreover, in their operation of local government, Pennsylvanians gave clear-cut expression to their goals of security, stability, and self-determination.

§

When Pennsylvania residents failed to create the closely knit townships that William Penn had envisaged as the basic unit of settlement in his colony, the county became the most important focal point for local government activities. Originally intended to be no more than secondary units of administration, the counties contained both large populations and land areas. When the northwestern backcountry areas of Bucks and Philadelphia were cut off from the old counties in 1752, Bucks still contained 16,500 residents on a land area of almost 400,000 acres, and Philadelphia had 39,000 people on an approximately equal area.[1] Because of their large size there were few counties, only eight in the province by 1755, five of which had been created west and northwest of the original three. As settlement had become more concentrated in the backcountry areas, residents petitioned the Assembly to set up new counties, and, when it judged that the population was large enough to warrant such action, the provincial government complied.[2] The legislators carved Lancaster out of western Chester in 1729; York and Cumberland out of western Lancaster in 1749 and 1750; Berks out of northwestern Philadelphia, and Northhampton out of northwestern Bucks, in 1752.

The most important symbol of county government was the courthouse, and it was because of the benefits bestowed by proximity to that institution that individuals petitioned for new counties. Both the establishment of firm title to real estate and the purchase or sale of real property required visits to the county office of the recorder of deeds; settlement of estates often necessitated prolonged dealings with the orphan's court; legal battles over real estate rights, suits for debt, and claims for damages constantly brought people to the county seat to file pleadings and affadavits with the prothonotary and eventually to appear before the court of common pleas. Citizen involvement in the process of law enforcement, whether it be in the apprehension, arrest, and prosecution of alleged criminals or as the victim of some crime, required trips to the jail or attendance at the court of quarter sessions. When law enforcement, civil suits, and the ordering of personal affairs entailed long absences and costly trips, "the benefit of many good and wholesome laws [was] almost, if not entirely lost."[3] The cost of compliance and the difficulties of enforcement encouraged confusion and license rather than regularity and order.

Along with the courthouse and the jail went the personnel that gave substance to the institutions of county government. With the establishment of a new county, backcounty inhabitants gained a full complement of judicial and administrative officials for an area that had formerly been only a section—and often a rather neglected section —of an already established county. At the creation of each new county, the governor appointed a clerk of courts, prothonotary, register of wills, and recorder of deeds to keep the records of all court business in the county and filled up a commission of the peace with a sufficient number of justices of the peace to serve the needs of local residents.[4]

As members of the three county courts, justices of the peace presided over criminal trials or civil litigation and performed various administrative duties during the four annual sittings of these courts. Most of their concerns as members of the orphan's court—settling intestate estates by appointing administrators, auditing accounts, dividing real estate, investing money for minors, appointing guardians—fell into the latter category, as did much of their work in the court of quarter sessions. The difference, of course, was that while estate settlements were private matters, the administrative tasks tended to by the quarter sessions court were of public concern. The quarter sessions bench, often sitting in consideration of some issue raised by the grand jury or after receiving a petition from interested parties, might appoint a committee to lay out a new road, decide on the site of a new bridge, regulate the number and operation of taverns, or create a new township.[5]

In addition to their duties as members of the regular county courts, justices of the peace performed important judicial and administrative functions, singly or with a fellow judge.[6] Single justices had summary jurisdiction over a wide range of causes, including offenses against the provincial game laws, the liquor sales regulations laws, and the flour inspection laws, and over actions for debt that did not exceed five pounds.[7] Any two justices had similar jurisdiction over offenses such as petty larceny and failure to comply with the provincial excise law.[8] At the same time they performed singly or in pairs important administrative functions such as assigning servants, authorizing overseers of the poor to levy township poor taxes, judging claims for bounties on predators, and performing marriage ceremonies.[9] The justices of the peace performed such a variety of important functions that it is readily apparent why backcountry residents wanted their own county unit with an appropriate number of judicial appointments.

Two other county officials who worked closely with the magistrates in the administration of justice were the coroner and sheriff. The coroner's principal function was to determine by inquest the circumstances of any death not obviously due to natural causes, but he was also empowered to relieve the sheriff of the trouble of executing some types of warrants.[10] Undoubtedly, the sheriff needed assistance of this kind on occasion, for his responsibilities were onerous. He attended all court sessions and was responsible for serving the legal instruments and executing the judgments of those courts; he was chief law enforcement officer, responsible for searching out violations of the law, arresting offenders, and maintaining the county prisoners.[11] Because of his crucial role administering and upholding the law, the sheriff was the most important single local official. With the creation of new counties he became much more accessible to backcountry residents.

Despite the rather limited aims of government in the eighteenth century, the performance of some public services did require a county revenue. The court buildings, prison, and workhouse had to be kept in good repair; bridges and causeways had to be built and kept serviceable; and the money for bounties on foxes, wolves, and other pests had to be appropriated. The officers who were responsible for performing these tasks and for raising the money to finance such activities were the three county commissioners and the six county assessors. These nine men were to meet each fall and estimate the public needs of the county for the next year. Once this had been done and the township constables had returned assessment lists of local residents to the assessors, they, alone, were to decide what the assessment rates should be and to appoint collectors for each county district to collect the tax. The commissioners were responsible for setting the tax rate and for hearing any appeals by residents against their tax, for seeing that the collectors performed their tasks, and for authorizing the expenditure of the sums collected.

While Philadelphia's assessors and commissioners respected the division of power that separated their responsibilities, those in the newer county of Lancaster often met together, with the assessors having some voice in determining what public works projects should be given priority. Where this blurring of distinction between the responsibilities of assessor and commissioner did take place, however, the operation of county government was not significantly affected. The commissioners and assessors were chosen by the same electorate and they had the same end in view—the maintenance and extension of county facilities and the efficient management of tax revenues.[12]

The procedure for laying and collecting county taxes, providing as it did for the township constables to draw up assessment lists and for tax collectors to be responsible for specific districts, suggests one important shortcoming of county government: the county was simply too vast to function as a basic unit of administration. Thus, the township continued to be useful as a fundamental administrative unit even after the county had gained its preeminence in local affairs. The most important township officials were the constable, the supervisor of the highways, and the overseer of the poor, all of whom were appointed by the court of quarter sessions. The constable was the sheriff's deputy, and his duties included drawing up assessment lists, aiding the tax collectors, enforcing laws, preserving the peace, arresting lawbreakers, and serving warrants and other legal papers; the supervisor of the highways was in charge of opening roads and maintaining them, for which purpose he could demand two days' labor per year from local residents; the two overseers of the poor were responsible for levying township poor taxes, providing relief for the poor and "impotent" who had established township residence, and warning off vagrants whose place of abode was outside the township boundaries. These were the officials who actually implemented many of the decisions county officials made on both public and private matters.[13]

In addition to the county and township, there was one other unit of local government in Pennsylvania that deserves note. Philadelphia, Chester, Bristol, and Lancaster were market towns with their own corporate identity; as such, they were able to exercise some legislative, administrative, and judicial control over their inhabitants. The one characteristic that they held in common was that officials in each town could issue ordinances to regulate economic affairs, maintain order, provide for public safety and welfare, and manage corporate property.[14] Beyond that their structure and powers varied considerably.

Philadelphia, the most important of the four, had its charter modeled after the closed English boroughs.[15] The members of the Philadelphia Corporation—the common councilmen, aldermen, mayor, and recorder—conducted all of the corporate business, determined if any new men should be recruited as common councilmen, and who among themselves should serve as aldermen and mayor during the forthcoming year.[16] But the officers of the Philadelphia Corporation were not as insulated as their system of closed elections might imply. Philadelphia was the colony's metropolis, and the corporation members were men of affairs, involved in business, politics, and a variety of social activities that were provincial in scope.[17] The mayor and aldermen automatically became justices of the peace in the mayor's court—an institution peculiar to Philadelphia—which, in its capacity as a quarter sessions court, attracted most of the legal business that fell within its jurisdiction from Philadelphia County and City.[18] Thus, the city officials were caught up in provincial affairs as the members of no other corporation could possibly be.

One apparent advantage that the Philadelphia Corporation enjoyed over the other three boroughs was the right to tax its inhabitants. In 1712 the Assembly made provision for six assessors, to be elected by all city residents qualified to vote in provincial elections. These officials were to levy taxes for the support of city government. Although the assessors were responsible for raising revenue, the members of the mayor's court had sole control over the appropriation of it. This division of authority between popularly elected and corporation officials proved to be virtually unworkable, and the corporation came to rely almost wholly on fines, forfeitures, revenue from corporation property, and credit from the provincial government to finance its various projects. Because of the form in which it was granted, the right to tax failed to bring the kind of vitality to corporation affairs that it seemed to promise.[19]

The other three Pennsylvania corporations—Bristol, Chester, and Lancaster—had their own peculiarities, but they were similar in that their situation, on virtually every count, was different from Philadelphia. Bristol and Chester were situated in the shadows of the metropolis and were proportionately diminished in stature; Lancaster, although the most important urban center in the hinterland through 1755, was out of the mainflow of provincial affairs simply because it was a backcountry town. Despite the fact that Chester and Lancaster were county seats,[20] corporate affairs were only peripheral to and somewhat detached from the framework of county politics and administration. None of the towns had their own courts, and despite the advantages that Chester and Lancaster gained by having their chief burgesses automatically commissioned justices of the peace, and by having the sheriff and other major officials either urban residents or situated close by, town affairs were only one small part of county business. Whereas in Philadelphia the mayor's court absorbed county affairs, county business overshadowed urban concerns in the outlying areas. Nor did the corporations enjoy the right of self-taxation that the metropolis did. Lancaster, for example, was restricted to the modest income the corporation could derive from fines, forfeitures and the management of corporate property. Apparently, Bristol did raise town levies even though it did not have the legal right to do so, but even a much more far-reaching program of public improvements than the town could finance would not have restored vitality to this urban center, which, like Chester, was overshadowed by Philadelphia and had "been long at a standstill."[21]

The one apparent advantage that the three small towns did enjoy over Philadelphia was that corporate affairs were open rather than closed. Town officials were elected by all town residents who could meet a very liberal property requirement and who wished to vote, and the borough charters provided for town meetings to ratify proposed ordinances. In the case of Chester and Bristol, however, town meetings were never convened, and in Lancaster they quickly died out from want of interest. Despite their opportunities to influence borough affairs, it is not at all clear that the residents of Bristol, Chester, and Lancaster stirred themselves enough to ensure more responsive town government than the citizens of Philadelphia gained from the members of that city's closed corporation.[22]

§

Among the proprietary prerogatives was the right to choose the clerk of courts, prothonotary, recorder of deeds, and register of wills for each county. These offices placed the incumbent at the very center of county affairs, his role as mediator between proprietary officials and county notables unquestioned, his knowledge of the local land market and the maneuverings of businessmen unequaled. Because of the status, the economic opportunities, and the certain income from fees these offices conferred, they were widely coveted. Consequently, when an appointment came up the governor's commission went to a man with connections whose claims on the proprietors were at least as strong as their expectations of his loyalty. In Philadelphia County the offices were usually split up among contending candidates: James Hamilton succeeded his father Andrew as prothonotary in 1733; Provincial Councillor Thomas Hopkinson followed in the footsteps of Councillor Charles Read when he became clerk of courts in 1737; merchant William Plumsted became register of wills in 1745 after merchant Peter Evans had held the post for thirty-three years. In the counties other than Philadelphia, proprietary practice was markedly different: one man usually held the four posts. From the early 1720s through the 1750s Joseph Parker of Darby filled the four Chester County offices that David Lloyd's influence had secured for him; from the establishment of Lancaster in 1729 until his death in 1743, Samuel Blunston held the four offices in that county. Thereafter, Thomas Cookson and Edward Shippen controlled the posts. Particularly in the outlying counties, then, the chief court officials were key proprietary appointments that made the influential and sometimes wealthy man even more so.[23]

In addition to the four county clerkships, the office of justice of the peace was the one major source of patronage the governor had at his disposal. Commentators have often argued that Thomas Penn and his chief executives tried to build up a political alliance in the counties on the strength of their judicial appointments. The evidence usually cited in support of this contention is the suggestion of Richard Peters, as secretary of the Land Office, to John Penn in October 1741 that the proprietors should try to strengthen the executive's position through judicious magisterial appointments, and the subsequent changes that Thomas Penn authorized in the new justice of the peace commissions that were issued in May 1741.[24] Thomas Penn, on the other hand, specifically denied using the commission for political ends. He wrote to John that the new May 1741 commission of the peace had "as many [Quakers] in [it] . . . as [had] been struck out only [I] have taken good men and left out the bad ones."[25] The truth, in this case, lies somewhere in between. In Lancaster County Penn had left out four Quakers, three of whom were popular political leaders, and had apparently added no others; in Chester he had replaced three Quakers with three other Quakers and added five non-Quakers; in Philadelphia and Bucks the number of Quakers may have been slightly reduced, but the changes were not large enough to alter, significantly, the composition of the commission. After Penn left the colony in August 1741, however, there were no other wholesale alterations in the composition of the commission through 1755. The long-range trend in Philadelphia and Lancaster was to reduce the number of Quaker justices, but this was a natural enough phenomenon, given the strength of the executive-proprietary supporters in Philadelphia and the small number of Quakers in Lancaster County. In Chester County there were as many Quaker justices in the 1750s as there had been twenty-five years earlier.[26]

There is one other trend in appointments of justices of the peace that might be used to demonstrate that the magistracy was increasingly composed of political appointments; the number of justices of the peace who also served as assemblymen dropped significantly over the years 1729-55.[27] It is possible that this change reflected a tendency on the part of justices to be out of sympathy with popular politicians, particularly in Philadelphia County,[28] and it undoubtedly owed something to the popular distrust of the magistracy that followed the 1740-42 period of political contention; but to relate this development solely to conscious political partisanship and a more polarized political atmosphere would certainly be wrong. An important and obvious reason for the increasing reluctance of justices of the peace to become directly involved in popular politics was that the burdens of their office were steadily increasing as the population grew and court business expanded. Specialization, both in politics and the law, was a natural outcome of economic expansion and demographic growth.

Despite Thomas Penn's changes in the 1741 justices' commission and the long-run drift of magisterial appointments away from Quaker politicians, there is no evidence that either he or his governors made a concerted effort to build a political power base in the counties by using the office of justice of the peace strictly as a political reward. One of the accepted qualifications for the office was that appointees should be "well affected to his Honor's person and government," but in fact this stipulation meant no more than that they should not be outspokenly hostile to the executive.[29] The governor himself could not possibly know how well disposed various residents of the outlying areas were towards executive and proprietary. Consequently, he depended on the existing justices and other leading county residents to inform him of men who would make suitable magistrates. In answering Richard Peter's request for recommendations for a magisterial appointment for East Nottingham, Presbyterian minister Samuel Finley replied with the words of most country advisers. He suggested the names of both a Presbyterian and a Quaker, the former "a man of strong judgement, firm purpose, strict justice and impartiality," the latter "a good natured, candid, sensible man." Finley went on to add, "my great desire [is] to have men of wisdom, probity and resolution employed, who [know] what [becomes] their place and how to maintain the due dignity of it by the proper exercise of authority. If we have such I care not what party they belong to."[30]

Equally revealing was the request of the eleven Chester County justices that Henry Pierce and John Crosby be stripped of their commissions for failure to attend court sessions and that Benjamin Fred and David Llewelyn, Jr., be appointed in their stead; they recommended the latter two as "men of good sense" and "plentiful estates."[31] There would always be freeholders who would deny that Pennsylvania's justices met the first requirement,[32] but certainly they could not deny that they fulfilled the latter. Of the forty-eight justices named in commissions between 1729 and 1755 in Chester County, 69 percent were in the top decile of the county's property holders, 11 percent at the 80 to 90 percent level, 14 percent at the 70 to 80 percent level, and the remaining 6 percent at the 60 to 70 percent level.[33] The justices of the peace in the outlying counties were always men of substance and, therefore, important members of the community in which they lived.

By all accounts the man who was nominated for the position of justice had to be successful, possess good judgment, and be of "good reputation among his neighbours."[34] What was unspoken was the acknowledgment that in order to be well regarded in the county an individual had to share some of the whiggish sentiments that dominated the countryside. Recognizing this, proprietary advisers such as Richard Peters accepted it and tried to turn it to advantage. Knowing that the office of magistrate was "very troublesome and expose[d the incumbent] to frequent clamors and rude insults" the proprietary men tried to find respected and popular men such as Quakers John Smith and John Churchman who would accept the post.[35] The strategy of the proprietary was not to weaken the courts by completely filling the commissions up with acknowledged proprietary-executive supporters, but to shore them up with the appointment of popular men. For this reason most of Pennsylvania's magistrates were highly regarded individuals who, as products of a rural environment, shared many of the interests and opinions of their country neighbors.

Of course, there were always a few outspoken friends of the executive who held the commission. William Moore of Chester and Thomas Cookson of Lancaster committed themselves to the kinds of changes Pennsylvania's governors wanted to effect, and other justices of the peace, such as John Parry, and Job Ruston of Chester County, were sympathetic to the governor's calls for warlike preparations in the 1740s and 1750s.[36] With one or two exceptions, however, those predisposed to accept the governor's interpretations of public affairs did so quietly. Regard for position and popularity in the community outweighed whatever loyalties to the governor an appointment as justice of the peace was thought to entail.

Elections for sheriff, coroner, commissioner, and assessors took place at the county seat on October 1, the same day that freeholders voted for assemblymen. Those who were qualified to vote delivered to the election judges one ballot containing the names of those candidates whom they wished to have elected to the Assembly, a second ballot containing the names of two persons for the office of sheriff and two for coroner, and a third ballot with the names of one person for commissioner and six for assessors.[37] In the case of sheriff and coroner, the presiding officer tabulated the returns and immediately sent them to the governor, for the chief executive had the power to choose one of the two top vote getters for each position. Although he usually picked the candidate with the highest number of votes, on occasion he did commission the second.[38] In the case of the third ballot, the governor had no option to exercise. The candidate for commissioner and the six for assessor who had received the greatest number of votes were elected and assumed their responsibilities at the next meeting of the Board of County Commissioners.[39]

Unique officeholding patterns existed for all four of these county offices. Once a sheriff had been elected and commissioned he was almost always returned to the post for the next two years. Even though after 1725 there were annual elections for the position, Pennsylvanians perpetuated a tradition, based on their Charter of Privileges, that the sheriff's term should extend over three years. Knowing and accepting this practice, legislators guarded against the possibility of one individual monopolizing this very important position by specifically prohibiting anyone from serving two consecutive three-year terms. This restriction was universally acknowledged, and where, as in Chester and Lancaster counties, an individual served more than one time, he did so only after waiting out the three-year term of another.[40]

To some degree, coroners served in a pattern similar to sheriffs. Generally, in Chester and Lancaster they were reelected twice, but there were significant exceptions. In Lancaster, about half the incumbents served for either one or two years, while in Philadelphia a very different tendency occurred. There long service was the norm; Owen Owen was reelected from 1729 to 1741 and Henry Pratt succeeded him for eight consecutive years.[41]

The conditions of tenure for county commissioners were much more clearly specified. The three county commissioners were to be elected for three-year terms, one to be replaced each year, and they were barred from succeeding themselves. Unlike the sheriff's office, however, the last condition was not invariably honored; in Chester County three individuals spent six consecutive years as commissioners and one spent nine years. Occasionally, in all the counties except Lancaster, an individual would wait out only a year or two before standing again for reelection.[42]

There were no limitations on the number of successive one-year terms assessors could serve, and there were significant variations from county to county. The lowest turnover rate in the colony was in Philadelphia County. Of the 156 (6 annual openings times 26 years) openings between 1729 and 1755, only 34 percent were filled with men serving their first term, compared with 40 percent in Chester County, 45 percent in the city of Philadelphia, and 64 percent in Lancaster County. No matter the office, the turnover of officials in Lancaster County was invariably higher than in any of the old eastern areas.[43]

The fact that elections for these four county offices took place at the same time that the freemen chose their Assembly representatives indicates the close connection between provincial and county affairs. Counties were the basic political unit, and all elected officials, whether they be assemblymen, sheriffs, or commissioners, were products of the same political milieu. The informal talks that preceded elections concerned candidates for all county posts. Consequently, the amount of scope for conciliation among different interests was very broad. At any time those disappointed of inclusion in the Assembly ticket might be touted as a candidate for assessor, a position that could in turn lead to eventual service as county commissioner or assemblyman. All of the county positions were desirable, status-conferring offices, for they carried important powers, and election denoted that a candidate had been judged worthy of the community's confidence. In Chester County, John Owen and John Parry served as assemblymen, then sheriff and, when ineligible for sheriff, again as assemblymen. John Davis jumped from the Assembly onto the Board of County Commissioners and back to the Assembly.

Given the common county base of all these electoral offices, it is not surprising that many of the same considerations that affected the choice of assemblymen were also important in the selection of other officials. The major political division that occurred on the provincial level of politics—the split between supporters of the assemblymen and executive or proprietary—most clearly affected elections for the office of sheriff. When in 1741 the governor and Assembly were deadlocked in a bitter dispute, Christopher Saur warned voters not only to return the old assemblymen but, because "the sheriff's office is of great impor-tance in this province and the very chief weight whereby all is moved and turned in the courts, let us be careful in this also."[44] In fact, it was the contest between John Hyatt, a man who sympathized with the advocates of defense in Philadelphia, and Mordecai Lloyd, a member of one of the old Quaker families, for the position of sheriff that "drew the greatest numbers to the [Philadelphia County] election" of that year.[45] Even in quieter times one of the important qualifications for a prospective sheriff in the outlying counties was a "good inclination to select a few persons that can oppose a certain interest if occasion shall require."[46] This consideration referred to the sheriff's function of summoning jurors to sit on cases in which the proprietary sued a squatter, a delinquent debtor, or some other unfortunate.[47] Concern about the candidate's regard for governor and proprietor was most obvious in the case of elections for sheriff, but it was often a factor in the selection of other officeholders as well.[48]

Other considerations that electors entertained before choosing the county officers were the obvious ones: a man's ability, judgment, family, religious views, estate, and experience.[49] Ability and judgment are, of course, impossible to judge on this level, but there is no evidence to indicate that county officials were particularly inept and a good deal to the contrary. It is readily apparent that many of the commissioners and assessors for Bucks, Chester, and Philadelphia were members of old, well-established families. In the old counties, but not in Lancaster, most of the officials were Quakers. In Chester, for example, eighteen of the twenty-one county commissioners elected between 1729 and 1754 were Quakers, ten of whom attended the Philadelphia Yearly Meeting and fifteen the Chester Quarterly Meeting at various times.[50] On the question of wealth, 78 percent of the county commissioners, assessors, and sheriffs in Chester County were in the top 20 percent of the county's property holders.[51] Like the assemblymen, virtually all had performed public service at the township level as overseer of the poor, supervisor of roads, or constable.

Although these general considerations applied to all the county offices, the nature of the office sometimes dictated other, more specific conditions. The sheriff had to reside somewhere near the county seat, be knowledgeable in the law, and feel free to execute all the functions of his office, something that not all Quakers could do with a clear conscience. It was desirable, too, that coroners reside in or near the county seat, and that they appear to have the qualifications and willingness to perform legal functions. These were more important considerations than those of wealth and education. County commissioners almost always came from the northeastern part of Chester, where the oldest, richest, and most influential residents lived.[52] Assessors were somewhat more evenly distributed, for they were to represent the various parts of the county. Although some were virtually disqualified because of their geographical location, voters did recognize that a good assessor was a natural candidate for county commissioner. In Philadelphia County nineteen of the twenty-three commissioners who served between 1729 and 1755 had gained experience as a county or city assessor; in Chester sixteen of twenty-one, and in Lancaster eight of fourteen, commissioners who held office between 1741 and 1755 had prior experience as assessor. No other office in Pennsylvania was so clearly a prerequisite to another as assessor was to county commissioner.

Although assemblymen, sheriffs, coroners, commissioners, and assessors were chosen concurrently, it was in the election of sheriff rather than in contests for other offices that small but significant changes in election behavior began to take place in the 1740s and 1750s. Election-day competition certainly took place among various interests over the filling of Assembly seats and the office of commissioner, but, with the exception of the two years 1740 and 1742, the contest for sheriff produced the greatest conflict in Philadelphia County.[53] Disappointed and angered by the governor's failure to choose him as sheriff, despite the fact that he had polled 804 votes to John Hyatt's 765 in the hotly contested election of 1741,[54] Mordecai Lloyd took the unprecedented step of inserting an advertisement in the *Gazette* six weeks before the 1744 election, thanking freeholders for their past support, announcing his intention to run again, and requesting their "interest."[55] One week later his opponent, Nicholas Scull, replied that "though it [had] not till [that] time been customary to request . . . votes in print, yet the method being . . . introduced" he, too, requested the citizens' votes.[56] Similar advertisements appeared at the expected three-year intervals in 1747 and 1750 and then in 1751 through 1754.[57] By the 1750s this practice had begun to spread in two different ways. In Philadelphia candidates for coroner as well as sheriff began to solicit votes in the *Gazette,* and men who were running for sheriff outside of Philadelphia County, in Chester and the three lower counties, did likewise.[58] What this development demonstrated was that candidates and members of the electorate were prepared to accept overt solicitation of a kind never before practiced. It represented a movement away from the informal process of influence mobilization and private accommodation toward a more forthright acceptance of direct appeals to the electorate.[59] At this point the change was not large, and it had not visibly altered the overall tone of election behavior, but it was harbinger of things to come.

Every spring, at the first sitting of each county court of quarter sessions, the presiding judges were to appoint those who would serve as township constables, overseers of the poor, and supervisors of the roads in the coming year. By law, the justices of the peace had the right to make these appointments, and apparently they exercised that right; for in Chester County, at least, there is a record of those appointments.[60] But by 1740 there were forty-nine townships in Chester alone, and to fulfill their responsibilities the justices in attendance had to name between two hundred and two hundred fifty local officeholders.[61] The obvious question is, How did they know whom to appoint?

James Logan provided a clue to the actual procedure of choosing local officers when in writing to the three Penn brothers he mentioned that township constables as well as county sheriffs were elected.[62] Although slightly misleading, Logan's statement is largely borne out by the surviving records of town meetings in the township of East Caln. Each year, three to ten days before the March sitting of quarter sessions, the town decided on a list of names of potential officeholders to be forwarded to the justices. Usually such a list consisted of two nominees for constable, two for supervisor, and four for overseers, and it was from this list that the justices chose the one constable, one supervisor, and two overseers that were to serve East Caln for the coming year.[63] The justices, then, had the right to appoint, but they did so from a list of alternatives probably decided on by vote but openly drawn up, at least, at a meeting of the township residents.

There are additional bits of tantalizing evidence that the township was more than a handy unit of administration in which local officers were solely accountable to outside authority. Township meetings were regularly held in Thornbury, East Bradford, and Goshen, as well as East Caln, and at these gatherings residents authorized payments for poor relief, discussed how their obligations to the poor could best be fulfilled, and divided up responsiblity for the upkeep of township roads.[64] In some counties, then—and it may have been only in the old Quaker areas of eastern Pennsylvania—the local officials were only nominally appointed by the justices of the peace, for they were chosen by, and worked largely under the direction of, their fellow "townsmen." But overall three things kept the township from becoming the vital social and political unit it might have become: the concentration of local taxing authority in county officials' hands; the lack of congruence between township boundaries and meeting, congregation, or parish membership; and the casual development of neighborhoods.

No matter the exact method of appointment, or the active interest of local residents in the officeholder's performance, service in such offices was an obligation rather than an honor. This was apparent from the turnover rate among officials.[65] Between 1726 and 1755, 71 percent of the annual appointments as constable, overseer, and supervisor in ten sample townships went to men who had seen no prior service in any of the three offices.[66] In townships where there was a good deal of residential stability, where the number of taxables was relatively small, and where there were strong Quaker meetings, the number of men who served two or three years as a township officer tended to be slightly higher than average. The usual pattern in the case of repeaters was for them to serve in one office and then in a different one or in different ones within the next three to eight years. Occasionally, an individual would serve in one office and follow it immediately with a second term in a different office; less frequently, one man, or in the case of overseers two men, might succeed themselves, but never for more than one additonal year; even more rare was the case of the individual who on the recommendation of the town meeting would serve two, or possibly all three, of the positions simultaneously. But again, never for more than a year.

Successive or multiple appointments, however, were clearly the exception; rotation in office was the rule. Rich or poor, old family member or recent resident, the town meeting made sure that every reasonably responsible man took his turn. If the consensus was that someone had been avoiding service the meeting would nominate him for two posts, aware that if the justices passed over him for one post they would likely choose him for the second. Nor were there marked distinctions between the appointees to the three offices; the "better sort" in a given township sometimes successfully avoided serving as constable by becoming overseer or supervisor instead, but this was only a slight tendency, and there were myriad exceptions. In large measure, the story of township officeholding in Pennsylvania is the story of the high turnover rate of incumbents; it is difficult to imagine eighteenth-century officeholding patterns that could have been more equalitarian.

The only other noteworthy group of officeholders were those chosen by qualified electors in the four corporation towns. As always Philadelphia was a special case, for not only was the corporation closed but city officials were intimately involved with provincial politics. Throughout the 1730s a few popular Quaker politicians and the Presbyterians and Anglicans with whom they cooperated worked together in their roles as common councilmen and aldermen.[67] During the 1740–42 provincial political crisis, however, those who supported the governor against the assemblymen and who constituted a majority of the common councilmen refused to admit any but fellow sympathizers to the corporation and to elect any of the popular group then in the common council to the office of alderman or mayor.[68] Thereafter, the corporation was obviously dominated by men who were sympathetic to the idea of a stronger executive, defense preparations, and the measures that identified them as friends of the proprietary and governor. While their wealth, social attitudes, and life style were not much different from their Quaker counterparts, corporation officials thus differed from successful county politicians in that they were usually executive supporters rather than allies of the assemblymen, and churchmen rather than sectarians.[69]

While the character of the personnel in the Philadelphia Corporation was largely determined by the circumstances of provincial politics, that of the other corporations did not depend upon these configurations. Town politics in Lancaster, Chester, and Bristol were clearly divorced from the issues and consequent patterns of provincial and county affairs, a point demonstrated most obviously by Lancaster. There Germans were included among town officials from the moment of its incorporation in 1742, and subsequently they held about one-half of the local offices. Moreover, town office often harnessed together men who in provincial affairs were bound to be antagonists. Thomas Cookson, for example, was chief burgess of Lancaster for six of the town's first seven years, yet because he was an avowed friend and agent of the proprietary he could never have gained elected county office. Adam Simon Kuhn, the most eminent German in the town and the man who succeeded Cookson as chief burgess, had similar political leanings, and this, if not his German origins, would have barred him from county affairs. But along with these men Lancaster benefited from the talents of others—men like Peter Worral, Calvin Cooper, and James Webb—who were influential Quakers and popular politicians. The same situation obtained in Bristol, where John Hall, a Quaker— sometime sheriff, assemblyman, and county commissioner—held the post of chief burgess for sixteen years and worked along, in corporate affairs, with churchman Abraham Denormandie, whose political sympathies lay with proprietor and governor.[70]

The most significant feature of the three Pennsylvania corporations, then, was the degree to which town affairs took place in a uniquely restricted political arena. Concerns were local, the powers of the corporations were relatively weak, and the frame of reference for borough politics was the town itself. The inability to tax, and the clear separation of town from county functions, insulated urban affairs from the kinds of divisions that rent government at higher levels. Among residents of the towns, certainly all applauded economic growth, and what divisions appeared were occasioned by local ordinances that bore no relationship to the larger issues of provincial and county politics. Within the confines of the urban arena, voters undoubtedly looked for the same general qualities that they valued in county affairs—proven ability, good judgment, a substantial stake in the town's future, and both the free time and the desire to serve the best interests of the town. But once town leaders had emerged and proven their capability, they were reelected, time after time, for residents were willing to trust authority in their hands.[71]

§

By 1726 the basic governmental institutions in Pennsylvania were well established, and a solid framework of laws and legal procedures had long been in operation. Residents had cooperated to support order-creating agencies, they had welcomed the introduction of administrative and judicial practices that provided certainty and regularity, and they had staked out the general limits of acceptable social behavior.[72] Given the solid existence of governmental institutions—or, for those who moved to the Pennsylvania backcountry, the expectation of establishing those institutions—and the existence of acceptable statutory guidelines for governmental officers, the chief concerns of local officials became those of enforcement and of recommending what adjustments were necessary to further the purposes of the government.

One of the basic purposes of government was to provide protection for person and property, and trying individuals who transgressed those rights occupied much of the time of the judges who sat on the court of quarter sessions.[73] Security of life and property was an essential prerequisite for the kind of self-determination provincial residents desired, and both law enforcement agents and members of the judiciary were determined to offer provincial residents the protection they expected. Security too was the purpose of other pieces of legislation that did not deal with acts of violence or larceny. Regulations governing the construction of bakers' and coopers' shops in Philadelphia, prohibiting the firing of chimneys in the city, and outlawing the firing of guns and the lighting of fireworks in urban areas were framed to protect urban dwellers and their property.[74] In pursuing such ends the assemblymen were assisted by county administrators who enforced their laws and by borough officials who evinced similar concerns. Philadelphia councilmen passed ordinances to regulate the public activities of Negro and white servants and appointed larger numbers of regulators to control street traffic; Lancaster officials ordered an end to horse racing and selling spiritous drinks in the streets and firing guns in the town.[75] Their overriding aim was to make the towns quiet, orderly centers in which inhabitants and visitors could safely mingle.

Attempts to encourage good order in places where people congregated were motivated by more than a mere concern for protection of persons and property. The aims of the borough officers included the creation of conditions that would best facilitate commercial exchange. Lancaster officials were determined to maintain free access to the town market; they ordered pigs and boys off the streets and prohibited the building of fences that might impede commerce.[76] The Philadelphia councilmen tried to keep wharves and market stalls in good repair, expanded the number of market stalls to meet growing needs, and tried to improve the conditions of city streets.[77] Out in the counties the thrust of much administrative work was directed towards complementary ends: commissioners paid bounties on pests in order to reduce their toll on the freeholders' crops and livestock and oversaw the construction and repair of bridges that allowed greater amounts of produce to go to market; justices of the peace laid out new roads that would ease commerce and saw to it that the township supervisor opened them up. Government officials provided these and other important services that allowed individuals to accumulate progressively larger hordes of worldly goods, while institutions like the court of common pleas and the orphan's court helped them to protect those goods and control their disposition.

There were, of course, the usual dissonant notes along with the harmonious chords of order. In deciding standards of acceptable behavior, legislators, judges, and juries designated certain behavior deviant and, therefore, antisocial or disorderly. Occasionally, citizens took it upon themselves to dispute a magistrate's decision as to where a road should be laid out, or the provincial legislators' decision that the building of fish dams across certain streams was unlawful. Together, acting as a mob, they forcibly prevented surveyors and constables from executing their orders.[78] Conflict arose, too, out of competition among government officials. In the 1730s the Philadelphia County commissioners were still wresting away from the quarter sessions justices their power to decide which of several needed public works projects deserved priority.[79] Such competition could have tragic consequences: while the overseers of the poor in two Philadelphia townships were arguing over whose charge he was, the distraught object of their charity, a poor blind man, hanged himself.[80] Conflict, contention, disorder, and irresponsibility were present as they always had been and always would be in Pennsylvania society, but by 1726 there existed strong local institutions, with officers who could play an effective role in resolving incipient social conflict, quieting disorder, reconciling their own differences, and acknowledging governmental responsibilities.

Despite the obvious concern among government officials for order and security, perhaps the most significant characteristic of public activities in Pennsylvania was their limited scope. In failing to demand a more active, innovative role on the part of their government officials, settlers were accepting eighteenth-century English standards of limited government,[81] while at the same time giving expression to their own predilection for individual freedom and economic opportunity insofar as it was consistent with good order and security. There was some recognition of the value of old European traditions that governed the marketplace in the interests of the community, and this recognition qualified to some extent the heavy reliance on economic laws and contractual relationships. In Lancaster, the town passed ordinances to maintain equitable conditions of competition and to protect the consumer; there were regulations against forestalling, huckstering from door to door, and selling before the appointed market hours; butchers were forbidden to "blow" meat (plumping it up by blowing air between the meat fibers); woodcutters were provided with a standard measure for a cord of wood; and bakers were instructed on the quality of bread.[82] Such regulations may not have been very effective and were certainly not very far reaching; but they did illustrate that in the early eighteenth century immigrants brought social ideas and a sense of responsibility that were not wholly those of "liberalism" and "privatism."[83]

Whatever the exact mix of social assumptions and aspirations in Pennsylvania, the overriding aim of local residents was to procure the maximum amount of economic and political self-determination consistent with that value structure. What symbolized this desire was the gradual growth in power of elected county officials at the expense of the appointed justices of the peace who in the early part of the century had completely dominated county affairs. Although the justices were very much men of the community, they were more susceptible to outside pressure than were elected officials. When county business came into the hands of elected officials—the commissioners and assessors—residents certainly felt that they were better able to control local affairs. With the securing of county government then, the greatest threats to self-determination were not of a kind that could be met successfully at the county level alone. The Baltimore claims to Pennsylvania land, proprietary lands policies, and the threats of expanding executive power were the most imminent dangers to continued enjoyment of peace, prosperity, freedom, and happiness, and they could be confronted effectively only at the provincial level of politics —as indeed they were.

CHAPTER 7

PARADIGMS OF PEACE
AND CONTENTION

§

The sources of political stability in colonial Pennsylvania did not lie only in the established patterns of political behavior and organization. They also lay in the social and political ideals that eighteenth-century colonists consciously shared, among the most highly regarded of which was political peace. Because of the high value placed on a harmonious body politic, contention was inhibited.

The desirability of political harmony notwithstanding, some forms of contention were recognized to be legitimate. While concord was the aim of all social relationships, colonials also held that liberty, happiness, and peace could be guaranteed only by a balanced constitution. Thus, as the events of the 1750s demonstrated, the defenders of executive and legislative powers occasionally felt they were compelled to disturb the public peace; the long-range goal of a harmonious, liberty-loving society justified temporary contention.

While contention between acknowledged spokesmen for each branch of the constitution was legitimate, divisions that did not fit this pattern were not. The most prevalent form of illegitimate contention was the kind of personal dispute that might spread to include friends and family. Such disagreements happened constantly and were deplored as evidence of self-interested behavior. But the real danger in these disputes was not what they were but what they might become. Should they grow and gain political expression they would become factional disputes, tearing the body politic apart as men madly pursued their selfish designs. Factionalism was a serious form of political deviation, and Pennsylvanians were acutely conscious of the illegitimacy of this type of behavior. Between 1726 and 1755 the only example of this kind of dispute was the Keithian factionalism of the late 1720s.

§

Most eighteenth-century Pennsylvanians agreed on the desirability of a peaceful, harmonious world. Despite their disagreements over the details of social organization, a combination of factors—psychological needs, the weight of tradition and authority, the decrees of a Christian God—prompted most men to accept the ideals of peace and concord. The only worthwhile relationships between men were peaceful ones, and, when individuals or groups of men did fall out, they recognized the obligation, no matter how hedged with conditions it might be, to resolve their differences. Their allegiance to this idea was constantly reflected in the value judgments that infused contemporary political rhetoric, didactic discussion, and private interchange.

A peaceful society in which social relationships were regular and harmonious was a powerful concept because, even considering the evil propensities of man, that goal never seemed to be entirely out of reach—at least not in Pennsylvania. God had molded nature in the "most perfect arrangement" according to the principles of order, harmony, peace, and concord—a model, "obvious to every capacity," for men to follow in their management of human affairs.[1] For those who rejected or were unacquainted with the concept of a mechanistic universe, the knowledge of an active intervening God, who proved his benevolence by providing for individual salvation, implied divine assistance in achieving ideal ends. The very powerful leavening influence of the antinomian sects—the Quakers, Moravians, and all the other German separatists—produced a widely shared, optimistic idealization of man's potential relationship with God and with his fellow man. Members of society had the opportunity and the obligation to live in harmony with their Maker, and one of the most important ways of demonstrating their success in doing so was to live in amity with their neighbors.[2]

Personal awareness of the ideals that God had provided for society was in itself a strong inducement for man to keep his affairs in good order. Equally important in nurturing long-range optimism about society was the certain knowledge that man, even without achieving any prior changes in the conformation of society or undergoing any structural alteration in his own character, had the capacity to become disinterested and thereby promote harmonious action.

The most basic general concept used to interpret society and man's activities in it was the idea of "interest." Fundamentally, a man's "interest" meant his concerns or, more appropriately, his stake in society. That stake included the whole complex of his affairs, such as his political rights, possessions, friendships, family, status, and expectations of future opportunity. Society was considered open, in the sense that men were expected to be ambitious, striving beings who would attempt first to construct and then to protect and expand their interests. Provided that individual efforts to attain personally satisfying goals did not deny, or threaten, the access of others to the same ends, such striving contributed directly to the public welfare, the general happiness, and the glorification of God. Thus, "disinterested" or virtuous actions were entirely consistent with the protection of one's "interests."

For example, in political affairs it was perfectly legitimate for men to convert the potential power inherent in their economic holdings, family relations, and status into actual power in the form of influence. Nor were individual happiness and the public welfare promoted only by individual actions. In the course of election management, individuals combined their "interests" to ensure the election of representatives whom they judged best fit to serve; residents of certain geographical areas united to pressure government into setting up new units of local administration; members of occupational groups such as coopers, tanners, merchants and ironworks owners cooperated among themselves to achieve ends that they judged consistent with their own best interests and the public welfare.

Viewed from the perspective of the individual's character rather than from the overall structure of society, the legitimacy of "interest" and actions based on its promotion were equally obvious. Motivation originated in man's affections, and good actions were a product of personal interest.[3] "Every passion, every view that men have is selfish in some degree, but when it does good to the public in its operation and consequence, it may be justly called disinterest in the usual meaning of that word."[4] The chief problem in society was to educate men to the fact that their true interest consisted of "mutual beneficence" and to teach them to value "serenity of . . . mind, the security of liberty and property, the good of . . . friends and relations, and the welfare of . . . posterity."[5] With the aid of reason, then, passions such as rashness, avarice, and revenge could be directed toward the general welfare, and thus become "so many virtues."[6] When zeal gave way to contemplation, affections that carried the taint of self-interest became true interests and men could unite together in harmony to pursue a common goal.[7]

Efforts to order society in an ideal way were bound to center on political affairs, for only in a country where life, liberty, and property were secure could man serve the ends of creation by properly glorifying God and living in happiness.[8] Consequently, the foremost concern of members of the body politic was to recruit politicians who could be trusted with the power that officeholding conferred. The man whom society universally agreed upon as a proper political leader was none other than the virtuous man—the man who had legitimate interests in society such as property, friends, and family, yet who could maintain a reasonable detachment and who had the capacity to discern what actions—public and private—promoted the general welfare. With such men as leaders, society could achieve order, harmony, and freedom that would produce human happiness and please God.[9]

Despite the power of God and the ability of man to channel his affections into virtuous acts, the goal of a happy, harmonious society was difficult to attain. Man's free will allowed him to choose short-term personal pleasure over long-term happiness, and passions of the moment were often so strong that they overpowered whatever cautions reason might add. At other times, hampered by the limiting perspective of their situation, men honestly mistook a self-interested consideration for the general good of society. In fact, the affections, which as the single source of human motivation were fundamentally amoral, had come to be a term of opprobrium, because they had so often appeared as vicious manifestations of self-interest. In contrast to the harmonious blending of reasoned statements about the overall nature of society, day-to-day experience produced many jarring and dissonant notes. Ambitious, domineering men who too often held the reins of political power periodically threatened the rights of others. Fortunately for all members of the body politic, there was an institutional check in colonial society that impeded the progress of those who wantonly followed the dictates of their passions; the provincial constitution provided basic protection for the rights and liberties of the freemen and thus was itself the single most important contribution to God's glory and the citizens' happiness.[10]

The one thing that Pennsylvania residents were most agreed upon was the superiority of their constitution. It sprang from the best possible root, the English prototype. Rather than slavishly duplicate that model, however, the Charter of Privileges and Frames of Government had met the pecularities of local conditions with appropriate innovations. Such adaptions as a unicameral legislature proved to be inordinately successful, for, in the years since the form of the constitution had been settled, Pennsylvania had visibly prospered. Obviously, the "great progress" that the province had made "within so small a compass of years, in improvements, wealth, trade and navigation" must be "principally and almost wholly owing to the excellency of the Constitution for it was an allowed maxim that whenever ability shone . . . people would naturally flock to bask in its beams."[11]

The "ability" of the Pennsylvania constitution to protect the liberties of private citizens, men believed, was entirely due to the fact that it was properly balanced. The powers of government had been carefully divided into executive and legislative functions, the former consisting of the administrative duties that gave substance to the magisterial powers and the latter consisting of the legislative rights that represented the individual's liberties. The purpose of each branch of government was to circumscribe the other and thus to duplicate in macrocosm the relationship between affections and reason that produced individual virtue; the legislature was to limit power to its proper uses, while the executive prevented liberty from degenerating into license. Because such a balance was institutionalized in the basic structure of provincial society, harmony could prevail in public affairs, despite the failure of individual men to govern their passions properly.[12]

§

Although contention was never desirable, there were times when it was not to be avoided. Because man's only hope for long-range happiness and harmonious living lay with a balanced constitution, he had to be prepared to fight for its preservation when the spokesmen for either branch of government threatened to encroach on the privileges of their counterparts. Of course, politicians hoped these times would be few and the strife would not be too intense, but mentally most were prepared for the test; they were well-acquainted with the regular episodes of conflict that took place between executive and legislature throughout the English colonies. Thus, beneath the formal structure of ideal values there developed a de facto acknowledgment of the legitimacy of that contention which arose from the defense of popular rights or magisterial authority.

Members of the Assembly most often gave expression to this logic because as popular politicians they had to seek the approbation of their constituents. In so doing they revealed a good deal about how they perceived executive-legislative conflict. Most importantly, they expected it to occur—not only because it had held such a prominent place in English history and in neighboring colonies but also because Pennsylvania was a proprietary colony in which the chief executive was accountable to a private interest. Although confidence in the proprietary family increased briefly in the late twenties and early thirties, Thomas Penn's policies soon convinced provincials that executive and proprietary designs continued to threaten their rights and privileges. But at the same time as they recognized their inability to discern exactly what plans the proprietary might follow, the popular politicians were confident of the outcome of the anticipated conflict.

They realized, as did their opponents, that, in the Assembly's control over the public purse and its own prorogation, they had much of the effective power of government in their hands. They knew, too, that the Penns would not push overly hard to achieve some political goal because the proprietors feared giving cause to the Crown for royal intervention. Finally, they felt that the world of contention between executive and legislature was a familiar world; their progenitors had fought the battles of that world and emerged unscathed. Moreover, these men had left sign posts to guide their heirs. What had once been won, Pennsylvania legislators were confident they could defend.

Executive supporters differed from their legislative counterparts in that they were neither so vocal in their claims nor so confident in the outcome. The tide of public affairs had steadily run against them. Despite these differences, however, they, too, grounded their claims in the logic of balance both when they responded to Assembly pressure for new powers and when they expected their own policies to draw public anger. The best example of how executive spokesmen appealed to the logic of balance and of how popular politicians reacted to that stance occurred in the 1750s, when Thomas Penn pushed for changes in proprietary policies in the appropriation of public revenue.

In order to set this instance of executive-legislative conflict in perspective, it is necessary to appreciate what a powerful legislative body the Pennsylvania Assembly had become. From its position in 1682 as the weaker lower house in a bicameral legislature with only the power of rejection or assent to proposed legislation, the Assembly had swiftly climbed to prominence in provincial affairs. By the late 1720s the upper house had been eliminated, assemblymen had established their right to declare their own adjournments, and the Assembly had gained a sizable revenue from the annual interest payments of those who held mortgages from the provincial Loan Office and from an excise tax on alcoholic beverages—a revenue it could appropriate on its own by simple legislative vote.[13]

When Thomas Penn came to his colony in 1732, he quickly realized that James Logan's earlier epistolary laments about the excessive amount of popular power were not exaggerated. Although Penn was conciliatory during the mid-thirties, he soon concluded that the proprietary had already conceded too much. The intransigence of delinquent debtors, the unwillingness of the elected sheriffs and local juries to act in the proprietary's favor, the annulment of Governor Keith's equity court, and above all the assemblymen's role in the heated 1740–41 disputes with Governor Thomas, convinced Penn that the balance of power had to be redressed. The chief executive needed both to resist further encroachment on the prerogative and to regain a portion of the lost influence. The establishment of a regular militia and the reconstruction of a proper equity court would increase the magistracy's ability to maintain order and uphold property rights, while the reestablishment of the executive's right to participate in the appropriation of all public funds would provide political power where it was most needed, in the Assembly.[14]

The spokesmen of the Assembly were not unaware of the difficulties a determined executive could cause, but the chancery court, militia, and a host of other changes might be pressed on the colony if the executive could gain the leverage that a veto power over all public expenditures would confer. And, although the Assembly enjoyed the sole right of appropriation of the income from the currency and excise acts, periodically the governor had to give his assent to that legislation.[15] The assemblymen first noted the importance of the governor's assent to the Loan Office and excise legislation in the late 1730s when, after Governor Patrick Gordon died in the summer of 1736, Pennsylvania was without a chief executive for two years. The excise tax, which from 1724 through 1733 had been renewed every three years, expired in January 1737, and the 1730–31 Currency Act, putting £69,000 in circulation specified that the currency should not be reemitted beyond October 1737.[16] For a year and a half there was no governor to sign the bills permitting continued collection of the excise taxes and allowing the Loan Office trustees to continue making new loans with the principal that existing mortgagors paid into their hands each year. Mainly because of this unfortunate conjunction of circumstances, the Assembly lengthened the term that the bills were to run. The 1738 Excise Bill was not to expire for five years, while the new £80,000 Currency Act, passed in 1739, specified that the money was to be reemitted continuously for the next ten years.

What Governor Gordon's death brought to attention, the 1740–42 political dispute magnified. Governor Thomas's ravings about the need to tether the Assembly were made more ominous by Thomas Penn's close identification with his chief executive and by the clear implications of his earlier success in using the threat of a veto power over currency legislation to pry quitrent compensation payments from the Assembly. The impact that these events had on the Assembly leaders was obvious. Biding their time carefully, the assemblymen waited until war with France made it unlikely that Governor Thomas would risk a break with them, and, after demonstrating their own cooperative spirit by voting £4,000 in mid-1745 to purchase supplies for the garrison occupying Louisbourg, they introduced a bill early in 1746 extending the reemission period of the £80,000 from the three remaining years to ten years. A few months later, when the British requested Pennsylvania troops to participate in an expedition against Canada, the excise was brought into line. Despite the fact that it, too, having been renewed in 1744, did not expire until 1749, the Assembly funded a £5,000 grant to the king's use on an excise extension that ran until 1756. In the only other legislation that directly affected the operation of the Loan Office, the Assembly affected a complementary change. After dutifully limiting the authority of the trustees who managed the office to four-year periods, the 1748–49 act renewed that authority for the customary time "and thence" until the Assembly made new nominations. Here was another attempt to remove all aspects of currency management from the executive's reach.[17]

With the existing currency and excise legislation in effect until 1756, there seemed no hope that the executive could cause trouble until that date. But with the expansion of the Pennsylvania economy in the 1740s, the £80,000 put into circulation by the 1739 act soon proved inadequate.[18] By the late forties even Thomas Penn agreed that the amount of currency should be increased by £20,000. At the same time, however, he warned the assemblymen not to draw attention to Pennsylvania by pushing such legislation, for there was a movement afoot in English mercantile circles to prohibit paper money as legal tender in the colonies.[19] When, in 1751, news that Parliament had responded to that merchant lobby by passing the restrictive Currency Act, but that it did not apply to Pennsylvania, the assemblymen concluded that there was no good reason for further restraint; in March 1752 the legislature drew up a bill adding £40,000 to the provincial currency.[20]

Knowing that Penn had designated joint executive-legislative appropriation of all revenue as the "great cause of all," Governor James Hamilton put off the issue on grounds that coming so soon after the 1751 Currency Act it might goad the British into extending those restrictions to Pennsylvania, and then wrote to Penn for explicit instructions.[21] By way of reply, Penn ordered Hamilton to limit the amount of new currency to £20,000 and to insist on joint appropriation of all revenue raised by the Act.[22] Shortly thereafter, he added an informal corollary that was to carry the weight of a full instruction: any continuation of the excise duties was to be subject to the same condition.[23]

On the opening of the January 1753 session, the assemblymen proceeded to frame a bill for the emission of £20,000 in new currency and the reemission of the old. Hamilton sounded out Chief Justice William Allen and Attorney General Tench Francis for their response to the proprietary instructions; both reacted with horror. Concluding that if these two would give no aid, none could be had, Hamilton submitted his resignation. At the same time both he and Richard Peters fired off letters to Penn, pleading their isolation and raising the specter of a total breakdown of government. With no support from his placemen, and thinking that the new bill provided only for an addition to and not a complete reemission of all Pennsylvania's currency, a reluctant Thomas Penn released Hamilton from his May 20, 1752, instruction.[24]

The Assembly was again pressing with the currency bill during its August sitting when Hamilton received Penn's note. But still the £20,000 bill did not pass. Hamilton felt that his proprietary instructions and a royal order of 1740 required that he assent only to that currency legislation which contained a clause suspending its operation until the crown had reviewed the act. Faced with Hamilton's insistence on the inclusion of a suspending clause, and viewing this demand as an attack on its rights, the Assembly adjourned in disgust. Two months later, when Penn realized that the Assembly wanted to use the £20,000 bill to reemit all of Pennsylvania's currency he, too, dug in his heels. In an additional instruction of November 1, 1753, he ordered Hamilton to hold out for joint executive-legislative appropriation of the proceeds of any new currency bill.[25]

Because it signified the proprietary determination to curtail the Assembly's power over provincial revenue, this instruction was to be of general importance during the following two years, but it played no direct part in the contention between the executive and the legislature. When the Assembly drew up a new £40,000 bill in February, Hamilton did not reveal Thomas Penn's additional instruction. He simply gave the bill an outright veto and suggested that, as the province was facing an emergency, he would waive a suspending clause if the Assembly would grant money to the king's use and sink it immediately.[26]

The emergency was that the French had occupied the Ohio country and that the British government had authorized any of the colonies whose territory they invaded to repel the enemy by force. Hamilton's initial request for military preparations to repel the French invaders was given further urgency when the Virginia forces, which the Assembly had failed to strengthen with Pennsylvanian aid, were expelled from the forks of the Ohio by a superior French force. In response to this news, the assemblymen did draw up a bill appropriating £10,000 to the king's use. They funded the grant, however, on a ten year extension of the excise, a tax that would yield approximately £30,000 revenue. Still bound by his verbal acknowledgment of Penn's July 13, 1752, informal instruction not to extend the excise without joint appropriation of the revenue, and knowing that Penn's additional instruction of November 1, 1753, had reaffirmed his determination not to have any currency bill that did not contain a similar proviso, Hamilton tried to accept the appropriation for defense on terms that would be consistent with the proprietary instructions but that would not reveal their substance. He amended the Assembly's act by shortening the duration of the excise tax, thereby participating fully in the appropriation of all the revenue that the excise would raise.[27]

In taking this tack, Hamilton set the course that the executive was to follow for the next two years. When Robert Hunter Morris succeeded Hamilton in October 1754, Penn informed him fully of the expedient Hamilton had devised—to maintain, yet to avoid direct disclosure of, the proprietary instructions. Of course, Penn furnished Morris with explicit formal instructions that reaffirmed his July 13, 1752, stand on the excise, but Morris had full discretion whether to disclose them or not. On receiving much the same kind of advice from the Philadelphia placemen that Hamilton had heard, Morris decided that his predecessor had adopted the proper course of action. In the months remaining before Braddock's expedition, the governor amended all three of the Assembly's bills granting money to the king's use so that the excise tax would exist only long enough to raise the money necessary to cover the amount of the appropriation.[28]

Braddock's defeat in the summer of 1755 was, in some ways, a major watershed in Pennsylvania's affairs. Among the circumstances affected was the dispute between executive and legislature. The excise tax was no longer sufficient to bear the expenses that the coming war effort would entail, and in July 1755 the Assembly drew up a bill appropriating £50,000 to the king's use to be funded on a general, inclusive land tax. With this measure, the Assembly forced Penn back onto the defensive. From the position of chief executive contending for joint appropriation of revenue in order to redress the balance in government, Penn moved to the position of a privileged landholder using his power over the executive to protect his immediate private interests. The moral and political equation had been altered, though the contending parties had not.[29]

Since Penn was, in a very real sense, the aggressor in the paper currency controversy, the question of why he embarked on such a course when he did is an important one. The proprietor had concluded that the balance of government needed to be redressed during his days in Pennsylvania. Yet more than a decade had elapsed since that time, and he had made no effort to strengthen the executive power. Even when he first returned to England in 1741, hot and determined, there is no evidence that he formulated any immediate plans to cut the Assembly down to size.[30]

Penn's failure to act in the 1740s stemmed from a number of circumstances. His elder brother John was still senior proprietor, and considerably more whiggish in outlook than Thomas. The financial exigencies of the Penn family, and the risk of English interference in a colony that was constantly squabbling during wartime, emphasized the desirability of peaceful executive-legislative relations in Philadelphia. And Governor Thomas's extension of the excise and paper currency reemission until 1756 left no good place to apply the necessary leverage. By the late 1740s, however, conditions had changed: Thomas had succeeded to John's half interest in the colony on the latter's death in 1746, the proprietary financial affairs were in better shape, and the French war had ground to a halt. But, even favored with these conditions, it is doubtful whether Penn would have stepped boldly forward to challenge the Assembly, for in Pennsylvania he had shown that he was not made of that mettle. What influenced him to seize the initiative in these new circumstances was his sensitivity to a changing British imperial policy and the vigorous promptings of his Philadelphia friends.

On the former count, it is not possible to establish just how much the ideas and activities of Lord Halifax and other spokesmen for a rejuvenated Board of Trade influenced Thomas Penn in the early 1750s. It is apparent, however, that they did offer him both a sympathetic ear and vocal encouragement. Significantly enough, while Penn sounded them for advice, he was careful not to rely on them too much nor to give them an excuse for interference. Faced with a Board of Trade deeply interested in colonial reorganization, Penn's problem was to act in harmony with the new British policy in such a way as to not discredit the proprietary form of government.[31]

The second source of encouragement, his placemen in Philadelphia, was certainly more persistent if somewhat less determined at the crucial moments. During the first three and one-half years of Hamilton's administration, he and Richard Peters bombarded Penn with complaints about the Assembly's "inveteracy . . . against the magistry."[32] The Assembly's bill to regulate the poor in Philadelphia encroached on the powers of the justices of the peace, as did a piece of legislation to erect workhouses and jails in the newly formed counties; the night watch bill for Philadelphia infringed on corporation rights, and the bill to change the process of probating wills severely disrupted settled administrative procedure; Chief Justice John Kinsey's irritating habit of removing cases from the regular county courts to the Supreme Court where he presided was another sore point. In answer to these cries of outrage, Penn first spoke his determination to move onto the offensive by demanding joint executive-legislative appropriation of the colony's revenue.[33]

Although Peters and Hamilton could not gather any local support for Penn's instructions in January 1753, they continued sending encouragement to Penn. To them, the fact that they were so beleaguered only heightened the obligations of the proprietor to persist somehow in his case. As Peters eloquently stated: "The good of the country calls for it—the authority of government cannot dispense with it."[34] The failure to attract support was a failure, not of right but of organization, and Hamilton attributed this to the fact that he was a Pennsylvanian by birth. Because they knew him as an old friend, the gentlemen who normally would have united their interest on the governor's behalf had failed to construct any sort of informal political alliance.[35] But, even without support, the one or two individuals who discerned the true state of affairs had an obligation to act. "A Governor must oppose their schemes to prevent the ruin of the country . . . though it is attended with the most disagreeable of all Engagements, contention."[36] When the cause was the balanced constitution, the prospect of disagreement should be no deterrent.

Despite the proprietary preparedness for contention, sharp public disagreement between executive and legislature did not break out until the latter part of 1754.[37] With the assumption of the governorship by Robert Hunter Morris, whose unsavory reputation as one of the proprietors of East New Jersey had long preceded him to Pennsylvania, and with the decision of the proprietary supporters to contest the 1754 election in several counties, Pennsylvanians began to line up openly behind governor or Assembly, depending on whom they felt was responsible for the defenseless state of the province.[38] Moreover, during the December 1754 session of the General Assembly, Morris's invocation of the 1740 royal instructions and the terms of the 1751 Currency Act to justify his refusal of a £20,000 grant to the king's use indicated that the proprietary instructions that had presumably bound Hamilton were still in force.

At that point the Assembly declared all-out war.[39] The exchanges between the governor and the Assembly were reported in the *Gazette*; the proprietary refusal to contribute to Indian affairs—which the Assembly had kept quietly in its hand for a year and a half—was published; and the assemblymen, their friends, and their relations spread word of the proprietary determination to use the present crisis to destroy their liberties.[40] By late 1754, then, the assemblymen openly espoused the same rationale as the executive spokesmen: they were *obliged* to contend for the rights of their branch of government in order to preserve the balance of the Pennsylvania constitution.[41]

§

Despite the ideals of peace and concord to which Pennsylvanians paid allegiance, there was, at any one time, always evidence of disputes between individuals, disagreements that rarely had anything to do with defending a balanced constitution. What one man felt to be his "interest" in a given set of circumstances others felt to be no more than "self-interest." And Pennsylvania was no different from other societies in that animosities between politicians often developed from private rather than public disagreements, and from personality conflict rather than matters of principle. The Norris-Allen family rivalry and the Andrew Hamilton–Governor Patrick Gordon disputes serve well as examples. In the former case an antagonism born of business rivalry became more bitter in the early 1730s. On one occasion William Allen killed seven of Isaac Norris's hogs when he saw them rooting in his meadow, only to find on closer examination that the frost in the ground had prevented them from doing any damage. Later, Isaac Norris, Jr., lost out to Allen in marriage suits for Peggy Hamilton, Andrew's daughter. This rebuff, and Isaac senior's altercation with Andrew Hamilton when Norris charged him with illegally raising his Philadelphia County prothonotary fees, contributed to Norris's decision to retire from law and politics to his country home. A coolness born of these circumstances continued to accompany dealings between Isaac Norris, Jr., and William Allen.[42]

Just as in the Norris-Allen case, the disputes between Andrew Hamilton and Governor Gordon in the early 1730s involved several different episodes. One of the governor's daughters charged James, Andrew's son, with unbecoming conduct, and when the accused denied it the two fathers joined the battle, for they both had "strong affections for their children"; furthermore, Hamilton disliked the men that Gordon relied on as administrative aides in the three Lower Counties and purported to see a number of slights in the actions of the governor's confidant and son-in-law, Robert Charles; and, finally, a series of unguarded comments Hamilton made about the governor's mental capacity brought on flurries of recriminations. Yet Hamilton and Gordon continued to maintain personal relations during the 1730s. After each falling away they patched up their differences and attended to the public business. The point is that such halting relationships could, and did, exist in a government chiefly distinguished by signs of concord and good harmony.[43]

No matter how peaceful and stable colonial society appeared at any given time, clashes between personalities who agreed completely on the importance of peace and amity were certain to be taking place. Such contention was always most intense near the centers of power, for ambitious men were drawn to the strategic centers like moths to a flame, and their myopia magnified the importance of minute changes in the distribution of power. Whether the fact that the second quarter of the eighteenth century was a period of relatively high deference, and expectations of deference affected the amount of personal contention in society, is a moot point. What may be said is that the peculiar configurations of individual conflict in and about Philadelphia were partially determined by the existence there of two general deference groups. Those who felt themselves at the very heart of English society in America because they were close to the executive, attended certain clubs, and belonged to the Anglican Church were not always treated according to their expectations. Others, men of rank as well as obvious inferiors, often considered the Quaker who spoke out for popular liberties to be far more worthy of respect. The subtle variations in deference criteria among members of the upper social strata provided a social context in which those bent on it could easily find an excuse for differences.

Usually the harmonious operation of society was not threatened by the kind of individual or family quarrels that occurred constantly in this and other early modern societies. Serious danger came when these types of disagreements developed into larger "party" disputes or when legitimate group activities changed into the zealous pursuit of some shared goal that seemed to conflict with the public welfare. Politically, self-interest could take the form of cooperative efforts to use positions of power to augment that power, or to effect some particular end in public policy or in political practice. Such factions did not have the uncontested right to speak for one branch of the constitution, either because there were no such widely accepted spokesmen, or because a respectable number of the established politicians were not included and were either indifferent or hostile to that group, or because the members of the cabal were attacking those established leaders. Thus, contention of this sort seriously threatened the normal operation of the executive or legislative branches of government. Because of the disruption it caused and the destructive bent of the self-seeking designs that underlay it, factionalism was clearly recognized as an illegitimate form of political behavior.

The one clear example of this type of factional conflict in Pennsylvania between 1726 and 1755 occurred immediately after William Keith's governorship. Keith had built up a personal following, largely in Philadelphia City, when as chief executive he had cooperated with David Lloyd in leading the advocates of paper currency against their foes, in denying the validity of proprietary instructions, and in contending that the Council members had no power other than the influence they wielded as personal advisers to the governor. When, in 1726, Patrick Gordon succeeded Keith and the latter decided to use his power base in Philadelphia to challenge David Lloyd's leadership of the Assembly, popular politics degenerated into self-interested factional warfare.

The bitterness between Keith and Lloyd was the bitterness of former allies, men who, despite differing emphases, had been co-spokesmen for an antiproprietary brand of politics and who now threatened each other's political existence. Keith coveted Lloyd's position as Speaker of the Assembly, and Lloyd ingratiated himself both with Keith's replacement and with his old proprietary enemies. Among the voting public, political allegiance depended on geographical location;[44] while Keith's popularity in the city of Philadelphia, and to a very limited extent in Philadelphia County, gained for him the confidence of the countrymen from Chester and Bucks.[45] In the October 1726 election Keith met with considerable success, winning his own seat and sweeping the other nine Philadelphia seats with his supporters. This was not good enough, though, for he could not match the fifteen votes David Lloyd could muster in the contest for the Speakership—and for Keith that contest was crucial.[46] If he were to extend his influence he would have to join the legislature as a popular leader within the framework of Assembly politics; yet his personal vendetta with Lloyd, and his obvious unwillingness to play second fiddle to a colonial, ruled out any possibility of a lieutenancy under the old Speaker.

Thus, once he had failed to get elected Speaker, Keith was reduced, at best, to the status of an ordinary assemblyman and, at worst, to a factional leader guilty of mounting a self-interested campaign against the established spokesman of the most prestigious institution in the colony. The final ironic touch was that, by signing the Currency Reemitting Act in his last days as governor, Keith had contributed to his own political impotence, for his legislation nullified the paper currency question as an immediate political issue that he might have effectively exploited in seeking additional support.[47]

If Keith failed to recognize the futility of his efforts immediately after the 1726 election, the 1727 results brought the message home. Again he nominally swept the Philadelphia elections, but in so doing he was only marking time. The outlying countrymen were solidly behind Lloyd; the Philadelphia County opposition was becoming more organized; and, if anything, his standing among fellow assemblymen had weakened.[48] Faced with the prospect of increased opposition at future elections and of attrition in the ranks of his Philadelphians, pursued by creditors, and hopeful of royal favor, Keith slipped surreptitiously out of Pennsylvania, boarded a ship in Delaware, and headed for England.

When Keith departed from Pennsylvania in March 1728, he left instructions with his followers: they were to maintain their allegiance while he was procuring a new commission, be extraordinarily vigilant in protecting their liberties, elect his nephew to the vacant Assembly seat, and work together to encourage demands for more paper currency.[49] It had been two years since the Reemitting Act had been passed, and men were voicing opinions that the £40,000 still in circulation was insufficient for the colony's needs. In addition, prospects looked good for some sort of confrontation with Governor Gordon on this issue: a letter from the Board of Trade stating that their Lordships would "certainly" be "obliged" to recommend disallowance of any further currency acts had reached Gordon before the colonists had despatched the Reemitting Act to England, and the board's continued silence on the fate of that legislation encouraged Keith to think that Gordon would not chance a further emission in the near future.[50] Continued contention in Pennsylvania might serve his cause well when he arrived in London.

Rather than the currency question, it was the election of a member in Sir William's stead that caused the most intense and disruptive period of factional strife. When, on April 17, 1728, a member from Philadelphia moved that a by-election be held, the House carried a countermotion that Keith's absence merely "be excused."[51] The following day the Assembly refused to rescind that resolve, and on April 20 all but one of the nine members from Philadelphia willfully absented themselves from further House proceedings.[52] Although the remaining fourteen failed to constitute a quorum, they did not publicly acknowledge this fact. They refused to accept any communiqué from the eight that was not delivered personally, ordered the delinquents to "repair" to the House, and finally, on the same day, adjourned until the governor should call them into session.[53]

When he did so, in mid-May, on the occasion of a crisis in Indian affairs, the eight members continued their absence.[54] Under Lloyd's direction the seventeen sitting assemblymen circumvented the obvious difficulty they faced in being one short of a quorum by a simple straightforward procedure: they unanimously adopted a resolution stating that they, "being a Majority of the whole representative body," possessed "the power of an Assembly."[55] Having taken this precaution, the seventeen set to work carrying out the normal Assembly business.[56]

Throughout the six-day May session and a two-week-long August sitting, the deadlock continued. The Lloydians persisted in acting together as a legal Assembly; the Keithians refused to heed the orders and later, the more conciliatory requests of the seventeen that the absent eight resume their duties in the legislature.[57] The point at issue remained in August what it had been in April: the Keithians contended, and the Lloydians denied, that the House could not bar a by-election, for when a vacancy occurred the Speaker had a duty to issue, "ex officio," a writ to the sheriff for the choice of a replacement.[58] In theory the Keithians had no case; in fact their intransigence was understandable and did serve a purpose. Even though the Assembly did have the power to do so, the Lloydian refusal to fill Keith's seat was an act of extreme political partisanship, for there could be no doubt that he was willfully absent and would not be back within the year.[59]

By quitting the Assembly in dramatic fashion, the Keithians drew attention to the injustice of their colleagues and thus curried favor with their constituents. For the Philadelphia assemblymen involved, the incident performed a service of even greater importance. The sense of persecution they felt helped to fill the void left by the absence of their leader. The Keithians, as their name indicated, were totally dependent on one man for political identity, and the feelings of persecution were the best possible surrogate for Keith's charisma.[60] As a political strategy, then, the Lloydian maneuver had certainly backfired, for it provided the means for the Keithians to prolong their existence as a distinct political faction.

Despite the immediate success of the Philadelphians' withdrawal from the Assembly, that action—negative and obstructionist as it was— foreshadowed the Keithians' fate. Although seven of the eight were reelected in the hotly contested election of 1728, the "ex officio" issue died with the appearance of a full slate of Philadelphia county representatives, and no new cause presented itself. The paper money issue did not precipitate the kind of contention that Keith had predicted, for even the old diehards—such as James Logan, who had originally opposed the use of a paper currency—now agreed that paper money was beneficial and that an increase in the amount circulating was sound ecenomics and expedient politics.[61] In May 1729 Patrick Gordon disregarded proprietary instructions ordering him not to sign any paper money bill that failed to exempt quitrents from the legal tender clause of the legislation and assented to an act that increased the supply of Pennsylvania's paper money by £30,000. With the passage of this legislation, and the publication of a proclamation ordering government officers to enforce the new Riot Act just passed by the Assembly, the mobs that had agitated Philadelphia in the fall of 1728 and again in the spring of 1729 melted away. Although a residue of high-tempered political contention lasted into the autumn months of that year, there was no clear polarization of political extremes during the annual election. And cool heads defused whatever explosive potential still existed by arranging election tickets acceptable to all.[62]

William Keith's ability to disrupt the normal patterns of politics sprang from a unique set of circumstances. Both prior to his appointment as governor and after he was dismissed, the chief executive of the colony was totally dependent on the proprietary, holding the post at his pleasure and always subject to written and in some cases verbal instructions. It was Keith's good fortune to gain his appointment just as William Penn's death had thrown proprietary affairs into confusion. This lapse in effective control by representatives of the Penn family allowed Keith to use his position as leading spokesman for the executive branch of government to protest proprietary controls and to gain for himself, as governor, a measure of popular support that ordinarily was reserved for Assembly leaders. But the events of 1726—Keith's dismissal from office and his failure to establish himself immediately as a major Assembly leader in a reasonably united House of Representatives—created a new and very different political equation.

The most important change, of course, was the alteration in Keith's status: in the early summer of 1726 he was the recognized spokesman for one branch of government; six months later he was leader of a political faction. As such he and his supporters fell afoul of a whole polemical tradition that branded them as dangerous, dishonorable, and subversive men. Equally significant was the new sense of certainty that this infused into Pennsylvania affairs. Governors, as everyone knew, were always unpredictable—the erratic William Keith provided irrefutable evidence of that—but factions were something else. When Pennsylvanians recognized a faction for what it was they had an interpretive framework at hand to fence it in. They knew what dangers factionalism presented, they knew how faction members would act, what their ends were, and what motivated them. When politicians gave way to their passions they were chained by them—still dangerous it was true, but part of a known political world. Moreover, history and experience had taught disinterested politicians how to deal with faction when it appeared: they should isolate the factious men and allow their passions to play themselves out. Simultaneously, they should draw their constituents' attention to the disgraceful display and expose that behavior for what it was.

These were essentially the tactics that David Lloyd and his country allies followed. After Keith's initial challenge in 1726, they quietly and confidently confined Keithian influence to the Philadelphia area. They grew impatient and pushed too hard in 1728, but that was only a momentary lapse and they recovered quickly. At the same time, they publicly branded the Keithians with the stigma of factionalism and appropriated for themselves the whole range of legitimizing political rhetoric that was available for popular politicians. They claimed a monopoly of virtue, disinterest, independence, integrity, ability, and capacity.[63]

The Keithians, on the other hand, made no concerted effort to establish their place within the "country" tradition. Prior to 1726 Keith—as governor—had no opportunity to employ on his own behalf the kind of political rhetoric that lent legitimation to popular politicians, and after that time he and his followers made no effort to do so. The Keithians concentrated on making vitriolic charges against the character and intentions of their opponents, reminding the electorate of old issues and bolstering their charges with new evidence of intrigue.[64] Beyond that they did suggest that they stood for principles of political practice that their opponents chose to ignore: they were responsive to the people, they would act as the freemen's delegates, they would encourage mechanics and freemen of all ranks to seek political office.[65] As appropriate as these positions might have been some years before, however, they were no longer viable by the late 1720s. The social standing of the members of Keith's own Assembly slate and the fact that he headed two distinct political groups—the Gentlemen's Club and a leather-apron group known as the Tiff Club—rather than one organization, proved them a mockery;[66] such postulates were out of tune with the political behavior in Pennsylvania and ran counter to the direction in which the province was moving.

The Keithian disturbances of the late 1720s were important because they illustrate that in Pennsylvania, as elsewhere in the colonies, factional strife did occur. Equally significant, however, is how it happened and how it came to an end. Keith, the central figure in the dispute, was an aberration, for he had acquired the kind of popularity normally accorded only Assembly leaders in his pre-1726 role as chief spokesman for the executive branch of government. When he lost that office and challenged David Lloyd, that popularity began to melt away—partly because of the electoral and in-House tactics he and his followers adopted, but mostly because his open challenge to Lloyd convinced the majority of politically aware Pennsylvanians that he and his followers constituted a faction. The most telling feature of this brand of contentious politics was not the shrillness of James Logan and a sprinkling of other proprietary men who had formed their Keithian fears in the strange triangular politics of the early 20s, but the heavy-handed confidence of David Lloyd's supporters. Right was on their side, and the Keithians had hobbled themselves by being so obviously "factious." It was simply a question of playing out the charade.

CHAPTER 8

THE QUAKER
CONTRIBUTION

§

More than any other group in Pennsylvania, Quakers were committed to the politics of peace. Of course Friends were not without their differences, but in no case did these differences develop into vitriolic public disputes. A whole set of values, procedures, and traditions operated to promote both good harmony between Quakers and those of different religious views and unity among Friends. Because many Quakers were deeply involved in secular affairs—as the members of any dominant elite must be—the chance that some serious conflict might break out among them was always present. But the very range of their interests, which under certain circumstances could work to divide their society, predisposed Quakers to prefer the peace of concession to the unity of sectarian purity. Nowhere was this more evident than in the case of meeting discipline on gravestones and that of defining the peace testimony. In their own peculiar ways the Quakers enriched the more general culture of social and political stability that all colonists shared.

§

Despite the growing disproportion of non-Quakers to Quakers in Pennsylvania between 1726 and 1755, the amount of power concentrated in Quaker hands was substantial. Members of the Society of Friends dominated elective offices, held a large number of appointive positions, and constituted a majority of the colony's economic and social leaders. As Pennsylvania had gained wealth and strength, so had members of the Quaker elite. There are a number of reasons why the

141

Quaker minority was able to dominate the province to such a degree: the Quakers' early arrival in Pennsylvania; their relatively extensive capital resources, overseas connections, and location on good lands near Philadelphia; their practices of mutual aid and experience in public office; the "Quaker economic ethic"; the popular perception of Pennsylvania as the Quaker colony; the identification of Quakerism with whiggish political views; the organizational advantages the meeting structure conferred; and the Assembly's systematic underrepresentation of the backcountry. All of these reasons for Quaker success in establishing and preserving their power were important ones and could be treated at length. One additional condition, however, was critical for the continuation of Quaker prominence in public affairs. That was unity. It was absolutely essential that the Quakers avoid fragmentation over religious and political issues if they were to maintain their power.

Between 1726 and 1755, Friends were not without their differences. Personal disputes arose among Quakers, just as they occurred among members of all religious persuasions and between representatives of different religious groups. In the summer of 1744, for example, Israel Pemberton, Jr., and Assemblyman James Morris became so angered at one another that Pemberton threatened to challenge four incumbent assemblymen representing Philadelphia County with four new candidates in the October election.[1] What resulted in this case also resulted in other instances where personal or family disputes broke out among Friends: cooler heads prevailed, and the threatened disruption did not noticeably affect the Quaker role in public affairs.

Group rivalries, however, were a somewhat more serious matter. Occasionally, one of the ordinarily innocuous and constantly shifting associational networks insisted on their conception of the society's true interest and thereby jeopardized the unity of Friends.[2] Between 1726 and 1728, for example, a number of Philadelphia Quakers cast their lot with dissident William Keith, while in 1739 a group of Chester County Quakers refused to join in the quitrent settlement with the proprietors. In 1740-42, Quaker leaders were divided into three recognizable, though ill-defined groups. At one extreme was a little group of legislative radicals who wanted to continue contending with Governor Thomas; they were balanced by a second small group whose members were not in the Assembly, but who wanted the legislators to appropriate money for military purposes; between these two extremes there was one large mass of moderate opinion with several, often indistinct, points of focus. Other differences among Friends took place in 1747-48 and 1754-55, when there was an apparent need for Quaker legislators to establish wartime policies. In addition to these specific examples of divisions among Friends, there lay the general difference in outlook that allegedly set city and county Quaker apart.

But aside from two incidents of open disagreement—in Philadelphia in the 1720s and in Bucks County in the 1740s—when a small number of Friends supported the executive, Pennsylvania's Quakers refused to allow their political differences to become public disputes. While some of these differences among Friends did have significance in the course of public events, most important from the broader perspective of Quaker affairs was the fact that disputes were few and were, with minor exceptions, contained within the Society of Friends. The ability of the Quakers to avoid serious contention was the single most important reason why Friends were able to dominate Pennsylvania politics to such a degree and why, in turn, politics were so stable.

That Quakers were able to contain their differences was in no small measure due to the cohesiveness that sprang from Friends' self-conceptions as a "peculiar" people. Outwardly, Friends expressed their solidarity by complying with certain modes of behavior that, although they had originated as statements of noncompliance with standard social practices, had become positive, established rituals in Pennsylvania. The plain style of speech and dress, the affirmation, aversion to games of chance, and refusal to remove the hat save in meeting publicly defined the Quakers as a distinct social group. But such symbols were only effective in preserving a sense of identity among Quakers because they were visible expressions of a distinctive and meaningful way of life.[3]

At the very heart of the Quaker way was the conception of the "inner light"—the notion that any man might, at any time, feel within himself the divine presence and that salvation was the actual working out of the spiritual impulse through the actions and thoughts of each individual. Because Quakerism developed, in part, as a reaction against excessive theological disputation, Friends made no attempt to emphasize other distinctive doctrines. More complete differentiation depended on the actions of Friends as they translated the spiritual impulse into actual behavioral patterns.[4]

Of the four categories of concern—equality, simplicity, community, and harmony—that best typified Quaker behavior over the centuries, the latter two were particularly important during the years 1726-55.[5] The first of those, community, included the strong sense of mutuality that permeated the meeting structure. Intrasociety benevolence, founded on the belief that as all men had embarked on the same pilgrimage, each deserved what aid and comfort his fellows could offer, created powerful bonds that imparted resilience to Quaker society. By fulfilling its functions as a "dispenser of poor relief, a loan office, a court of arbitration in economic matters, an employment agency, and a source of advice to new arrivals on the management of their affairs," the meeting structure created a sense of community that resisted tendencies toward serious fragmentation.[6]

Closely connected to the Quaker concern for community was the active pursuit of peace and harmony. Because the character of one imminent and revelatory God and "the very nature and design of the Gospel" dictated that "all should be of one mind and become as one family," the achievement of unanimity among Friends was as much an end as the attainment of more specific goals.[7] The fundamental nature of the urge for unity was evident not just in the day-to-day performance of mutual aid activities but in the very structure of Quaker behavior inside the meeting house. The relationships among Friends were conceived as consensual, and in meeting decisions were made in such a way as to facilitate the maintenance of a consensus among members. In the process of transacting business, dealing out discipline, or elaborating religious premises into Advices, "the supremacy of a majority over a minority was completely dispensed with."[8] The conception of compromise was as alien to the meeting as the idea of voting. Decision making was an "organic" procedure in which opinions were offered and synthesized by orderly group discussion. The clerk of the meeting was responsible for guiding this discussion and for gathering the sense of the meeting. Often, important questions lay in limbo for months, if not years, for differences were commonly met with the tactics of delay. The development of meeting unity could not, and hence need not be instantaneous, for opinion formation was just that—a process. Inability to arrive at a clear conclusion simply indicated the need for more concerted effort on the part of individual members in an attempt to isolate the distortions that human conscience and reason had produced in reflecting the inner light.[9]

Of course, Quaker acceptance of a consensual framework for decision making should not be construed as evidence that participating Friends had an equal voice in the formulation of policy. As Frederick B. Tolles has pointed out, Quakers shared fully in eighteenth-century beliefs that social ranking among men was perfectly natural and desirable, and in each meeting there were "weighty" members whose voices were the crucial ones in any attempt to settle an item of business.[10] These were the men whose names turned up again and again in meeting minutes, as members in charge of dealing with delinquents, as elders of the meeting, as representatives to the quarterly meeting, and as overseers of the Quaker poor. Thus, deference reinforced consensus. In situations where most of the "weighty" Friends agreed, formation of an acceptable consensus was undoubtedly expedited. In situations where they did not, it was clear where the greatest need and responsibility for self-examination lay.

Despite the potential for fragmentation inherent in the latent individualism and equalitarianism of the "inner light," the combined weight of consensus and deference repressed such tendencies. Individual Quakers were to work out the implication of their spiritual experiences in a group context, and, particularly in situations where no clear-cut Quaker testimony governed the matter, the Friends' first duty was to consult men of weight.[11] But to overstress the coercive side of Quakerism would certainly be wrong. Concession rather than repression was the norm, for Friends clearly agreed that deferential relations were proper, that the consensual framework was divinely sanctioned, and that the existing meeting structure best promoted the peace and harmony that was an essential characteristic of right relationships among men.

In addition to the cohesion that Friends derived from their identity as a religious sect and from the strong commitment to the values of community and harmony, unity among Friends was also promoted by the peculiar situation of the Pennsylvania Quakers: they were part of a larger international organization at the same time as they enjoyed a very special—and dominant—position in the Penn colony. The benefit that membership in an international brotherhood conferred was the advantage of perspective; the danger of Quakers being completely caught up in a local dispute without realizing the larger significances of their actions was considerably lessened. Yet, at the same time, Quakers drew strength from the historical interpretation they gave to their own peculiar past in Pennsylvania. Choosing to forget the un-Quakerlike contention that had marked Pennsylvania's first years, they celebrated the early period as a golden age of harmony and liberty under a perfect constitution. As the true spiritual descendants of William Penn, the great lawgiver, Quakers were obliged to protect the gifts that their self-sacrificing progenitors had bequeathed.

What endangered these rights and the specific Quaker privileges that accompanied them was that Friends had become a minority group in Pennsylvania—a development that they had related directly to the Keithian schism. George Keith's defection from the Society during the early 1690s had visibly weakened the Friends' position, and future splits could only work to the advantage of non-Quakers. Aware of their precarious position as a privileged minority group, determined to fulfill their role in Pennsylvania history by maintaining that position, and sensitive to dangers of dissent to which they, as a religious group with a powerful dissenting tradition, were particularly susceptible, the

Quakers were determined to prevent further fragmentation in their ranks.[12]

Two characteristics that distinguished social relationships among Friends facilitated fulfillment of the urge for unity implicit in Quaker separation, organizational values, and interpretation of the past. First, despite the fact that formally the Quakers designated the family a miniature meeting, in common usage that metaphor was often turned around, and what appeared early as a figure of speech came, after two or three generations, to have a ring of truth. Quaker emphasis on marriages within the meeting, the tendency to have large families, and the natural predilection of children to pick their spouses from among close acquaintances led to the formation of large kin groups.[13] These ties cut across the boundaries of both the monthly meeting and the city and county,[14] so that the strength spawned by the widespread respect for kinship ties was diffused among Society members.[15]

Second, the Quaker ministry and visiting elders played exceedingly important roles as ambassadors of good will, moving from meeting to meeting, creating a sense of inclusion, and soothing ruffled feelings that might produce serious differences within the Society. Men like Mordecai Yarnall, William Brown, Michael Lightfoot, John Churchman, and Peter Worrall, who first gained their reputations as country ministers, became influential Friends in Philadelphia as well. Accompanied by a city Friend such as Daniel Stanton, Robert Jordan, one of the Pembertons, or perhaps by a visiting English minister, these leaders constantly made the rounds of Pennsylvania's meeting houses. They were, truly, the cement of Quaker society.[16]

Although Quaker principles set Friends apart as a unique social group, members of the meeting still could not avoid the problem that every religious fraternity had to face: how to order day-to-day life in accordance with their religious beliefs. The monthly meeting made decisions about what constituted compliance and noncompliance with the canons of Quaker behavior, and openly forged the discipline of Quakerism.[17] From records of this disciplinary action emerges a clear understanding of how the Quakers of Pennsylvania defined deviant behavior, how they treated errant members, and, consequently, what operative imperatives Friends actually assumed.[18]

Tradition has assigned to the Quakers a set of exterior symbols, such as plainness of dress and speech, and a set of straightforward principles, such as pacifism and refusal to take oaths, that have served to represent all of the values and beliefs and presuppositions commonly designated "Quaker." But these commonly known characteristics were rarely, if ever, mentioned during the monthly meetings. The tables in appendix V.2 clearly show where the brunt of disciplinary activity by the monthly meeting fell. With the single exception of marrying outside the meeting, the crimes that drew the most attention were the same type of actions that the society at large had declared unacceptable: the sins of fornication, fighting, indebtedness, assault, and cursing.[19] This very congruity between Pennsylvania's criminal records and the disciplinary actions of its Quaker meetings points out why Friends were inclined to focus their attention where they did. About the nature of these crimes there existed a broadly based consensus that they were indeed wrongs. The chances of any deep-seated split in Quaker meetings over these issues was nonexistent, for the individual dissidents were automatically isolated; the wrong was so obviously antisocial and so well known to all that a man could gain no support and little sympathy for his position as a fornicator, a blasphemer, or a drunk.

In this context, it is clear why marriage outside the meeting received as much attention as these obvious forms of deviance. Because it struck at the very roots of the religious organization, it was an obvious social wrong.[20] When two Friends were married by a minister or magistrate, the most basic unit of social organization—the family —was born in defiance of discipline, and the meeting was unlikely to have much success in asserting control over that partnership in the future. When a Friend married a non-Quaker, reasoning was much the same. Friends and contemporary spokesmen for other religious groups agreed that exogamous marriages "in all Ages hath been hurtful to the People of God," for they prevented husband and wife from uniting to build a harmonious household and to support each other in the proper education of their children.[21]

The monthly meeting records of disciplinary action, centering as they did on certain widely acknowledged wrongs, gave members of the meetings that sense of mutuality and group solidarity that all social groups sought. Moreover, by defining their parameters as they did, Friends defused the explosive potential inherent in their religious basis. As long as the need to define was satisfied by identifying perpetrators of generally recognized social wrongs, then the chance of a serious disputation within the meeting diminished. Quaker leaders felt the importance of this steady stream of predictable wrongs even if they did not completely understand the reasons for it.

The accepted norms of conduct were anchor points for the whole existing structure of social relationships, and when these were threatened a muted tone of anger and outrage seeped into the normally bland record of monthly decisions. When Josiah Lewis, who was married to Martha Allen but cultivating the impression that he was only cohabiting with her, refused "to make it appear that he [was] married," he was guilty of a crime much more serious than mere fornication. According to the Christian dogma and social convention, the state of marriage had been sanctioned by God and was, therefore, a definite good; cohabitation out of wedlock was, conversely, an evil, and the practitioner thereof should acknowledge this wrong and immediately rectify it. Married, yet refusing to appear as a married man, Josiah Lewis was hopelessly destroying the clarity between right and wrong, between the categories of action that justified righteous feelings and those that demanded manifestations of guilt and ultimate expiation. Quaker spokesmen felt that such puckish manipulation of social conventions was malevolence of the most destructive kind. No wonder the Chester Monthly Meeting determined that if Josiah Lewis could not be convinced "that he ought to make it appear that he [was] married if it [was] so," the "proper measures [would] be taken to compel him to it . . ."[22]

The impulse to protect the accepted criteria for deviance not only appeared in such incidents but also lay behind the common ritual that had to be performed by all penitent deviants. Each errant person who wished to remain under meeting care had to appear before the appropriate monthly meeting and sign an acknowledgment of guilt, the substance of which condemned the crime in general and his specific lapse in particular. This acknowledgment was then read in public at the breakup of the next preparative meeting.[23] The purpose of the public ritual was plain: it reaffirmed the established divisions between acceptable and nonacceptable behavior, and it produced constant and needed reassurance that the defined boundaries were the right boundaries.

The need to define operated as a group imperative among Quakers just as it did in other societies, but in Quaker society a whole series of habits and procedures operated to ensure the least amount of conflict and division consonant with the necessity of defining the limits of behavior. The bulk of the meeting's disciplinary action focused on commonly accepted social and religious wrongs, so that the formulation of a consensus was not a difficult matter. Even in the case of the most grievous sins, however, Friends were too much aware of the weight of old habits and the appetites of unregenerate flesh to demand the immediate ostracism of all offenders. Besides, strict adherence to the principle of immediate and unequivocal disownment meant the shattering of the concord that they were trying to create. To deal with members for stepping outside the acceptable limits of Quaker discipline, then, "persuasion" and "gentle dealing" was to be the practice. Only when that court had obviously failed should Friends resort to disownment.[24]

One of the most important functions of the meeting elder was to visit Friends whom he judged to be stretching the limits of acceptable behavior, in the hopes of persuading them to desist.[25] "Weighty members" of any meeting shared a similar responsibility in relationship to any of their fellows.[26] Evidence exists, too, that, before the members of the preparative meetings brought a complaint against one of their neighbors, they often attempted to persuade him of the evil consequences of his present course.[27] Once an individual had been reported to the monthly meeting, a concerted effort was made to reclaim the sinner. Patience and tolerance characterized the procedures set in motion by the meeting.[28] Committee after committee might be appointed "to deal" with the offender in the hopes that they could bring him to acknowledge his wrong.[29] When a difference appeared between the brothers Robert and Patrick Miller (Patrick defamed Robert's character), the Bradford Monthly Meeting spent a full year talking them into a reconciliation.[30]

In the case of habitual offenders, the meetings were equally lenient. Thomas Arnold was the object of three complaints within an eight-year period. Each time the meeting, after "solid consideration," agreed to accept his acknowledgment condemning the overuse of strong liquors. The fourth time, however, Arnold, undoubtedly as tired of the charade as were his fellow Quakers, told the committee that they "might do as they please."[31] Arnold's remark and the quick disownment that followed isolates very well what the meetings looked for in their dealings with a deviant. The phrase "a pretty good disposition of mind" appears with some regularity in the meeting records and adequately conveys the sense of remorse and contrition that the Friends expected to find in those who had committed some wrong.[32] Of course, such feelings were expected to be sincere, but if there was some doubt on this score, the benefit of it often went to the deviant.[33]

When an individual refused to repent, which happened approximately 40 percent of the time,[34] the meeting members conceived of the disownment not as an act of ostracism but as a public declaration that the sinner had turned his back on them. When John Salkeld joined the Church of England, the Chester Monthly Meeting reported that "he hath disjoined himself from our community."[35] Because, in the disownment process, volition was attributed to the deviant, the Quakers logically held that a penitent offender could by a sincere ackowledgment be "joined in fellowship" again.[36] Every statement of disownment included the same message: the deviant was to remain outside the society until "by unfeigned repentance and amendment of life" he had found God's mercy and condemned the evil to "the satisfaction of the meeting."[37] The door of reentry was always ajar, and a considerable number took advantage of the opportunity it afforded.

In addition to muting the conflict that was a necessary product of the process of creating mutuality, Friends strove to smother the discord that naturally arose from the great areas of religious, social, and political concern. On the organizational level alone, certain procedures helped restore harmony. For example, if two individuals disagreed, the person who felt wronged approached his opposite and explained the situation as he saw it. If no accommodation could be reached, neutral Friends met with the antagonists. Failing results, the parties at odds chose arbitrators and agreed to abide by the decision. If this was not done, the matter was referred to the monthly meeting where the "dealing" procedure came into operation.[38]

The whole process of appeals within the Quaker organization was another lubricant designed to ease legitimate disputes between the members. If an individual felt he had been wronged by his peers at the monthly meeting level, he could appeal to the quarterly meeting and ultimately to the yearly meeting; if, in the process of considering a problem, a monthly meeting found itself deeply divided, it would pass the onus of making a decision on to the quarterly meeting rather than make a majoritarian ruling;[39] if two meetings could not work out an agreement over the maintenance of a poverty-stricken member, for example (though most often they could), the quarterly meeting would be asked to apportion the financial responsibility;[40] if a meeting was disturbed by internal disagreements or stresses of any kind, a member of that meeting might ask for an advisory visit by leaders of a neighboring meeting or representatives of the quarterly meeting.[41]

These procedural techniques were important in the easing of tension, but no more so than the relationship that existed between the yearly meeting and the monthly meetings. In theory it was a hierarchical relationship, and at first glance it would appear that the yearly meeting, in charge of defining discipline, would unequivocally demand the implementation of that discipline. In fact, that was not so; they sent out policy statements but created no machinery to ensure adherence to that policy. In 1743 a set of queries about meeting practices, which could have been used to measure monthly meeting disciplinary standards, was drawn up by the Philadelphia Yearly Meeting.[42] These questions, however, were sent out without any such design in mind; they were simply to be read at least four times a year by each monthly meeting as an aid of self-examination at this, the tertiary, level. When in other instances the Yearly Meeting did send out its periodic epistles, instructions about behavior were set out in general terms.[43] Dress was not to be "out of mode"; "vicious company" was to be shunned; the "taking of Tobacco" should not be "unseemly"; the perfect model for emulation should be the "sincere and humble" man.[44] It was entirely up to the different monthly meetings to interpret those standards and to import substance to them. In actual practice that was what Quaker discipline depended upon: the type of practical accommodation that could best be achieved at the local level. And behind each pragmatic decision there loomed very large the steadfast conceptual allegiance to the values of peace, harmony, and stability.

The case of Caleb Harrison best illustrates the tone of Quaker disciplinary activity during these years. In October 1732 the Chester Monthly Meeting brought a complaint against Harrison "for refusing to come to that meeting though he hath been in a friendly and tender manner treated with," for "showing his dislike publically of keeping on his hat," and for "going out of Meeting when a friend under our notice was in prayer." For the next five months a series of committees were appointed to deal with him, but by April 1733 the Friends appointed could only report that Caleb was "obdurate, justifying himself and charging the Monthly Meeting and Chester Preparatory Meeting for not putting the rules of discipline in practice." Faced with this stalemate, the members of the monthly meeting appealed to the quarterly meeting to intervene. In May the committee from that meeting reported that "Caleb hath let in resentments" against the members of the lower meetings and that he should acknowledge his guilt. Two months later, when Caleb still refused to "make any satisfaction," several appointees of the quarterly meeting agreed that, "although it [was] yet their Judgement he ought to make satisfaction, yet in regard to his family and the nature of the offence not being of Public Scandal . . . they request[ed] . . . that he [might] be continued under friends care . . . which this meeting agree[d] to."[45]

Once the initial complaint had been made against Caleb Harrison, he threatened to cause difficulties because Friends were divided over his case. A rigid and strict application of Quaker discipline was simply not worth the division and discontent that it would produce. Because the nature of his offense was not of a scandalous nature, failure to censure Caleb would not adversely affect the society's public reputation. In the absence of this factor there could be no argument: the preservation of peace and harmony among members of the society was more important than a narrow, fragmented but pure meeting (if Caleb and others were forced to leave) and was certainly preferable to a continuation of the existing state of dissension.

§

The conditions and attitudes of mind that promoted unity among Friends were of crucial importance for the political success of the Quakers because members of the society were so deeply involved in worldly concerns. The Society of Friends was filled with men of diverse interests, and the centrifugal tendencies that arose out of these differences had to be overcome if the Quakers were to retain their position of dominance in public affairs. Yet, assuming these differences could be reconciled (as they were in the first half of the eighteenth century), this diversity could become a political advantage. Not only did the inclusion of a large number of different personalities and interests in the Society allow a wide range of problems to be compromised under the special facilitative conditions that Quakerism entailed, but it also allowed Quakers to identify and espouse public issues on which members of society could agree.

Thus, the concern for unanimity was a distinctive outward-looking kind that sprang mainly from the peculiar role of the Quakers as economic, political, and social leaders and from their determination to maintain their positions of power. What helped to legitimatize this position was a belief, shared by both Friends and members of other religious groups, that Quakers were best suited to safeguard provincial liberties and a recognition by Friends that Quaker ideals of community and harmony should govern their relationships with all men outside the meeting house.[46] This Quaker characteristic gained concrete expression in the widespread practice of birthright membership,[47] in the halfway disownment procedure that allowed former Friends to attend meeting for worship,[48] in the close relationship that Friends kept with former meeting members,[49] and in the willingness of Friends to listen to the spokesmen of other religious persuasions and, occasionally, to attend their services.[50]

Most important of all, however, the concern for unity was translated into an active avoidance of any self-definition that would have been likely to produce strife and division. On the local level, Friends disciplined those whose actions were overwhelmingly conceived to be wrong. But almost without exception they refused to enforce Advices that had the faintest air of controversy about them: on the provincial level, leading Quakers doled out the same type of general advice from year to year, refusing to set the Quakers more clearly apart as practitioners of a superior and uniquely righteous way of life.

Quaker history is rife with examples of how, as matters of principle, Friends preferred the peace of concession to the unity of sectarian purity. In matters of "pride and vanity," almost all of the disownments from the society lay outside the years 1710-55.[51] Despite strictures of plainness, Friends' houses, artifacts, and apparel differed but slightly from their non-Quaker contemporaries'.[52]

One illustration of the Quaker way of handling a question of unity was the accommodation worked out on the use of gravestones. In the three years from 1706 to 1708, the Yearly Meeting spelled out in plain fashion the Quaker discipline on "Gravestones and Monuments." Existing ones should be torn down, no more should be put up, and any that opposed the policy should be dealt with as "disorderly persons."[53] The advice was clear and uncompromising; compliance was not. By 1729 there were still many gravestones in Quaker burying grounds, and more were being put up. In response, the Yearly Meetings of 1729, 1730, and 1731 urged new efforts against this form of declension.[54] Results, however, had already been foreshadowed.

Chester Monthly Meeting was the one unit that had made a concerted effort to follow the Yearly Meeting's directives. The response among member preparative meetings was mixed at best. Providence removed all of their gravestones, Chester and Middleton took down some, and Springfield had them but refused to do anything about them.[55] Goshen Monthly Meeting simply reported that some stones had been removed and that others remained.[56] Nottingham avoided the whole problem by reporting that they were "clear therein so far as we know."[57] The silence of the other meetings, at least some of which did have gravestones,[58] undoubtedly meant that what had been the prevailing practice continued to take place.

Faced with such diversity, the Yearly Meeting could only put the best possible face on a difficult situation. For the sake of the continuity of policy, and for the sake of those who believed in the traditional stand, marks of distinction were condemned, yet not so far "as to direct the denying of those who so oppose[d]—(in hopes that further dealing and patient waiting [might] answer the end without that severity)."[59] But the point of the whole controversy was clear: on that particular issue decisions about discipline were really in the hands of the local meeting members, and, because diverse practices and opinions prevailed on that level, the yearly meeting would not apply any pressure that would lead to open disagreement and possible fragmentation.

Matching Friends' unwillingness to enforce some tenets of existing discipline was their reluctance to redefine old testimonies to fit new circumstances in Pennsylvania. The best illustration of this point is the history of the peace testimony. Pacifism has always been associated with Quakerism, but during the seventeenth and eighteenth centuries it was not always clear what Quakers felt that commitment to the principle entailed. The peace testimony Pennsylvania Friends drew on as a guide for their pacifism was advice that their English predecessors had elaborated in the latter half of the seventeenth century as an expression of their wish not to be directly involved in or responsible for violent .actions of any kind. Because English Friends were unable to hold more than minor civil office, they did not concern themselves with the hypothetical case of a government official but tailored their advice to fit the circumstances of the ordinary Quaker citizen: he could not participate directly in fighting of any kind, but he could, in a situation of war, perform tasks such as keeping watch over prisoners or helping to erect defensive works that would aid others in the performance of their military duties. In Pennsylvania, however, the traditional Quaker peace testimony was no longer adequate, for, by filling government office, Quaker politicians were obliged by their own pronouncements on the duties of government to suppress deviant behavior in society and to protect the body politic from outside aggression. Thus, William Penn's Friends were faced with the "dilemma" of reconciling their duties as magistrates and members of the legislature with the intent of the peace testimony.[60]

During the first four decades of Pennsylvania's history, when circumstances of war forced the Quakers to come to grips with their conflicting obligations, appropriate guidelines did emerge. First, as in England, there was to be no direct participation by Friends in actual military activities. Second, Friends refused to act in their capacity as legislators to frame a bill that would compel any man to participate in a provincial militia. Third, in keeping with their obligations as governors and as members of the British Empire, they were willing to grant a sum of money to the monarch; when the crown gave specific orders to provide money, men, or stores for some military venture that by virtue of its being outside of Pennsylvania was clearly a part of imperial, not domestic, defense, they could reply with a grant to the "King's use." The responsibility to apply that money was the crown's, not theirs. The vote of money was considered a declaration of loyalty —giving to Caesar what was Caesar's.[61]

Although testimony and precedent had established these guidelines, not all Quakers agreed with the decisions, and certainly the rules themselves did not cover all forseeable circumstances. The most widely accepted principle was that Friends should not take a direct hand in military activities. But, when conditions of war prevailed at any time during the century, a few always would disregard this testimony. On the opposite side of the fence, those who took most seriously the spirit of the peace testimony raised an objection to a practice that was unquestioned in England and generally accepted in Pennsylvania. Thomas Maule and a few others argued in 1711 that Friends should not pay a tax that was levied specifically to fund military expenditures. Lastly, although Friends had refused to pass a militia act in 1693 and again in 1709, certainly not all Quakers were convinced that this self-imposed limitation was reasonable for Quaker legislators to accept. If in a real emergency those who believed in the right to defend the state wanted such legislation, why should Quakers, who as conscientious objectors would not have to serve, deny others their privileges? Muted disagreement on the issue presaged more serious differences on the closely connected but larger question of what general measures Quaker legislators should take if, either in the absence or presence of specific royal orders to defend Pennsylvania, they were convinced of real danger to the province.[62]

With the end of Queen Anne's War in 1713, Quakers quickly turned away from this potentially disruptive issue, and for twenty-six years they were able to ignore it. Consequently, when King George's War broke out in 1739, the old question of what the assemblymen's exact obligations in wartime were was still not entirely resolved. Although most Quaker assemblymen were prepared to respond to the royal orders of 1741 commanding Pennsylvania to provide supplies for the Cartagena expedition by voting a sum to the king's use, there may have been a sprinkling of "tender consciences." More obvious were the disagreements among Friends about the acceptability of a provincial militia law and appropriations for military defense. James Logan, Robert Strettle, and a number of other Friends wanted to have this issue canvassed at the Philadelphia Yearly Meeting in 1741. But when Strettle argued in Meeting that Logan's open letter "To Robert Jordan and others . . ." raising these questions should be read and discussed he was told, euphemistically but decisively, to sit down and keep quiet. Most influential Quakers were determined to avoid any formal discussion of this thorny problem, for once it had been opened up differences would surface, animosities would develop, and the process of clearly redefining the peace principle would likely have produced fragmentation.[63]

Although the Quaker advocates of defense preparations kept a relatively low profile after 1741, there were other wartime problems that the assemblymen had to confront. Between February 1745 and June 1746 New England officials sent three separate requests to Pennsylvania for military aid, and twice the English government commanded Pennsylvania to support the war effort against the French. In the former cases, when there were no specific royal orders commanding obedience, Quaker assemblymen did argue that their consciences forbade compliance, but at the same time they did not unequivocally state that they refused to send help to the New Englanders for religious reasons. Rather than make a decision on what their religious principles did entail when there were no direct orders from the crown, the Quakers straddled the fence. They alluded to the difficulties their religious principles caused, but only after listing a whole series of practical reasons, including the lack of royal direction, for their noncompliance. In the latter two cases, the Quaker response was quite different. In these instances neither religious objections, the relative merits of the campaign, the needs of their allies, nor the imminence of danger apparently carried much weight. The important consideration was the existence of royal orders commanding support for the war effort. In 1745 the Quaker assemblymen quickly granted £4,000 to the king's use, and the next year they followed up with a vote of £5,000.[64]

As unpredictable as in former colonial wars, the French were not to let the Quakers off so easily. In 1747 and 1748 enemy privateers concentrated in or near the Delaware River, posing a threat both to Pennsylvania's commerce and to the safety of the colonial residents who lived along the Delaware Bay. Panic momentarily swept eastern Pennsylvania in mid-July 1747 when news reached Philadelphia that a raiding party from a French privateer had landed near Bombay Hook, approximately fifteen miles below New Castle, and had plundered two plantations. Because Governor Thomas had resigned his commission and departed for England six weeks prior to this incident, and because the Assembly was not in session, the Provincial Council under President Anthony Palmer called on John Kinsey and four other Philadelphia members of the Assembly to advise them what the legislature would be willing to do. Kinsey referred to the difficulties Quaker religious principles raised, implying that there would be no initiative from the legislature, and then added in characteristic fashion that while, on the one hand, the Assembly "would always show so much regard for what was intended for the benefit of the province that they would make compensation" for what the Council judged necessary to be done, on the other, such compensation would depend on the nature of those actions.[65] When the Assembly met in August and again in October its spokesmen followed Kinsey's example: they pointed out that there were, indeed, difficulties of conscience in this case, but by arguing, too, that there were military and financial reasons why the Assembly should not commit itself to financing a privateer or providing for other defensive measures, they kept open the possibility of some Assembly action if circumstances should change.[66]

Although there were no further attacks along the Delaware River in the fall of 1747, rumors persisted that the French were preparing privateers in the West Indian ports to cut off Pennsylvania's shipping and attack Philadelphia. Determined to channel apprehensions into constructive channels, Benjamin Franklin and a few of his confidants of the moment hatched a scheme to form a voluntary militia. The general response to Franklin's famous pamphlet *Plain Truth* is well known. Many Pennsylvania residents who were not conscientious objectors formed regiments of what was called the Voluntary Association, providing the province with a modest militia until the end of the war. As for the Quakers, their spokesmen warned all Friends that testimonies on pacifism forbade the bearing of arms, and the monthly meetings disowned those few who did join the association. Quakers did not, however, use the occasion to state any more clearly what the exact obligations of Pennsylvania legislators were in wartime, and they were quick to recognize the rights of non-Quakers to band together in militia units. In fact, their assertions of tolerance were so far from grudging admissions that they came very close to tacit encouragement—a situation that undoubtedly owed as much to self-interest as to charity.[67]

Despite the pressure that the formation of the Voluntary Association took off Quaker assemblymen, their problems were not quite over. During late May and early June 1748, French and Spanish ships blockaded the Delaware. Twice during this crisis the Provincial Council requested that the Assembly provide funds sufficient to outfit a man-of-war to send against the enemy. The responses they received were varied: a referral by the assemblymen to an earlier statement about their tender consciences and a denial of the practical wisdom of what the Council proposed; a private assurance from Speaker of the House John Kinsey that even if the Council were to commit the government to "any Expense, tho' it might happen in such an instance as the Assembly would not have advised," the legislature would make an "adequate provision . . . for the support of Government"; finally, an Assembly statement that it would bear the expense of whatever "reasonable" obligations the executive incurred during an emergency but that it thought the cost of fitting out and maintaining a ship of war was prohibitive. In the case of the assemblymen's last objection events proved them good prophets, for privateering activity dropped off in June, and in July news of preliminary peace negotiations reached Philadelphia.[68]

During the year of danger, from July 1747 to June 1748, Quakers were clearly undecided and confused about where their obligations lay. Not only had the current generation of Friends never before considered the province to be in serious danger, but they had also never before granted money for military purposes without an express order from the crown. Presumably, some of the sixty-odd Quakers who signed a petition to the Assembly in November 1747 requesting defense appropriations were prepared to do as Benjamin Franklin suggested in *Plain Truth*: vote a sum to the king's use without an express order from the crown, and leave it to others to oversee its expenditure. But, as a group, Quaker legislators rejected this step as being too innovative. What they did say was that, during periods of emergency when they were not sitting, they would honor council expenses as executive orders comparable to a royal command, subject only to the sometimes stated and sometimes implied proviso that these be reasonable.[69]

Behind the maneuvering of the Quaker assemblymen it is clear that different Friends leaned in different directions—and that some changed their position over the years. It is impossible, however, to enumerate points of view or estimate the number of adherents to each. Specific stands were usually the result of individual action or of some circumstance that forced isolation. Yet some individual experiences were revealing, for example, that of the well-known Philadelphia Quaker, John Smith. Although Smith was one of the most vociferous Quakers in denying that there was any special category of "defensive war" that allowed conscientious objectors some freedom to pursue warlike policies, in the May–June crisis of 1748 he apparently changed his mind. Taking John Kinsey at his word that the legislature would make "adequate provision . . . for the support of government" even if the executive council made commitments the "Assembly would not have advised," Smith started a private subscription that was to pay for the outfitting of a privateer.[70] His understanding, of course, was that when the Assembly next met it would reimburse himself and whoever else had contributed to the fund. Smith's action momentarily found a leading Quaker instigating a military action on the mere belief that Quaker legislators who had no direct orders from the crown would support that action. Needless to say, Smith concocted the scheme himself, and, although another well-known Quaker James Pemberton joined with him, that was as far as the subscription went. Other Friends convinced them to withdraw their pledges and canvass no more.[71]

As significant as Smith's erratic wanderings was what he wrote on being reprimanded by his peers. "Friends," he recorded, "in such cases ought as much as possible to stand still . . ."[72] In a situation where no consensus was readily apparent, where Friends were confused, uncertain, and showing signs of disagreement, the right course of action was the "expedient" one.[73] Among Quakers, temporization was conceived of as a positive form of action so long as it was combined with a determined effort to keep open as many options as possible. This was exactly the course of action Friends followed. Seeing no clear way, they opted for delay, and in 1747–48 time was on their side.

Once the immediate danger to Pennsylvania had receded, provincial residents were quick to let the defense issue drop, and the Quakers in particular were relieved to be able to turn their backs on a problem that had threatened to divide them. After the tensions of 1747–48, Friends were determined to keep peace among themselves, as well as with the executive, and in large measure they succeeded.[74] But the continued rivalry between Britain and France, which presaged a return to hostilities, could not be ignored for long. In the summer of 1753 the French began their advance into the Ohio country, and the following spring they routed the Virginia forces sent to fortify and protect the Ohio-Allegheny area.[75]

Despite the fears occasioned by the French success, demands for vigorous wartime policies by the governor and his allies, and General Braddock's preparations for his march to Fort Dusquesne, circumstances favored Friends' efforts to keep members of the Society from openly disagreeing on what policy the assemblymen should follow.[76] The Quakers' normal concerns for unity were reinforced by their suspicions of Governor James Hamilton, who, in vetoing the Assembly's vote of £10,000 to the king's use, funded on a ten-year excise extension, refused to grant an extension of the excise that would raise more money than the bill specifically appropriated.[77] Although Quaker leaders were not aware of what lay behind Hamilton's actions, they were afraid that the executive was trying to use the crisis to discredit them. As always, when the prospect of executive-legislative contention loomed ahead, Quakers counseled unity.

The second advantage the Quakers enjoyed was that from early 1754 until Braddock's defeat in July 1755, the Assembly had direct orders from the crown specifying what military aid the king expected Pennsylvania to provide.[78] Even though the royal orders involved the defense of Pennsylvania rather than some distant imperial venture, Quakers apparently considered the precedent of giving aid in answer to a direct order from the monarch broad enough to cover these new circumstances. Although some members of the Assembly refused to grant an appropriation for the defense of the Ohio country in the spring of 1754, events of that summer quickly changed their minds.[79] When the crown sent orders for military aid in the fall of 1754, a vote of £20,000 passed "almost unanimously."[80] In early 1755 such a well-known and conscientious Quaker as James Pemberton busied himself gathering provisions for Braddock's campaign. The Philadelphia Quarterly Meeting, whose membership included a number of Pennsylvania's most "weighty" Friends, sent an epistle to the London Meeting of Sufferings expressing the opinion that Quakers should continue to participate in government in order to protect their rights, and pointing out that they had provided, and would continue "to provide for the exigencies of government."[81] As late as May and June 1755, then, the vast majority of Friends accepted past votes to the king's use as precedents that covered the present situation, and this stand had provoked no outright dissent.

With Braddock's defeat in July 1755, however, the avoidance of dissent was no longer possible. Pennsylvanians knew they were in a war they would have to fight. If one of the obligations of government was to protect the province's citizens, then a militia would have to be formed and large sums of money would have to be raised, appropriated, and administered. This time there would be no explicit royal orders to hide behind; Pennsylvania's legislators were on their own.

In the late summer and early fall, those ministering Friends who had been reluctant to speak out openly about the obligations of assemblymen in early 1755 found their voices.[82] They and like-minded Quakers, some of whom had accepted the actions of the Assembly prior to Braddock's defeat, joined together to revive the spirit of the peace testimony by defining it anew. In publicly proclaiming their refusal to pay taxes they would support activities "inconsistent with the peace testimony," they finally broke the unity of Friends.[83]

For Pennsylvania's Quakers there had proved to be no long-run solution to their dilemma. The world would not leave them alone. But, during the entire early history of Pennsylvania, and most obviously during the fifteen years prior to Braddock's defeat, Quakers used to great advantage the political tactics of temporization. They accepted votes to the king's use as a minimal concession to their obligations as governors and refused to air the differences latent among them. Thus, on strength derived from the absence of a clear-cut definition of a fundamental testimony—the peace principle—Friends were successful both in retaining their political power and in practicing the politics of peace.

EPILOGUE

§

Between 1726 and 1755, Pennsylvania passed through a period of relative political stability. In large measure, Pennsylvania's politicians were successful in resolving, or accommodating themselves to, whatever differences stood between them, and thus the politics of peace predominated during those three decades. Of course, throughout the years of peace there were constant shifts in power relationships and endless incidents of minor conflict, but these were mainly of a routine nature that need be incorporated into any realistic model of a functional political system. Only in the late 1720s, when the Keithian disputes took place, the early 1740s, when Governor Thomas and the Assembly fell out, and again in 1754–55, when Thomas Penn initiated his challenge to the assemblymen's power of revenue appropriation, did outright political dissension wrack the province. While in each of the first two cases it is true that contention did bring important changes in the configurations of politics, the striking thing is how quickly those upheavals settled down into what were simply new variations of old patterns.

Throughout the thirty years of predominantly peaceful politics, the inner world of the politicians reflected that tranquillity. Provincial politics were governed by a widely accepted set of norms that restricted competition for office, put a premium on the accommodation of political differences, and tended to perpetuate the careers of established political leaders. Moreover, politics in Pennsylvania consisted mainly of traditional processes carried on within known parameters; the existing allocations of power were time sanctioned, and politicians knew, in most situations, both what their allegiances were and what they could expect from others. Even during times of anger, fear, and contention, the various forms of possible political action were familiar and the stance of the contending parties often predictable. Thus, the politician's world was a well-known one, characterized more by its stability than by its uncertainty.

Political stability—like instability—does not occur without reason, and, despite the caveats that must accompany all historical explanations, it is possible to identify some of the more important conditions that contributed to stability in Pennsylvania. There were, of course, the relatively obvious kinds of causes that were simply the responses of Pennsylvania politicians to public issues as they saw them. In the late 1720s and early 1730s fear of an external enemy—Maryland—drew Pennsylvanians together. Mindful of the disadvantage that a contention-ridden Pennsylvania would be at during the dispute with Maryland, tired of the political factionalism that William Keith had inspired, sensitive to the welcome the provincials had extended to William Penn's sons when they arrived in their colony, and aware that it was through the proprietary that they could best protect themselves from the aggressive Marylanders, Pennsylvania's politicians made an effort to reconcile their differences and prevent the surfacing of whatever disaffections developed in the larger community. In the 1740s and early 1750s different circumstances promoted the same ends. After 1742 the proprietary-executive supporters were so weak politically that they could not even challenge the electoral supremacy of the Quakers and their allies. Moreover, throughout the entire period, there was no important alteration in the relative distribution of power between the executive and legislative branches of government. Although Thomas Penn threatened at various times to try to regain some of the lost proprietary powers, he did not actually move in this direction until the 1750s, and only in 1754–55 did the uncertainty this effort was bound to entail begin to develop.

Beneath this level of explanation, however, there is another. The political stability that mid-eighteenth-century Pennsylvania experienced rested on a whole series of social, economic, political, and cultural conditions that were deeply embedded in the structure of provincial society. There were, for example, no social conflicts so divisive as to find serious political expression. In the cases of German immigration and the Great Awakening, where such conflict was possible, the danger was averted. Pennsylvania's open, pluralistic community structure was capable of absorbing changes in cultural composition and religious enthusiasm without undergoing drastic dislocation. Moreover, the structure of community in Pennsylvania worked to prevent the generation of indigenous social tensions; it was, simultaneously, flexible enough to accommodate the fluidity of a dynamic society, and cohesive enough to produce the type of community life that would satisfy the deep-felt needs of provincial residents.

Economic conditions, too, conspired to produce a society in which social discontent stayed at low levels. Pennsylvania's prosperity was widely shared, both economic dislocation and the social dislocation that could follow economic development were at a minimum, and upward mobility was visible. Preoccupied, as they were, with taking advantage of unprecedented economic opportunity, and sharing, as they did, a certain range of acquisitive norms, Pennsylvania's residents failed to find social differences among themselves that might have found expression in political affairs. Prosperity was a social lubricant and acquisitive norms a bond that together promoted unity in Pennsylvania society.

On the political level, of course, there were circumstances that made a more obvious contribution to the maintenance of political stability. The rough equilibrium that existed between executive and legislature throughout the second quarter of the eighteenth century was only the most evident of a sizable number of formal and informal political relationships that together promoted that end. On one hand, the existence and widespread acceptance of differential patterns in politics and the tight networks of influence that controlled access to elected office insulated politicians from their constituents; on the other, annual elections, the petitioning process, and the representatives' recognition of a responsibility to their constituents kept the legislature open and responsive. Similarly, although the degree of voter participation proved that Pennsylvania was not a highly politicized community, the timing of fluctuations in the level of voter interest indicated that electorate opinion could be, and was, effectively asserted through the ballot box. Thus, while social beliefs and political practices tended to keep Pennsylvania free of the kind of broadly based competitive style of politics that would have prevailed in a more democratic society, the political system was open enough to reflect changing ideas, attitudes, and interests. Narrow, yet responsive, Pennsylvania's political system kept power in the hands of the few while retaining the confidence of the many.

As might be expected in a society where informal patterns of political behavior were well established, governmental organization and administrative procedures were orderly as well. By 1726 the institutionalization of government had proceeded to the point where over the ensuing thirty years there were only minor changes in governmental organization and administrative affairs. This development was of importance not only in the old counties, where the existence of these time-sanctioned patterns promoted social order, but also in the new. In a fast-growing society like Pennsylvania, residents of newly settled areas had only to look to the old counties to find an acceptable model for the organization of county and township government. Thus, it was through the establishment of standardized administrative and governmental procedures, as well as through the representation of new areas in the provincial legislature, that Pennsylvanians promoted the kind of horizontal integration of provincial society that tended to retard the development of serious regional differences and the rivalries that those differences would entail.

As prominent as the structural features of political and governmental organization must be in any explanation of political stability, they alone are not equal to the task. As much as political procedures and institutional patterns mold men, so are men responsible for the shape those political procedures and institutional patterns take. If members of the politically active community value political stability enough, they will achieve that goal, at least part of the time. If they genuinely dislike political contention they will devise procedures that will normally resolve conflict that arises. In mid-eighteenth-century Pennsylvania, provincial residents did share a strong commitment to the kinds of values that promoted political stability. Generally, men believed that peace and concord should govern political relationships and that all contention, except that which was entered into to protect Pennsylvania's balanced constitution, was illegitimate. What reinforced the efficacy of these values was the peculiarly intense allegiance Quakers swore to those ideals. Friends strove for harmony among themselves, counseled conciliation with their neighbors, and tried to avoid any self-definition that would provoke serious dissension. In their worldly way, this generation of Friends worked for social and political unity both within the meeting house and without, thus promoting order and stability in political affairs.

The existence of this period of political peace and stability in Pennsylvania raises several important questions: Were the predominantly peaceful politics of Pennsylvania some kind of strange aberration—or were they duplicated elsewhere? Taken together, were those quiet years only a momentary calm in a world of political chaos—or were colonial politics more restrained than many believe? Was this period of stability *sui generis*, of virtually no meaning at all in the broader context of colonial history—or did it reflect similar trends elsewhere? In short, what does the Pennsylvania experience signify?

The answer to such questions lies in the realm of comparative politics and thus, without the benefit of a full-scale investigation, must be skeletal. That, however, need not make it tentative. Even a cursory glance at other colonies, such as South Carolina, Virginia, and Massachussetts, establishes that political peace occurred over long periods of time in the eighteenth century and that many of the basic patterns of political behavior in these colonies were of an enduring kind.[1] Moreover, many of those features of Pennsylvania society that comprised the bases of political stability were well-known components of political life in the other mainland colonies—certainly not in the same proportion, often in a different guise, sometimes with new variations, but nevertheless recognizably there.

The existence of periods of relatively stable politics in colonies other than Pennsylvania means, of course, that the political conditions of mid-eighteenth-century Pennsylvania are much more than a curiosity. They reflect general tendencies in early American politics, tendencies that because of prevailing preoccupations with the apparent disfunctions of colonial politics have been largely ignored. If historians are to understand the world of the eighteenth-century politician, if they are to fathom the early forms of American political behavior, there will have to be even further clarification of the range of political behavior in early America and a more complete elaboration of the kinds of conditions that supported or undermined stable political relationships. To this end, the Pennsylvania case can be of some help. It suggests, both implicitly and explicitly, a whole range of criteria useful in determining the extent of political stability in any society.[2]

For example, in recent years there has been renewed interest in conflict models of social analysis, and colonial historians, sharing this interest, have cast about considerably for evidence of social tensions in eighteenth-century America. In fact, part of the case for the prevalence of acute political instability in the colonies rests on the assumption that in societies in which social tensions exist the political structure *must* be fragile. As the Pennsylvania experience illustrates, however, in situations where serious social disfunction reputedly exists, and where there is no clear-cut evidence of consequent political disruption, such categorization deserves a hard look. Social tension and conflict exist in any society whether it be politically stable or not. The crucial question is how, or to what degree, conflict is resolved and tension eased. Moreover, it is clear that in many instances the social conflict that appears to disrupt parts of society simultaneously serves as an integrative force in others. The point, then, is that while it is obviously true that social malaise may produce political instability, the mere existence of social tensions does not automatically demonstrate that the political structure is particularly unstable.

In addition to reexamining eighteenth-century societies with these reservations in mind, it will also be necessary to look more critically at political leadership in the various colonies with an eye to determining what the actual patterns of leadership reveal about the relative degree of political stability in a given period. What is important here is not only to ask the right questions but to ask enough of the right questions. It will not do simply to ask if political contention exists; the historian must go on to examine the extent of the contentions he finds, the character of the dissension, and the tolls of the conflict on the political leadership's effectiveness. It is not enough simply to ask if there is evidence of intraelite conflict; the historian must go on to investigate how conflict is resolved, if the turnover in leadership implies anything more than a simple replacement of existing elite members, and what sorts of continuities and discontinuities appear in the associations that politicians form. Again it is not enough simply to catalogue evidence of political change; the historian must go on to explore the apparent effects of that change. What does increasing or decreasing politicization of the electorate mean for the politicians? What alterations in the character and behavior of the political elite do new methods of choosing political leaders actually produce? How do new circumstances affect the relationship of the political elite to the different geographical areas in the existing political unit? How does collective violence, when it occurs, affect the established political leaders? Drawn on piecemeal, as they often are, these kinds of questions will only serve to perpetuate old biases, but used together they can lead to the establishment of reliable indicators of the degree of leadership stability, or instability, that a society enjoys.

There is one final type of consideration that constitutes crucially important, but often overlooked grounds for judging the overall level of political stability in any society. This is the stability, not of political leadership within a given regime, but of the regime itself. One determinant of regime stability, of course, is the durability of a given set of constitutional relationships. If the constitutional framework of any society remains intact over a relatively long period of time, that in itself is evidence of a considerable degree of political stability; if it does not, it can be ultimate evidence of political instability. But it is not enough, especially in the case of the eighteenth-century American colonies, simply to distinguish between societies that experience numerous constitutional changes and those that do not, for within the life span of any regime there will be variations in the stability of the established constitutional framework. More importantly, there could be distinct changes in the regard that members of a political community accorded the established regime. Thus, the legitimacy of a regime—the capacity of that regime "to engender and maintain the belief that the existing political institutions are the most appropriate ones for the society" may vary over time, and in doing so affect the degree of political stability.[3] If the level of legitimacy of a regime is high, so will stability likely be high; if low, so will stability likely be low.

But again, the important point is not that there are categories of opposites, in this case of legitimacy and illegitimacy, but that there are levels of legitimacy. Too often, for example, commentators on Pennsylvania have smelled the smoke of illegitimacy and, without turning to see if it came from candle flame or forest fire, proclaimed the presence of deep-seated political instability in that colony.[4] True, in 1741-42, just as in the early 1720s and between 1755 and 1765, there was protest against the proprietary form of government, but the only significant change Pennsylvanians envisaged for their provincial constitution was the termination of the proprietary role in government. Beyond that, they expected no more than a confirmation of the existing political situation—a dominant Assembly, a weak chief executive, a reasonably independent judiciary, and widespread enjoyment of traditional popular rights.

As the Pennsylvania situation illustrates, there are criteria by which the degrees of legitimacy in different societies may be judged: for example, the sources of illegitimate feeling, the extent of vocal and written protest against the constitution, the ability of the political elite to fulfill the functions assigned to it under the existing set of constitutional relationships, and the incidence, kind, and purpose of collective violence. In addition to these kinds of criteria, however, there is also in the case of eighteenth-century America one special circumstance that has a very important bearing on the possible levels of legitimacy. Illegitimacy and political instability, it might be argued, were bound to be omnipresent in the colonies, for the colonial relationship itself was profoundly unsettling, and the later colonial years are most profitably viewed as a prelude to independence. There is a certain plausibility to this reasoning, and thus, it has done good service in the hands of those who stress the peculiar instability of colonial American society.[5] On close examination, however, it is clear that this kind of generalization—that the colonies shared an extravagant amount of political instability because they were incomplete societies—is not soundly based, for it simply assumes what needs to be proven. And to prove that, may, indeed, be difficult, for even the most fleeting glance at *autonomous* European societies during the early modern period reveals many symptoms of political instability—perhaps more than existed in the dependent American societies. Moreover, there is a good deal of evidence that other early modern and modern colonial societies have passed through periods of relative political stability despite their lack of autonomy.[6] While it may be that colonial status reduces to some extent the chances of a society experiencing extremely long periods of political stability and complicates, to some degree, the problems of political leadership, there is no reason to believe that members of a colonial society cannot resolve their conflicts and find the tensions under which they live eased to the point where they can sustain stable political relationships over a significant period of time.

To say that historians need to inquire more closely into the conditions and origins of political stability in the American colonies is not to say that political instabilities were somehow absent from colonial society. Of course they were present, as the uncertainties of political contention in mid-eighteenth-century Pennsylvania point out. But such uncertainties, as well as the conflict that underlay them and the state of mind that accompanied them, are misleading if they are taken by themselves and wrenched out of context. The unstable factionalism and paranoic suspicion that Bernard Bailyn has emphasized may have dwarfed all other American political characteristics after the mid-1760s, but only because they were triggered by the very real and observable changes in British imperial policy. Prior to that time they were much less prominent, only one facet of a very complex political world. If students of early America are to understand that world, they must accept it in its totality and strive to reproduce it in its true proportions. In a world in which there was political calm as well as crisis, there must be room for both.

As always, there is the question of emphasis, and here again Pennsylvania has something to say. Although there was political faction and contention in mid-eighteenth-century provincial politics, this was not the most prominent feature. Rather it was the peaceful activities of first, second, and third generation Americans—as they worked out political compromises, accommodated themselves to each other, and created the means of resolving conflict, all in the interest of perpetuating the political harmony they so clearly valued. In a new, expanding society, which was susceptible to the tensions that growth could bring as well as those which often accompanied colonial status, what was truly remarkable was the prevalence of political peace. Pennsylvanians were determined to have a stable politics, and they succeeded despite the obstacles that stood in their way. That, of course, should not be surprising. Despite the many and various kinds of instabilities that the new world allegiance to growth and change has entailed, America is widely acknowledged to be one of the three or four societies which has experienced the most political stability in modern history. What Americans were to do again and again in the future, Pennsylvanians had accomplished in the mid-eighteenth century. That was what was inherently American about the Pennsylvanian experience.

APPENDICES

APPENDIX I.1

RELIGIOUS COMPOSITION OF THE ASSEMBLY BY YEAR, 1729-54

Bucks Co. (8 seats)	1729-30	1730-31	1731-32	1732-33	1733-34	1734-35	1735-36	1736-37	1737-38	1738-39	1739-40	1740-41	1741-42	1742-43	1743-44	1744-45	1745-46	1746-47	1747-48	1748-49	1749-50	1750-51	1751-52	1752-53	1753-54	1754-55
	Q	Q	Q	Q	Q	Q	Q	Q	Q	Q	Q	Q	Q	Q	Q	Q	Q	Q	Q	Q	Q	Q	Q	Q	Q	Q
	Q	Q	Q	Q	Q	Q	Q	Q	Q	Q	Q	Q	Q	Q	Q	Q	Q	Q	Q	Q	Q	Q	Q	Q	Q	Q
	Q	Q	Q	Q	Q	Q	Q	Q	Q	Q	Q	Q	Q	Q	Q	Q	Q	Q	Q	Q	Q	Q	Q	Q	Q	Q
	Q?	Q?	Q?	Q?	Q?	Q?	Q?	Q?	Q?	Q	Q	Q	Q	Q	Q	Q	Q	Q	Q	Q	Q	Q	Q	Q	Q	Q
	DR	Q	DR	Q	Q	Q	DR	DR	DR	Q	Q	Q	Q	Q	Q	Q	Q	Q	Q	Q	Q	Q	Q	Q	Q	Q
	P	DR	P	DR	Q	Q	P	P	P	Q	Q	Q	Q	Q	Q	Q	Q	Q	Q	Q	DR	DR	DR	DR	Q	Q
	P	P	P	P	Q	P	P	P	P	Q?	Q?	Q	Q	Q	Q	Q	Q	Q	DR	?	NQ	NQ	NQ	NQ	DR	DR
	NQ	NQ	P	NQ	Q	DR	NQ	NQ	NQ	P	P	Q?	DR	DR	DR	DR	Q	DR	NQ	DR	NQ	NQ	NQ	NQ	NQ	NQ

continued . . .

APPENDIX I.1 – continued

Chester Co. (8 seats)

Year	Seat 1	Seat 2	Seat 3	Seat 4	Seat 5	Seat 6	Seat 7	Seat 8
1729–30	Q	Q	Q	Q	Q	Q	Q	Q?
1730–31	Q	Q	Q	Q	Q	Q	Q?	A?
1731–32	Q	Q	Q	Q	Q	Q	Q	Q
1732–33	Q	Q	Q	Q	Q	Q	Q	Q?
1733–34	Q	Q	Q	Q	Q	Q	Q	A
1734–35	Q	Q	Q	Q	Q	Q	A	B
1735–36	Q	Q	Q	Q	Q	Q	A	B
1736–37	Q	Q	Q	Q	Q	Q?	A	B
1737–38	Q	Q	Q	Q	Q?	Q?	A	B
1738–39	Q	Q	Q	Q	Q	Q?	Q?	A
1739–40	Q	Q	Q	Q	Q	Q?	Q?	A
1740–41	Q	Q	Q	Q	Q	Q	Q?	Q?
1741–42	Q	Q	Q	Q	Q	Q	Q?	Q?
1742–43	Q	Q	Q	Q	Q	Q	Q?	Q?
1743–44	Q	Q	Q	Q	Q	Q	Q	Q?
1744–45	Q	Q	Q	Q	Q	Q	Q	Q?
1745–46	Q	Q	Q	Q	Q	Q	Q	Q?
1746–47	Q	Q	Q	Q	Q	Q	Q	Q?
1747–48	Q	Q	Q	Q	Q	Q	Q	Q?
1748–49	Q	Q	Q	Q	Q	Q	Q	Q?
1749–50	Q	Q	Q	Q	Q	Q	Q?	P
1750–51	Q	Q	Q	Q	Q	Q	Q	Q?
1751–52	Q	Q	Q	Q	Q	Q	Q	Q?
1752–53	Q	Q	Q	Q	Q	Q	Q	Q
1753–54	Q	Q	Q	Q	Q	Q	Q	Q
1754–55	Q	Q	Q	Q	Q	Q	Q	Q

continued . . .

APPENDIX I.1 - continued

Year	Philadelphia Co. (8 seats)								Philadelphia City (2 seats)	
1729-30	Q	Q	Q	Q	Q	B	B	?	A	A
1730-31	Q	Q	Q	Q	A	P	NQ	?	A	A
1731-32	Q	Q	Q	Q	Q	A	A	P	Q	A
1732-33	Q	Q	Q	Q	Q	Q	A	P	Q	A
1733-34	Q	Q	Q	Q	Q	Q	A	P	Q	A
1734-35	Q	Q	Q	Q	Q	Q	A	P	Q	A
1735-36	Q	Q	Q	Q	Q	Q	A	P	Q	A
1736-37	Q	Q	Q	Q	Q	A	P	NQ	Q	A
1737-38	Q	Q	Q	Q	Q	Q	A	P	Q	A
1738-39	Q	Q	Q	Q	Q	Q	A	P	Q	A
1739-40	Q	Q	Q	Q	Q	Q	Q	A	Q	A
1740-41	Q	Q	Q	Q	Q	Q	Q	A	Q	A
1741-42	Q	Q	Q	Q	Q	Q	Q	A	Q	?
1742-43	Q	Q	Q	Q	Q	Q	Q	A	Q	?
1743-44	Q	Q	Q	Q	Q	Q	Q	A	Q	?
1744-45	Q	Q	Q	Q	Q	Q	Q	A	Q	?
1745-46	Q	Q	Q	Q	Q	Q	Q	A	Q	?
1746-47	Q	Q	Q	Q	Q	Q	Q	A	Q	?
1747-48	Q	Q	Q	Q	Q	Q	Q	A	Q	?
1748-49	Q	Q	Q	Q	Q	Q	Q	Q	?	A
1749-50	Q	Q	Q	Q	Q	Q	Q	Q	?	A
1750-51	Q	Q	Q	Q	Q	Q	Q	A	Q	A?
1751-52	Q	Q	Q	Q	Q	Q	A	A	Q	D
1752-53	Q	Q	Q	Q	Q	Q	Q	A	Q	D
1753-54	Q	Q	Q	Q	Q	Q	Q	A	Q	D
1754-55	Q	Q	Q	Q	Q	Q	Q	A	Q	D

continued . . .

APPENDIX I.1 - continued

	1729-30	1730-31	1731-32	1732-33	1733-34	1734-35	1735-36	1736-37	1737-38	1738-39	1739-40	1740-41	1741-42	1742-43	1743-44	1744-45	1745-46	1746-47	1747-48	1748-49	1749-50	1750-51	1751-52	1752-53	1753-54	1754-55
Lancaster Co. (4 seats)	Q	Q	Q	Q	Q	Q	A	A	Q	Q	Q	Q	Q	Q	Q	Q	Q	Q	Q	Q	Q	Q	Q	Q	Q	Q
	A	Q	A	A	A	P	P	P	P	P	Q	Q	Q	Q	Q	Q	Q	Q	Q	Q	Q	Q	Q	Q	Q	Q
	P	A	P	P	P	P	P	P	P	P	A	Q	Q	Q	Q	P	P	P	Q	Q	Q	Q	Q	Q	Q	Q
	?	?	P	?	P	P	P	P	P	P	A?	A?	Q	Q	P	P	P	P	P	P	P	P	P	P	P	P
York Co. (2 seats)																					Q	Q	Q	Q	Q	Q
																					P	?	?	NQ	NQ	NQ
Cumberland Co. (2 seats)																						P	P	P	P	P
																						?	NQ	NQ	P	NQ
Northampton Co.																								M	M Q?	M
Berks Co.																								Q	Q	Q

Symbols: Q – Quaker, NQ – not a Quaker but religion unknown, DR – Dutch Reformed, P – Presbyterian, A – Anglican, B – Baptist, D – deist (used only in Benjamin Franklin's case), M – Moravian, ? – unknown, symbol and ? – likely but some doubt.

PROFILE OF CHESTER COUNTY ASSEMBLYMEN, 1729-54

Name	Relative Wealth Holdings[x]	Religious Affiliation[*]	Religious Office[o]
Ashbridge, George, Jr.	Top 10%	Q	QM, YM
Brinton, Joseph	Top 10%	Q	QM, YM
Chandler, Thomas	80-90%	Q (?)	--
Cowpland, Caleb	Top 10%	Q	QM, YM
Cummings, Thomas	70-80%	Q	QM, YM
Davis, John	Top 10%	Q	QM, YM
Dicks, Peter	Top 10%	Q	QM, YM
Evans, John	Top 10%	Baptist	--
Gibbons, James, Jr.	Top 10%	Q	QM
Gibbons, Joseph	Top 10%	Q	QM, YM
Gilpin, Samuel	80-90%	Q	--
Grubb, Nathaniel	Top 10%	Q	--
Harvey, Joseph	Top 10%	Q	QM
Hayes, Henry	Top 10%	Anglican (?)	--
Hayes, Richard	Top 10%	Q	YM
Hockley, Henry	Top 10%	Q	--
Howell, Jacob	70-80%	Q	QM, YM
Hughes, William	Top 10%	Q (?)	--

continued . . .

APPENDIX II.1 - continued

Name	Relative Wealth Holdings[x]	Religious Affiliation[*]	Religious Office
Hunt, Roger	Top 10%	Presbyterian	--
James, James[+]	70-80%	Q	--
James, Joseph	Top 10%	Q	QM
Lewis, Evan	Top 10%	Q	QM, YM
Lewis, Robert	Top 10%	Q	QM, YM
Levis, Samuel, Jr.	Top 10%	Q	QM, YM
Lewis, Samuel	Top 10%	Q	QM
Lloyd, David	Top 10%	Q	QM
Moore, William	Top 10%	Anglican	--
Owen, John	80-90%	Q	QM
Parry, John	Top 10%	Q	--
Pennock, Joseph	Top 10%	Q	QM, YM
Pennock, Nathaniel	Top 10%	Q	QM
Peters, William	Top 10%	Q	QM, YM
Pierce, Henry	Top 10%	Q	--
Starr, Jeremiah	60-70%	Q	QM
Tatnall, Thomas[+]	Top 10%	Q	QM
Taylor, John	Top 10%	Q	--
Thomas, Thomas[+]	Top 10%	Q	--
Webb, William[+]	Top 10%	Q	QM
Worth, Thomas	Top 10%	Q	QM, YM
Yarnal, Francis	80-90%	Q	QM

continued . . .

APPENDIX II.1 - continued

^x Relative to other county residents. This information is based
on an analysis of three tax lists: 1730, 1740, and 1751. I located
the legislators on the one of these three lists which came closest to
the midpoint of his term in office.

[*] In cases where I am not entirely certain about affiliation,
or where affiliation may have changed during the twenty-five year period
I have added a (?).

^o Includes only service by Quakers as Quarterly or Yearly Meeting
representatives (QM - Quarterly Meeting, YM - Yearly Meeting).

⁺ Disowned after having served in the Assembly.

PROFILE OF BUCKS AND PHILADELPHIA ASSEMBLYMEN,
1729-54

Name	Religious Affiliation	If Quaker – Attendance at Yearly Meeting
Bucks County		
Biles, William	Q	
Brown, Samuel	Q	YM
Canby, Thomas	Q	YM
Canby, Thomas, Jr.	Q	YM
Chapman, Abraham	Q	YM
Child, Cephas	Q	YM
Eastburn, Samuel	Q	YM
Fell, Joseph	Q	
Field, Benjamin	Q	YM
Growdon, Lawrence	Q	
Hall, John	Q	
Hamilton, Andrew	Presbyterian	
Hampton, Joseph	Q	
Hoge, William	Q	
Hogelandt, Derrick	Dutch Reformed	
Hughes, Mathew	(?) (Non-Quaker)	
Ingham, Jonathan	Q	YM
Jones, Benjamin	Presbyterian	

continued . . .

APPENDIX II.2 - continued

Name	Religious Affiliation	If Quaker – Attendance at Yearly Meeting
Kirkbride, Joseph, Jr.	Q	YM
Kirkbride, Mahlon	Q	YM
Langhorne, Jeremiah	Q (?)	
Logan, George	(?)	
Marriot, Thomas	Q	
Mitchell, Richard	Q	
Owen, Griffith	(?) (Non–Quaker)	
Paxon, William	Q	YM
Shaw, Joseph	Q	YM
Smith, William	Q	YM (?)
Vanhorne, Christian	Dutch Reformed	
Vansant, Garret	Dutch Reformed	
Walker, Richard	(?) (Non–Quaker)	
Watson, John	Q	YM
Watson, Mark	Q	YM
Woolston, John	Q	YM

Philadelphia City and County

Allen, William	Presbyterian	
Cadwalader, John	Q	YM
Callender, William	Q	YM

continued . . .

APPENDIX II.2 - continued

Name	Religious Affiliation	If Quaker — Attendance at Yearly Meeting
Clymer, William	Anglican (?)	
Evans, Hugh	Q	YM
Evans, Owen	Q	YM
Farmar, Edward	Anglican	
Fox, Joseph	Q	
Franklin, Benjamin	D	
Goodson, Job	Q	YM
Horne, Edward	Q	
Jones, John	Q	YM
Jones, Robert	Q	YM
Kearsley, John	Anglican	
Kinsey, John	Q	YM
Leech, Thomas	Anglican	
Monington, William	Q	
Morgan, Evan, Jr.	Anglican	
Morris, James	Q	
Morris, Joshua	Q	YM
Morris, Morris	Q	YM
Norris, Isaac, Sr.	Q	YM
Norris, Isaac, Jr.	Q	YM
Pawling, Henry	Anglican	
Peele, Oswald	(?)[*]	

continued . . .

APPENDIX II.2 - continued

Name	Religious Affiliation	If Quaker – Attendance at Yearly Meeting
Pemberton, Israel, Sr.	Q	YM
Pemberton, Israel, Jr.	Q	YM
Pemberton, James	Q	
Potts, David	(?)	
Roberts, Hugh	Q	
Robeson, Jonathan	Q	
Robinson, Septimus	(?) (Non-Quaker)	
Rutter, Thomas, Jr.	Baptist	
Smith, John	Q	YM
Stretch, Joseph	Q	
Swift, John	Baptist	
Tress, Thomas	Anglican	
Trotter, Joseph	Q	
Warner, Edward	Q	
White, John	(?) (Non-Quaker)	

*
 Married to a Quaker, was disowned but buried in a Quaker cemetery.

APPENDIX II.3

ANNUAL TURNOVER IN ASSEMBLY MEMBERSHIP,
1727-55

Year	No. of New Men	No. of Men Returning After Break in Service	Total Turnover	Total House Membership
1727-28	5	3	8	26
1728-29	4	1	5	26
1729-30	9	6	15	30
1730-31	8	3	11	30
1731-32	5	4	9	30
1732-33	4	5	9	30
1733-34	5	3	8	30
1734-35	4	4	8	30
1735-36	5	4	9	30
1736-37	1	2	3	30
1737-38	2	5	7	30
1738-39	3	7	10	30
1739-40	7	4	11	30
1740-41	3	1	4	30
1741-42	3	1	4	30
1742-43	-	-	-	30
1743-44	3	2	5	30
1744-45	-	2	2	30
1745-46	4	-	4	30

continued . . .

APPENDIX II.3 - continued

Year	No. of New Men	No. of Men Returning After Break in Service	Total Turnover	Total House Membership
1746–47	5	1	6	30
1747–48	3	1	4	30
1748–49	3	1	4	30
1749–50	9	5	14	32
1750–51	10	3	13	34
1751–52	6	1	7	34
1752–53	8	3	11	36
1753–54	4	2	6	36
1754–55	1	1	2	36
TOTALS	124	75	199	860

     Reasons for the turnover in membership were not solely poli-tical. In 19 different cases it was clearly old age, illness or death that ended an incumbent's career. In 10 other situations explicit com-ments by contemporaries indicated that assemblymen refused to serve any longer because of personal affairs or other public obligations. In addition, the turnover rates increased, artificially, when the Assembly added new seats--in 1729-30, 4 new members appeared for Lancaster County (one of whom had served before for Chester County), in 1749-50, 2 from York, in 1750-51, 2 from Cumberland, in 1752-53, 1 from Northampton and 1 from Berks.

APPENDIX II.4

GEOGRAPHICAL DISTRIBUTION OF CHESTER COUNTY
REPRESENTATIVES, 1727-55

Township	No. of Assembly Years Represented	Within 24 Mile Radius of Philadelphia
Aston	5	X
Birmingham	22	X
East Bradford	3	
East Caln	1	
Charlestown	7	X
Chester	21	X
Lower Chichester	7	X
Concord	4	X
Darby	4	X
Gosen	12	X
Haverford	10	X
Kennett	9	
London Britain	5	
London Grove	6	
East Marlborough	2	
West Marlborough	14	
East Nantmeal	4	
Nether Providence	7	X
Newtown	1	X

continued . . .

APPENDIX II.4 - continued

Township	No. of Assembly Years Represented	Within 24 Mile Radius of Philadelphia
Radnor	2	X
Ridley	19	X
Springfield	19	X
Thornbury	10	X
Westtown	18	X
Willistown	12	X
TOTAL	224	180

NUMBER AND DISTRIBUTION OF ASSEMBLY LEADERS

Year	Phila-delphia (County)	Phila-delphia (City)	Bucks	Chester	Lan-caster	York	Cumber-land	North-ampton	Berks	Total No. of Leaders	No. of Assembly Seats
1727-28	2	2	4	3						11	26
1728-29	2	2	4	3						11	26
1729-30	3	–	3	2	1					9	30
1730-31	3	1	2	2	1					9	30
1731-32	3	1	3	2	–					9	30
1732-33	2	2	3	–	1					8	30
1733-34	4	1	3	–	–					8	30
1734-35	3	2	3	1	1					10	30
1735-36	4	1	2	2	1					10	30
1736-37	3	2	3	1	1					10	30
1737-38	3	2	2	1	–					8	30
1738-39	3	1	3	1	1					9	30
1739-40	5	2	–	1	1					9	30
1740-41	4	1	1	1	–					7	30
1741-42	4	1	1	1	1					8	30
1742-43	5	1	1	1	1					9	30

continued . . . .

185

APPENDIX II.5   Table A (continued)

Year	Philadelphia (County)	Philadelphia (City)	Bucks	Chester	Lancaster	York	Cumberland	Northampton	Berks	Total No. of Leaders	No. of Assembly Seats
1743–44	4	1	1	1	1					8	30
1744–45	6	2	–	–	–					8	30
1745–46	5	2	2	–	–					9	30
1746–47	5	1	1	1	–					8	30
1747–48	6	2	–	1	–					9	30
1748–49	6	2	1	1	–					10	30
1749–50	4	2	–	1	1	1				9	32
1750–51	5	1	1	1	1	1	–			10	34
1751–52	4	2	1	1	1	1	–			10	34
1752–53	4	1	1	1	1	–	–	1	–	9	36
1753–54	3	3	1	1	1	–	–	–	1	10	36
1754–55	4	2	1	1	1	–	–	1	1	11	36
TOTALS	109	43	48	32	17	3	–	2	2	256	860

APPENDIX II.5   TABLE **B**

PERCENT OF COMMITTEE LEADERSHIP COMPARED WITH
PERCENT OF REPRESENTATION

Electoral Unit	Leaders	% Leadership	% House Seats
Philadelphia Co.	109	42.5	26.0
Philadelphia City	43	17.0	6.5
Bucks Co.	48	19.0	26.0
Chester Co.	32	12.5	26.0
Lancaster Co.	17	6.5	12.0
York Co.	3		
Cumberland Co.	–	2.5	3.5
Northampton Co.	2		
Berks Co.	2	——	——
TOTALS	256	100.0	100.0

APPENDIX II.6

LEGISLATIVE RECORD OF THE ASSEMBLY, 1726-54

A. No. of petitions per year.[a]

B. No. of issues raised in petitions that required legislation.[b]

C. No. of issues answered by legislation.[c]

D. No. of acts passed in response to petitions.[d]

E. Total no. of acts passed.

Year	A	B	C	D	E
1726–27	23	7	4	4	6
1727–28	10	8	5	–	–
1728–29	26	13	8	6	8
1729–30	19	8	3	4	11
1730–31	20	7	4	4	8
1731–32	6	4	1	1	4
1732–33	6	–	–	–	–
1733–34	21	9	3	2	5
1734–35	17	8	3	2	5
1735–36	13	6	3	2	4
1736–37	5	–	–	–	–
1737–38	16	2	1	1	3
1738–39	21	11	3	5	6
1739–40	20	8	–	–	–
1740–41	4	–	–	–	–

continued . . .

APPENDIX II.6 - continued

Year	A	B	C	D	E
1741–42	3	–	–	–	–
1742–43	31	7	2	2	6
1743–44	26	3	–	–	2
1744–45	22	6	–	–	1
1745–46	21	6	2	3	9
1746–47	33	3	2	1	1
1747–48	7	1	–	–	–
1748–49	25	11	6	2	7
1749–50	43	10	7	6	7
1750–51	25	10	6	4	5
1751–52	39	21	7	7	8
1752–53	20	3	–	–	–
1753–54	23	8	–	–	–
TOTALS	545	180	70	56	106

[a] In occasional instances a rash of redundant petitions have been recorded in the legislative journals as "sundry petitions." For purposes of tabulation I have assigned these the value of one. The Assembly year ran from October 14th to October 1st of the following year.

[b] In deciding what was an "issue" I used the criterion of what would be a meaningful separation of items in legislative terms. Since many petitions were redundant and others contained several requests, it is necessary to deal with "issues" rather than petitions.

[c] Issues raised by petition have been counted as being answered if the appropriate legislation was passed within 4 years of the tabling of the petition.

[d] Some acts dealt with several issues as well as with matters that had not been raised by petitions.

CASES HEARD BY COURT OF QUARTER SESSIONS
IN CHESTER COUNTY, 1726–1755

Year	Assault & Battery	Disturbing the Peace and Riot	Forcible Entry & Jailbreaking	Larceny	Fornication, Adultery Rape, & Bastardy	Counterfeiting & Forgery	Selling Liquor without a License	Keeping a Disorderly House	Contempt of Authority	Unidentified	Miscellaneous[x]
1726	4			1	3				1		
1727	2			7	3			1			
1728	6			3	2						
1729	6			2	2						
1730	8	3		3	1		3	1			1
1731	7	12		4	2						
1732	5			2	4						
1733	4			5	3					2	
1734	6			8	7		1			6	
1735	5			3	3					5	
1736	9	4		2	4		2		2	3	
1737	2	4		3	2		1		1	1	2
1738	12			3	2		3		1	5	
1739*											
1740	4			6	3	2	1		1		
1741	1			6	4						
1742	7	1	1	3	6	2	2	1	2		

continued . . .

APPENDIX III.1 - continued

Year	Assault & Battery	Disturbing the Peace and Riot	Forcible Entry & Jailbreaking	Larceny	Fornication, Adultery, Rape, & Bastardy	Counterfeiting & Forgery	Selling Liquor without a License	Keeping a Disorderly House	Contempt of Authority	Unidentified	Miscellaneous[x]
1743	6			9	6		1			5	4
1744	4	5	1	6	8					5	7
1745	17		3	7	4		1		1	2	2
1746	6			7	7	2				11	
1747	12	1		6	16	1	1	1		5	1
1748	3			2	13					6	
1749	9			7	10			1		3	
1750	3			5	13	1		2		1	
1751	10			8	4					2	1
1752	10	1		6	12					6	2
1753	4			5	7			1		3	1
1754	11			5						7	
1755	9	—	1	10	8	—	—	—	—	15	7
TOTALS	192	31	6	144	159	8	16	8	9	93	28

[x] Miscellaneous charges included scandalizing, inhuman and barbarous treatment of wife, bigamy, nuisance, cutting a gelding's tongue out, killing a gelding, cheating, speaking seditious words, publishing seditious words, trespass and murder.

* Records missing.

APPENDIX IV. 1

A NOTE ON PROVINCIAL FINANCES

A. The Loan Office

Pennsylvania's Loan Office began its activities in March 1723, when, inspired by the currency experiments of other colonies and prodded by a serious economic depression, the legislature framed an act calling for the printing of £15,000 in bills of various denominations, which were to be made available as loans to provincial residents. Individuals could borrow between £12.10.0 and £100 at an interest rate of 5 percent per annum, principal and interest repayable in equal yearly payments over an eight-year period. The trustees in charge of the operation were to accept as security lands, at least twice the value of the loan; houses and lots, at least three times the value of the loan; and plate valued at five shillings per ounce. The realty had to be held in fee simple, with no encumbrances other than proprietary quitrents. Each year, whatever currency was returned as a part of the annual payment was to be destroyed and the amount of hard money received that was over and above the total interest due was to be used to redeem paper currency that current holders wished to turn in. Of course, an individual could pay off his entire mortgage at any time, but, assuming that this was not done with any regularity, approximately one-eighth of the paper currency would be removed from circulation each year. In this legislation, as in all future acts, the currency used to pay public debts was to be funded mainly by an excise tax on retailed liquor, while money loaned to the counties was to repaid from funds raised in the annual county levies.

Nine months after the original legislation had been passed, Pennsylvanians decided that the £15,000 in circulation was insufficient, and the Assembly passed an act adding £30,000 more. This piece of legislation was much the same as the initial currency bill but there were some significant changes. The ceiling was set at £200 rather than half that amount, and the term was twelve and one-half years rather than eight. The only other noteworthy change was that there was a provision for the reemission of currency when mortgages were paid off early. Such loans were to be paid off within the original twelve-year time limit, and payments were to be proportioned according to the number of years left within that period when the loan was taken out.

By the end of 1725 the shortcomings of these acts were apparent. The £15,000 act had run two and one-half years and over one-fourth of the currency had been sunk, while the two-year passage of time since the enactment of the £30,000 act meant that one-sixth of that sum had been removed from circulation. Of the £45,000 printed in 1723, only £38,889.15.0 remained. In order to prevent any further reduction in the currency supply, the Assembly passed a reemission act stipulating that none of the outstanding currency should be sunk but that all quotas should be reemitted as loans until January 1732. These loans were to be paid off within the twelve-year period stipulated by the December 1723 act, and payments were to be proportioned according to the number of years left within that time period at the moment the loan was contracted.

In the fall of 1726, before officials had sent the Reemitting Act to England, Governor Gordon received a letter from the Board of Trade warning colonial officials that members would "certainly think themselves obliged to lay them (any future currency acts) before His Majesty for disallowance." In reply the Governor sent a letter and the Assembly a representation supporting the Reemitting Act and requesting that it be confirmed. By the autumn of 1728, however, the Board of Trade had still not sent a reply, and local opinion was strong for more currency. Despite the apparent lack of support in England and a proprietary instruction that the governor should annex a clause suspending the operation of any future currency act until it received the royal approbation, Gordon concluded that it was politically expedient to increase the supply of currency, and in May of 1729 he signed an act providing for the immediate emission of £30,000. This sum was to be emitted over sixteen years (through 1744) at 5 percent interest.

A year and a half later, Loan Office officials were to start sinking the £38,889 that remained from Pennsylvania's first two currency acts. In addition, since the legislature had made no provision in the last £30,000 act for reemission, that sum, too, would contract with each annual sinking. Consequently, the legislature passed the Reemitting Act of February 1731, which authorized the reemitting of all of Pennsylvania's £68,889.15.0 until October of 1737, on loans running up to 1744.

When the reemission period was over, Pennsylvania had no governor, and consequently no act continuing the life of the currency could be passed. But even when Governor Thomas reached the colony one year later, in 1738, no reemission legislation was rammed through. Thomas Penn was in the colony, and the only conditions under which he would allow Governor Thomas to sign legislation reemitting or augmenting the currency supply was if it contained a clause stipulating that, if payments of quitrents that had been contracted prior to 1732 were made in Pennsylvania currency, they should be paid at the current rate of sterling exchange. Eventually, a compromise was struck, and a new emission was added to bring Pennsylvania's currency up to £80,000. These bills, to be emitted on loan over a sixteen-year period (until 1755) were to be reemitted constantly until 1749, at which point the six years remaining in their life would constrict demand so much that another reemission would likely be needed.

The Assembly, however, did not wait until 1749 before reemitting the currency. Political considerations and possibly hints of Governor Thomas's intention to retire, which awakened memories of the two-year delay (1737–39) in renewing currency legislation after Governor Gordon's death, prompted the legislature to reemit the £80,000 in March of 1746. The terms of this act were similar to the 1739 legislation: the currency was to be reemitted for a 10-year period from 1746, on loans that were to run until 1762 (sixteen years) at the standard 5 percent interest.

That same year, the governor also granted a special emission of £5,000, which was to pay for military expenditures and which was to be sunk over the following ten years. *Statutes at Large*, 3: 324-38, 389-407; 4: 38-51, 98-116, 199-208, 344-59, 420; 5: 7-22. *Votes*, 2: 1791-92, 1827-32. Board of Trade Papers, Proprietaries, 14: T25.

B. The Excise

Public expenditures by the Assembly, both prior to the emission of paper money and thereafter, were financed by a provincial excise tax. Until 1734 that tax had been six pence per gallon on any wine, rum, brandy, or spirits retailed in quantities under thirty-five gallons. In that year it was reduced to four pence per gallon on spirits retailed in any quantity under seventy gallons and on wine retailed in any quantity under thirty-five gallons. Prior to 1738 the excise had never been enacted for more than three years' duration, but in August of that year it was renewed for a five-year term. In May of 1744 it was again renewed for five years and in June of 1746, when it was used to fund a grant of £5,000 to the king's use for the Canada expedition, the collection of excise duties was authorized for the next ten years. *Statutes at Large*, 3: 408-17; 4: 68-77, 157-71, 238-48, 308-19, 395-407; 5: 45-49.

C. The Trustees of the Loan Office

Loan Office activities were placed under the care of four trustees prior to 1739 and five trustees thereafter. Of these, one "acting trustee" was in charge of managing financial affairs, while the others were responsible for estimating the value of the property the mortgagor offered for security. The two 1723 acts emitting currency and the 1728-29 Currency Act appointed the same four trustees. In 1730, however, the Assembly, suspecting that William Fishbourne had embezzled Loan Office funds, removed the incumbents and named replacements. After an investigation the Assembly resolved that the trustees should be changed every four years. In 1738 the Assembly passed an act for precisely that purpose, and one year later, when the £80,000 act was introduced, it contained a clause demanding that trustees serve no longer than four years.

Thereafter, the Assembly only partially complied with its announced policy. In 1744 and again in 1749 the Legislature replaced the regular trustees but allowed John Kinsey, who as "acting trustee" had the management of Loan Office affairs totally in his hands, to keep this position for thirteen years. After Kinsey's death in 1750 changes were made in the Loan Office personnel, but formal acts of the Assembly were no longer used to do so. In order to remove from the governor's hands another possible source of bargaining power, the Assembly provided in the 1749 Act that trustees could stay in office after their four-year term until the Assembly provided replacements. This was to be done by Assembly resolution. *Statutes at Large*, 3: 324-38, 389-407; 4: 98-116, 189-94, 304-308, 344-59, 407-15; 5: 54-61: *Votes*, 3: 2201.

APPENDIX V. 1

A NOTE ON CITY AND COUNTRY QUAKERS

Quaker historians have always distinguished between city and country Friends, and provided that such a categorization is tempered by an awareness that these two types are extremes and that most members of the society existed in between, sharing some of the characteristics of each, then it is a valid distinction. Occasionally, some hint of the metropolitan contempt for the hinterland appeared in the mid-eighteenth century. For example, in the fall of 1752 James Pemberton charged that the county meetings were "all but destitute when the few holy elders are removed," but significantly enough he mentioned that the situation was not too bright in Philadelphia either, and of the four competent ministers he named (Michael Lightfoot, Mordecai Yarnall, Daniel Stanton, and Sally Morris) the former two were Chester County products who had moved to Philadelphia (James Pemberton to John Pemberton, 18, November 1752, PemP).

On the other hand, one may suppose that just as some city residents were slightly contemptuous of country ways, countrymen were suspicious of the worldliness that Philadelphia represented. The important point, however, is that there is little evidence of contention along these lines, and certainly there was no sound basis for representatives of either city or country to claim a monopoly on righteousness, for both produced notable religious leaders, and both had their share of the ignorant, the uncharitable, and the worldly. What differences did exist between city and country Quakers were exactly the same differences that set apart non-Quaker residents of town and country.

Just as city and country Quakers shared the normal biases of urban and rural residents, so did they share the ties that drew metropolis and hinterland together. Business relationships, casual friendships, common political interests, perceptions of common threats, appreciation of mutual benefits, and common acknowledgment of a whole series of values forged strong bonds between city and country. In addition to these links, Quakers shared peculiar ones of their own. Kinship ties did cut across urban and rural boundaries to some extent; the meeting structure brought together men of different areas, the peculiarities of their sect creating a sense of mutuality; membership in a larger, international organization reduced in importance minor irritants; the feeling of isolation brought on by the rapid increase in the non-Quaker population was a source of unity; the sense of history Quakers shared was a common bond, and possession of political power and social prestige another. In addition, the freedom that monthly meetings had to work out their own compromises on discipline, and the general tolerance Quakers displayed in their mutual relationships, helped to avoid any build-up in intra-Society tension.

But the most important solvent for differences between city and country was the fact that the country produced a number of the Quakers' most respected leaders. William Brown, John Churchman, Jane Hoskins, Elizabeth Ashbridge, Michael Lightfoot, and John Wright either lived in the country or were products of the country, and despite the fact that in the late 1740s and early 1750s Philadelphia Friends seemed to appropriate them as their own (a phenomenon that says a great deal about the psychological needs of the Philadelphia merchants like the Pembertons), the country ministers constantly made trips back into the hinterland, often in company with some other respected religious leader. In the achievement-oriented world of Quakerism, those local products were a source of pride to the countrymen who had first recognized their talents, and their prominence, along with city-reared ministers and elders, created a unifying synthesis of city and country on the crucial level of religious leadership.

RECORD OF DISCIPLINARY ACTION IN THREE
MONTHLY MEETINGS

A. CHESTER MONTHLY MEETING

TABLE I

CHARGES LAID BY MONTHLY MEETING

Year	Marrying out of Meeting	Fornication, Bastardy, Adultery or Incest	Drunkenness	Fighting, Quarreling, Backbiting or Slander	Swearing	Debt	Resort to the Law	Disregarding Meeting Procedures	Meeting Inattendance or Loose Conversation	Unknown or Miscellaneous*	Total Charges	No. of Individuals Charged	No. of Individuals Disowned
1727	3	2	2		1						8	7	2
1728	6	4	2			1		1			14	11	4
1729	1		1			1		1		1	5	4	2
1730	7	2	2						1	2	14	11	4
1731	3		1							1	5	4	4
1732	3	2	3					1	1	1	11	10	6
1733	5	3	2							2	12	12	4
1734	2	4	3			1	1	1			12	9	2
1735	5	4	1								10	8	4
1736	2	1		1							4	3	-
1737	8	1	2					1	2	2	16	12	4
1738	7	5				1		1			14	12	3

continued . . . .

TABLE I - A. CHESTER MONTHLY MEETING - continued

Year	Marrying out of Meeting	Fornication, Bastardy, Adultery or Incest	Drunkenness	Fighting, Quarreling, Backbiting or Slander	Swearing	Debt	Resort to the Law	Disregarding Meeting Procedures	Meeting Inattendance or Loose Conversation	Unknown or Miscellaneous *	Total Charges	No. of Individuals Charged	No. of Individuals Disowned
1739	5	1									6	6	1
1740	7	2	4							1	14	13	4
1741	9	1	1		1			1	1		14	12	4
1742	6	5			1			1	1		14	11	4
1743	6	2									8	7	2
1744	8	7	1		1				1	1	19	14	4
1745	2	1									3	2	1
1746	5	2	2								9	8	5
1747	2	2						1			5	3	2
1748	1	1	3	2						1	8	6	1
1749	5	4									9	7	1
1750	6	4	2		1			1		1	15	12	5
1751	4	4									8	7	4
1752	6	1	3		1				2		13	9	2
1753	5		3	1					3	2	14	11	8
1754	6	2	1								9	6	1

continued . . . .

TABLE I - A. CHESTER MONTHLY MEETING - continued

Year	Marrying out of Meeting	Fornication, Bastardy, Adultery or Incest	Drunkenness	Fighting, Quarreling, Backbiting or Slander	Swearing	Debt	Resort to the Law	Disregarding Meeting Procedures	Meeting Inattendance or Loose Conversation	Unknown or Miscellaneous*	Total Charges	No. of Individuals Charged	No. of Individuals Disowned
1755	3	4	3	1		3		3	2	3	22	13	8
1756	1	1	2	2	4			2	2	2	16	10	4
TOTALS	139	72	44	7	5	12	1	15	16	20	331	260	100
%	42.0	21.8	13.3	2.1	1.6	3.6	.3	4.5	4.8	6.0	100.	100.	38.4

* Known miscellaneous charges include 1 of dereliction of familial responsibility, 2 of schismatic activities, and 1 of administering an oath.

TABLE II

DISOWNMENTS

Reason for Disownment	No.
Marriage out of Meeting	36
Fornication, Bastardy, Adultery or Incest	20
Drunkenness	19
Debt	8
Meeting Inattendance or Loose Conversation	8
Fighting, Quarreling, Backbiting or Slander	4
Dereliction of Familial Responsibility	1
Schismatic Activities	1
Swearing	1
Unknown	2
TOTAL	100

B. DARBY MONTHLY MEETING

TABLE I

CHARGES LAID BY MONTHLY MEETING

Year	Marrying out of Meeting	Fornication, Bastardy, Adultery or Incest	Drunkenness	Fighting, Quarreling, Backbiting or Slander	Swearing	Debt	Resort to the Law	Disregarding Meeting Procedures	Meeting Inattendance or Loose Conversation	Unknown or Miscellaneous*	Total Charges	No. of Individuals Charged	No. of Individuals Disowned
1727	1		2								3	3	1
1728													
1729													
1730		2									2	2	
1731		1	1	1							3	2	2
1732													
1733	3										3	3	1
1734				3							3	3	
1735	1		1								2	2	
1736													
1737													
1738	1	1	2	1							5	5	2
1739										1	1	1	
1740	2	1		1							4	4	
1741	3									1	4	3	1
1742	2		1								3	3	2

continued . . . .

TABLE I – B. DARBY MONTHLY MEETING – continued

Year	Marrying out of Meeting	Fornication, Bastardy, Adultery or Incest	Drunkenness	Fighting, Quarreling, Backbiting or Slander	Swearing	Debt	Resort to the Law	Disregarding Meeting Procedures	Meeting Inattendance or Loose Conversation	Unknown or Miscellaneous *	Total Charges	No. of Individuals Charged	No. of Individuals Disowned
1743	1	1	1								3	3	2
1744	2	1	2		1	1					7	4	1
1745				1						1	2	2	1
1746	2		1							1	4	4	2
1747	3									2	5	5	1
1748		1								1	1	1	1
1749	2									1	3	3	1
1750								1		1	2	2	1
1751	3		1			1					5	5	2
1752										3	3	3	
1753	3	2				1		1			7	5	2
1754	2	1						1			4	3	1
1755	2	2	1								5	4	3
1756	3		1						1		5	4	3
TOTAL	36	13	14	6	2	3		3	1	11	89	79	30
%	40.4	14.6	15.7	6.8	2.3	3.4		3.4	1.1	12.3	100	100	38.0

*Known miscellaneous charges include 2 of participating in military activities, 1 of gambling, and 6 of attending irregular weddings.

TABLE II

DISOWNMENTS

Reason for Disownment	No.
Marriage out of Meeting	9
Fornication, Bastardy, Adultery or Incest	7
Drunkenness	6
Debt	3
Participating in Military Activities	2
Swearing	1
Disregarding Meeting Procedures	1
Attending Irregular Marriage	1
TOTAL	30

C. <u>SADSBURY MONTHLY MEETING</u>

TABLE I

CHARGES LAID BY MONTHLY MEETING

Year	Marrying out of Meeting	Fornication, Bastardy, Adultery or Incest	Drunkenness	Fighting, Quarreling, Backbiting or Slander	Swearing	Debt	Resort to the Law	Disregarding Meeting Procedures	Meeting Inattendance or Loose Conversation	Unknown or Miscellaneous*	Total Charges	No. of Individuals Charged	No. of Individuals Disowned
1738	1		1	1					1	1	5	3	
1739	1			3							4	4	
1740	1		1		1						3	2	2
1741	2						1				3	3	1
1742	3										3	3	2
1743	4	1					1			2	8	8	5
1744				4							4	4	1
1745	5						1				6	6	3
1746	4		1			1				1	7	7	3
1747	3			2	1					3	9	9	4
1748	2										2	2	1
1749	5	2								2	9	9	6
1750	10	1								1	12	11	7
1751	3	1		6						1	11	10	2
1752	1										1	1	–
1753	7		1	1		1		1		2	13	12	3

continued . . . .

TABLE I - C. SADSBURY MONTHLY MEETING - continued

Year	Marrying out of Meeting	Fornication, Bastardy, Adultery or Incest	Drunkenness	Fighting, Quarreling, Backbiting or Slander	Swearing	Debt	Resort to the Law	Disregarding Meeting Procedures	Meeting Inattendance or Loose Conversation	Unknown or Miscellaneous *	Total Charges	No. of Individuals Charged	No. of Individuals Disowned
1754	3									1	4	4	2
1755	5	2		2						3	12	9	5
1756	7	1	1							1	10	8	5
TOTALS	67	8	5	17	2	4	3	1	1	18	126	115	52
%	53.2	6.3	3.9	13.5	1.6	3.2	2.4	.8	.8	14.3	100	100	43.5

* Known miscellaneous charges include 2 of attending forbidden entertainment, 2 of gambling, 7 of attending irregular wedding, 1 of dereliction of familial responsibilities.

TABLE II

DISOWNMENTS

Reason for Disownment	No.
Marrying out of Meeting	35
Fornication, Bastardy, Adultery or Incest	5
Debt	3
Drunkenness	2
Fighting, Quarreling, Backbiting or Slander	1
Swearing	1
Resorting to the Law	1
Gambling	1
Loose Conversation	1
Attending an Irregular Wedding	1
Miscellaneous	1
TOTAL	52

Source for Appendix V.2 - Records of Monthly Meeting Disciplinary Activity in the Society of Friends, compiled by Jack D. Marietta. Quaker Collection, Haverford College Library. I am indebted to Professor Marietta and to Mrs. B. Curtis of Haverford College Library for allowing me access to this material.

ABBREVIATIONS

§

CCCH	Chester County Court House
CCHS	Chester County Historical Society
CR	*Minutes of the Provincial Council of Pennsylvania*
FHL	Friends Historical Library
Franklin Papers	*The Papers of Benjamin Franklin*
Gazette	*Pennsylvania Gazette*
INLB	Isaac Norris Letterbook
JHLB	James Hamilton Letterbook
JLLB	James Logan Letterbook
JSLB	James Steel Letterbook
LCCH	Lancaster County Court House
LCHS	Lancaster County Historical Society
LCP	Library Company of Philadelphia
Mercury	*American Weekly Mercury*
MM	Monthly Meeting
PA	*Pennsylvania Archives*
PH	*Pennsylvania History*
PHC	Penn-Hamilton Correspondence
PHS	Presbyterian Historical Society
PMHB	*Pennsylvania Magazine of History and Biography*
PcmP	Pemberton Papers
PPOC	Penn Papers, Official Correspondence
PvB	Penn versus Baltimore
PYM	Philadelphia Yearly Meeting
QM	Quarterly Meeting
RPLB	Richard Peters Letterbook
Statutes at Large	*The Statutes at Large of Pennsylvania from 1682 to 1801*
TPLB	Thomas Penn Letterbook
Votes	*Votes and Proceedings of the House of Representatives of the Province of Pennsylvania*
WMQ	*William and Mary Quarterly*

NOTES

§

PROLOGUE

1. Jack P. Greene, ed., *The Reinterpretation of the American Revolution* (New York, 1968), pp. 3-17.

2. Jack P. Greene, "The Role of the Lower Houses of Assembly in Eighteenth-Century Politics," *Journal of Southern History* 27 (1961): 451-74; idem, *The Quest for Power, The Lower Houses of Assembly in the Southern Royal Colonies, 1689-1776* (Chapel Hill, N.C., 1963); idem, "Political Mimesis: A Consideration of the Historical and Cultural Roots of Legislative Behavior in the British Colonies in the Eighteenth Century," *American Historical Review* 75 (1969): 337-67.

3. Robert E. Brown, *Middle-Class Democracy and the Revolution in Massachusetts, 1691-1780* (Ithaca, N.Y., 1955); J. R. Pole, "Historians and the Problem of Early American Democracy," *American Historical Review*, (1962): 626-46; Richard Buel, Jr., "Democracy and the American Revolution: A Frame of Reference," *William and Mary Quarterly*, 3rd ser., 21 (1964): 165-90 (hereinafter cited as *WMQ*); Michael Zuckerman, *Peaceable Kingdoms: New England Towns in the Eighteenth Century* (New York, 1970).

4. Jesse Lemisch, "The American Revolution seen from the Bottom Up," in Barton J. Bernstein, *Towards a New Past: Dissenting Essays in American History* (New York, 1968), pp. 3-45; James A. Henretta, *The Evolution of American Society, 1700-1815: An Interdisciplinary Analysis* (Lexington, Mass., 1973), pp. 111-12.

5. Bernard Bailyn, "Political Experience and Enlightenment Ideas in Eighteenth-Century America," *American Historical Review* 67 (1962): 339-51; Jack P. Greene, "Changing Interpretations of Early American Politics," in Ray Allen Billington, ed., *The Reinterpretation of Early American History* (New York, 1966), pp. 151-84.

6. Bernard Bailyn, *The Origins of American Politics* (New York, 1968) p. 64.

7. Ibid., pp. 53-58.

8. Bernard Bailyn, *The Ideological Origins of the American Revolution* (Cambridge, Mass., 1967).

9. M. Eugene Sirmans, *Colonial South Carolina: A Political History, 1663-1763* (Chapel Hill, N. C., 1966); Stanley N. Katz, *Newcastle's New York, Anglo-American Politics, 1732-1753* (Cambridge, Mass., 1968); Gary B. Nash, *Quakers and Politics: Pennsylvania, 1681-1726* (Princeton, 1968); Patricia U. Bonomi, *A Factious People: Politics and Society in Colonial New York* (New York and London, 1971).

10. The major monographic literature of Pennsylvania politics includes the following: William R. Shepherd, *History of Proprietary Government in Pennsylvania* (New York, 1896); C. H. Lincoln, *The Revolutionary Movement in Pennsylvania, 1760-1776* (Philadelphia, 1901); Winfred T. Root, *The Relation of Pennsylvania with the British Government, 1696-1765* (Philadelphia, 1912); Theodore Thayer, *Pennsylvania Politics and the Growth of Democracy, 1740-1776* (Harrisburg, Pa., 1953); Roy N.

Lokken, *David Lloyd, Colonial Lawmaker* (Seattle, 1959); Dietmar Rothermund, *The Layman's Progress: Religious and Political Experience in Colonial Pennsylvania* (Philadelphia, 1962); William S. Hanna, *Benjamin Franklin and Pennsylvania Politics* (Stanford, Calif., 1964); Nash, *Quakers and Politics*; Hermann Wellenreuther, *Glaube und Politik in Pennsylvania, 1681-1776: Die Wandlungen der Obrigkeitsdoktrin und des Peace Testimony der Quäker* (Cologne, 1972); James H. Hutson, *Pennsylvania Politics, 1746-1770: The Movement for Royal Government and its Consequences* (Princeton, 1972); Benjamin F. Newcomb, *Franklin and Galloway: A Political Partnership* (New Haven, 1972).

CHAPTER 1

1. For a more complete treatment of some of the themes in this chapter, see *Journal of the Lancaster County Historical Society* "Proprietary Affairs in Colonial Pennsylvania, 1726-1739" (forthcoming, 1978).

2. The derivation of the Penn title is an exceedingly complicated matter. For further information see Shepherd, *Proprietary Government*, pp. 183-204; Howard M. Jenkins, "The Family of William Penn," *Pennsylvania Magazine of History and Biography* 20 (1896): 1-29, 158-75, 370-90, 435-55; ibid. 21 (1897): 1-19, 137-60, 324-46, 421-44 (hereinafter cited as *PMHB*); William B. Rawle, "The General Title of the Penn Family to Pennsylvania," *PMHB* 23 (1899): 60-68, 224-40; Hannah Benner Roach, "The Family of William Penn," *Pennsylvania Genealogical Magazine* 25 (1967): 69-96.

3. Of the five commissioners of property appointed by William Penn in 1711, two—Edward Shippen and Samuel Carpenter—had died by 1725. In that year Hannah and Springett Penn reconfirmed the three survivors—James Logan, Isaac Norris, Sr., and Richard Hill—as commissioners and added Ralph Assheton and Thomas Griffith. When Penn's will was confirmed in 1727, the Penns commissioned the four surviving trustees of the will—James Logan, Richard Hill, Isaac Norris, Sr., and Samuel Preston as commissioners so that they could execute their trust. John H. Martin, *Martin's Bench and Bar of Philadelphia* (Philadelphia, 1883), p. 172.

4. For the procedure in obtaining a patent, see Shepherd, *Proprietary Government*, pp. 31-36.

5. James Logan to John Penn, 23 June 1726, Penn Papers, Official Correspondence, vol. 1. (hereinafter cited as PPOC); James Logan to John Penn, 16 May 1728, Logan Papers, James Logan Letterbook, vol. 3 (hereinafter cited as JLLB); James T. Lemon, *The Best Poor Man's Country: A Geographical Study of Early Southeastern Pennsylvania* (Baltimore, 1972), p. 23; James Logan to John Penn, 23 September 1727, 22 October 1727, JLLB (1717-43); 11 September 1728, PPOC, vol. 2; 21 July 1729, JLLB (1726-32). Unless otherwise stated, all manuscripts are in the Historical Society of Pennsylvania.

6. As proprietary secretary, commissioner of property, and trustee of the Penn estate, Logan was mainly responsible for the management of proprietary affairs. He worked closely with Surveyor General Jacob Taylor and with Acting Receiver General James Steel. Martin, *Bench and Bar*, pp. 172-74.

7. James Logan to James Steel, 18 November 1729, PPOC, vol. 2; *Pennsylvania Archives*, 2nd ser. 7: 129-30, 19: 721-66 (hereinafter cited as *PA*).

8. Between 1724 and 1732 the Land Office issued only forty-nine patents. Patent Book #A6 (1724-35), Pennsylvania Department of Internal Affairs Land Records, Philadelphia City Archives.

9. James Logan to John Penn, 26 June 1727, JLLB (1717-43); idem, 18 October 1728, JLLB (1726-32); idem, 14 May 1729, PPOC, vol. 2.

10. James Logan to John Penn, 26 June 1727, JLLB (1717-43).

11. James Logan to Elisha Gatchell, 4 December 1727, JLLB (1726-32).

12. James Logan to James Steel, 18 November 1729, PPOC, vol. 2; *PA*, 2nd ser. 7: 136; James Logan to Samuel Blunston, JLLB (1726-32); James Logan to Jacob Taylor, 20 November 1730, JLLB (1726-32).

13. James Logan to Hannah Penn, 1 January 1726, PPOC vol. 1.

14. Ibid. James Logan to John Penn, 25 November 1727, JLLB (1717-43); idem, 13 August 1729, PPOC, vol. 2; James Logan to Samuel Blunston, 13 March 1731, JLLB (1726-32).

15. Samuel Hazard, ed., *Register of Pennsylvania*, 18 vols. (Philadelphia, 1828-36), 12 (1833): 342. Of the different improvement rights, possession of a survey, or warrant and survey, was the most secure. Ibid. 13 (1834): 320; *PA*, 3rd ser. 2: 167-235.

16. *Register of Pennsylvania*, 13 (1834): 355, 356. Administrators of estates sold "improved and even warranted and surveyed land, as mere chattels, without any order of the Orphan's Court." Ibid., p. 320.

17. *PA*, 2nd ser., 7: 229-31.

18. James Steel to John Thompson, 13 April 1731, Logan Papers, James Steel Letterbook, 1732-42 (hereinafter cited as JSLB). James Steel to Patrick Moor and Thomas Melsop, 11 January 1732, ibid.

19. James Logan to Jacob Taylor, 19 September 1728, 15 March 1731, JLLB (1726-32); James Logan to Elisha Gatchell, 20 May 1730, ibid.; James Logan to James Anderson and Andrew Galbraith, 2 March 1731, ibid.; James Steel to Proprietaries, 21 May 1731, JSLB (1732-41); James Steel to Samuel Blunston, 21 January 1732, ibid.; James Steel to John Carnahan, 11 January 1733, ibid.; James Steel to John Hare, 6 October 1733, ibid; James Steel to Edward Farmer, 2 January 1734, ibid.

20. For background material on the boundary dispute, see Shepherd, *Proprietary Government*, pp. 117-33; Nicholas B. Wainwright, "The Missing Evidence: Penn versus Baltimore," *PMHB* 80 (1956): 227-35; idem, "Tale of a Runaway Cape: The Penn-Baltimore Agreement of 1752," ibid. 87 (1963): 251-93.

21. *PA*, 2nd ser. 7: 44-45.

22. Ibid., 45-46; Governor Gordon to Governor Ogle, 15 May 1736, PPOC, vol. 3; James Logan to John Penn, 18 October 1728, JLLB (1726-32).

23. James Logan to Elisha Gatchell, 4 December 1727, JLLB (1726-32); Elisha Gatchell to James Logan, 28 November 1727, PPOC, vol. 1.

24. James Logan to James Steel, 18 November 1729, PPOC, vol. 2.

25. At one point, Logan succinctly stated the proprietary dilemma: "Honest men cannot take people's money for a precarious title and to refuse it is dangerous because it seems a tacit confession of the invalidity of your [Penn's] right or claim." The only "expedient" was to grant titles above the disputed land and work out an understanding with those who settled below the forty-degree latitude. James Logan to John Penn, 26 June 1727 JLLB (1717-1743); James Logan to John, Thomas, and Richard Penn, 29 July 1728, ibid.

26. James Logan to John, Thomas, and Richard Penn, 29 July 1728, ibid.; James Logan to John Penn, 16 May 1728, ibid.

27. James Logan to John Penn, 26 June 1728, 17 October 1730, PPOC, vol. 2; James Logan to Joshua Gee, 2 June 1731, JLLB (1717-1743); James Logan to John, Thomas, and Richard Penn, 29 July 1728, ibid.

28. James Logan to John Penn, 24 November 1725, PPOC, vol. 1.

29. James Logan to John Penn, 25 November 1727, 28 June 1728, JLLB (1717-43); idem, 2 August 1731, PPOC, vol. 2. The Penn letters in reply to Logan demonstrate how badly the three sons misunderstood the proprietary problems. For example, see John Penn to James Logan, 11 November 1728, Gratz Coll., Governors of Pennsylvania, case 2, box 33a.

30. James Logan to Henry Goldney, 8 April 1723, PPOC, vol. 1; Patrick Gordon to Springett and John Penn, 1 October 1729, ibid., vol. 2; James Logan to John Wright and the Justices of Lancaster County, 13 April 1730, JLLB (1726-32); James Logan to Elisha Gatchell, 9 July 1730, ibid.; *PA*, 2nd ser. 16: 28-29; Mabel P. Wolff, *The Colonial Agency of Pennsylvania, 1712-1757* (Lancaster, Pa., 1933), pp. 16-17.

31. In the 1732 agreement, Baltimore theoretically gained five miles over the old understanding that had placed his northern boundary twenty miles south of Philadelphia. In fact, "Lord Baltimore's line" was not that far south. "A Map of Parts of the Provinces of Pennsylvania and Maryland with the Counties of Newcastle, Kent and

Sussex on Delaware," *PA*, 2nd ser., vol. 16, appended; Wainwright, "Tale of a Lost Cape," p. 256.

32. Wainwright, "Tale of a Lost Cape," pp. 259-65; Samuel Hazard, ed., *Minutes of the Provincial Council of Pennsylvania*, (Philadelphia and Harrisburg, 1852-53), 3:497-500 (hereinafter cited as *CR*); Report of Commissioners, 24 November 1733, Penn-Bailey Mss.

33. The best summary of events in London is in Wolff, *Colonial Agency*, pp. 59-71.

34. Abdel Ross Wentz, "The Beginnings of the German Element in York County, Pennsylvania," *Proceedings of the Pennsylvania German Society* 24 (1913): 69-87.

35. Thomas Penn to Samuel Blunston, 8 August 1734, 29 July 1734, 14 February 1737, Penn Papers, unbound mss.; Thomas Penn to Tobias Hendriks, 6 May 1736, Penn Papers, Additional Misc. Letters, vol. 1; Wentz, "Beginnings of the German Element," pp. 48-50.

36. *PA*, 1st ser. 1:295, 311-14, 330-31, 350-51, 352, 353-63, 399, 410-23; Governor Gordon to Governor Ogle, 21 February 1732, 25 June 1735, PPOC, vol. 2; *CR*, 3:542-43; John Hendriks to Thomas Penn, 22 February 1734, Penn Papers, unbound mss.

37. *PA*, 1st ser., 1:489-93, 518-28; 7:213-16. Also *CR*, 4:56-58, 61-65, 68, 69, 71, 76-79; James Logan to John Penn, 20 May 1737, PPOC, vol. 3; Samuel Blunston to Thomas Penn, 13 January 1737, Lancaster County Misc. Papers.

38. *CR*, 4:100-18; *PA*, 1st ser. 1:500-503, 505-19; James Logan to John Penn, 28 November 1736, PPOC, vol. 3; Thomas Penn to Samuel Blunston, 4 February 1734, 10 January 1735, Penn Papers, unbound mss.; Charles P. Keith, *Chronicles of Pennsylvania from the English Revolution to the Peace of Aix-la-Chapelle, 1688-1748* (Philadelphia, 1917), pp. 763-64. By the summer of 1735, Thomas Penn had let it be known that Cresap's arrest was worth a fifty-pound reward. Thomas Penn to Samuel Blunston, 9 June 1735, Penn Papers, unbound mss.

39. *PA*, 1st ser. 1:316-20, 529-33; *CR*, 4:116-18, 147-56, 160-61, 188-89, 228-32, 250-52; Samuel Blunston to Thomas Penn, 7 March 1737, Penn Papers, unbound mss.

40. *CR*, 4:116-18, 121-24, 130, 143, 144-47, 253-55, 263, 298-301; Gertrude Mackinney, ed., *Votes and Proceedings of the House of Representatives of the Province of Pennsylvania*, *PA*, 8th ser. (Harrisburg, 1931-35) 3:2420-23 (hereinafter cited as *Votes*); John and Richard Penn to Thomas Penn, 25 February 1738, Hazard Family Papers; John Penn to James Logan, 6 September 1737, 5 May 1738, John Penn to Thomas Penn, May 23, 1738, ibid.; Penn Papers, Thomas Penn Letterbook, vol. 1 (hereinafter cited as TPLB). *PA*, 2nd ser., 1:556-61, 568-76; Papers of the Board of Trade and Plantations, Proprietaries, 13: 589, 14: T1, T7; *Pennsylvania Gazette*, 10 January 1738, 7 September 1738 (hereinafter cited as *Gazette*).

Those who had settled under Maryland or Pennsylvania rights, but under the agreement were situated on the wrong side of the boundary, were to remain under the authority of the colony under which they had settled until chancery handed down a decision. The final decree was not issued until October 1750, when the court ordered performance of the 1732 agreement.

41. James Logan to John Wright, 3 May 1729, JLLB (1726-32); James Logan to John Paris, 29 December 1731, ibid.; James Logan to John Penn, 20 July 1727 ibid. (1717-43); Thomas Penn to Samuel Blunston, 5 May 1735, Penn Papers, unbound mss.; *CR*, 3:595-96.

42. *PA*, 1st ser. 1:330-31, 428-35, 461-88; *CR*, 3:566-68, 4:202-203; Wolff, *Colonial Agency*, pp. 59-72. Patrick Gordon held the post of governor of Pennsylvania from 1726 to 1736.

43. *PA*, 1st ser. 1:532-33.

44. Shepherd, *Proprietary Government*, p. 34; a letter of instructions to Thomas Penn on his going to Pennsylvania, 20 May 1732, TPLB vol. 1. The three Penns believed that even though Baltimore had repudiated the 1732 agreement it would eventually prove binding. Consequently, they were willing to grant lands north of the fifteen mile boundary. John Penn to Thomas Penn, 31 August 1733, TPLB, vol. 1.

45. *Register of Pennsylvania*, 13 (1834): 317-20; 12 (1833): 361-62; Wentz, "Beginnings of the German Element," pp. 69-87; Thomas Penn to Richard Peters, 30 May 1750, Penn Papers, Saunders-Coates.

46. *Register of Pennsylvania*, 13 (1834): 318; John Penn to Richard Penn, 10 March 1735, TPLB, vol. 1; William H. Kain, "The Penn Manorial System and the Manors of Springettsbury and Maske," *Pennsylvania History*, 10 (1943): 227 (hereinafter cited as *PH*).

47. *Register of Pennsylvania*, 13 (1834): 319; Thomas Penn to Samuel Blunston, 14 February 1737, 3 November 1737, Penn Papers, unbound mss.; Samuel Blunston to Proprietaries, 10 May 1736, Penn-Bailey mss.

48. Thomas Penn to Samuel Blunston, 14 February 1737, 9 December 1737, Penn Papers, unbound mss.; *Register of Pennsylvania*, 13 (1834): 316; *PA*, 2nd ser. 7:229-31.

49. *PA*, 3rd ser. 8: 24; Thomas Cookson to Thomas Penn, 13 November 1742, Cadwallader Coll., Thomas Cadwallader, Coates List #28; *Votes*, 3:2117-20; John Swift to John White, 20 September 1747, John Swift Letterbook.

50. James Logan to Elisha Gatchell, 4 December 1727, JLLB, (1726-32).

51. James Logan to James Steel, 18 November 1729, PPOC, vol. 2.

52. At least, some were willing to take the depreciation of Pennsylvania currency into account and pay £15.10.0 and 1 shilling per hundred acres. Samuel Blunston to Thomas Penn, 9 April 1735, Cadwallader Coll., box 2, Thomas Penn Letters; Thomas Penn to Samuel Blunston (?), 22 December 1735, Penn Papers, unbound mss.

53. The three proposals were: (a) £16.15.0 and 1 shilling quitrent per hundred acres, (b) £15 and 2 shillings per hundred acres, (c) £6.10.0 and 1 penny per acre quitrent. Penn felt that these terms should be adequate, for the inhabitants had been "settled 12 or 15 years" and had "paid no consideration for that favor." Thomas Penn to (?), 23 January 1733, Penn Papers, unbound mss.

54. Thomas Penn to Samuel Blunston, 5 May 1735, 9 June 1735, Penn Papers, unbound mss; Thomas Penn to Samuel Blunston, 24 January 1735, Penn Papers, unbound mss.

55. Benjamin Eastburn to John Taylor, 20 April 1736, Taylor Papers, Taylor's Surveys; James Steel to John Taylor, 5 June 1734, JSLB (1732-41); Samuel Blunston to Thomas Penn, 3 February 1734, Lancaster County Misc. Papers (1724-72).

56. Thomas Penn to Samuel Blunston, 8 July 1738, Penn Papers, unbound mss.

57. Thomas Penn to Samuel Blunston, 9 December 1737, ibid.

58. Governor Thomas' proclamation announcing the 1738 Order-in-Council appeared in the *Gazette* on September 7.

59. *Register of Pennsylvania*, 13 (1834):316.

60. Ann Bezanson et al., *Prices in Colonial Pennsylvania* (Philadelphia, 1935), pp. 318-19.

61. *British Statutes at Large* (London, 1769), 4: 324-25.

62. Keith, *Chronicles*, p. 790.

63. James Logan to Thomas Penn, 5 December 1733, Misc. Mss.; *PA*,2nd ser. 7:163-64, 176-77, 185-86; Clement Plumsted to John Penn, 4 October 1736, PPOC, vol. 3.

64. James T. Mitchell and Henry Flanders, eds., *The Statutes at Large of Pennsylvania from 1682-1801* (Harrisburg, 1896-1915), 4:198 (hereinafter cited as *Statutes at Large*).

65. Instructions to Colonel Thomas, 11 August 1737, Penn Papers, Penn vs. Baltimore, 1739 (hereinafter cited as PvB).

66. *Votes*, 3:2427-28, 2460-63, 2465-66, 2469-71.

67. Ibid., pp. 2464, 2467-69, 2472-74, 2474-75.

68. Ibid., pp. 2482-83, 2484, 2485, 2486.

69. *Statutes at Large*, 4:322-26. For a summary of paper money legislation between 1726 and 1755, see appendix IV.1.

70. Thomas Penn to John and Richard Penn, 16 August 1738, Penn Papers, Small Letterbook.

71. *Gazette*, 28 June 1739.

72. See generally Lokken, *David Lloyd*, pp. 208-35; Thomas Wendel, "The Keith-Lloyd Alliance: Factional and Coalition Politics in Colonial Pennsylvania," *PMHB* 92 (1968): 289-305; Thomas Wendel, "The Life and Letters of Sir William Keith, Lieutenant-Governor of Pennsylvania and the Three Lower Counties, 1717-1726" (Ph.D. diss., University of Washington, 1964).

73. James Logan to John, Thomas, and Richard Penn, 30 April 1739, PPOC, vol. 2. For the division between Keithians and Lloydians in the Assembly, see chapter 7. The peaceful elections of 1729 and 1730 signified the end of the Keithian disturbances Patrick Gordon to Springett and John Penn, 15 November 1729, 16 October 1730, PPOC, vol. 2; John Penn to Colonel Gordon, 20 January 1730, TPLB, vol. 1.

74. See chapter 7.

75. For background on Hamilton, see Burton Alva Konkle, *The Life of Andrew Hamilton, 1676-1741* (Philadelphia, 1941); James Logan to John Penn, 10 May 1727, PPOC, vol. 1; Patrick Gordon to John Penn, 1 January 1728, ibid., vol. 2.

76. Thomas Penn to Samuel Blunston, 4 February 1733, Penn Papers, unbound mss.; Governor Gordon to Governor Ogle, 15 May 1736, PPOC, vol. 3; Clement Plumsted to John Penn, 4 October 1736, ibid.; Governor Gordon to Governor Ogle, 14 May 1734, Gratz Coll., Governors of Pennsylvania, case 2, box 32; James Logan to Proprietaries, 25 March 1735, Gratz Coll., Chief Justices of the Supreme Court of Pennsylvania; *Votes*, 3:2117-119, 2120, 2196-97.

77. James Logan to John Penn, 23 June 1726, PPOC, vol. 1.

78. James Logan to John Penn, 17 November 1734, Logan Papers, vol. 10, Additional Letters and Business Papers; *American Weekly Mercury*, 13 September 1733, 20 September 1733, 27 September 1733, 4 October 1733, 18 October 1733, 21 December 1733, 29 December 1733, 8 January 1734, 5 February 1734 (hereinafter cited as *Mercury*); Leonard W. Labaree, ed., *The Papers of Benjamin Franklin*, (New Haven, 1959-), 1: 333-38, 2:327-28 (hereinafter cited as *Franklin Papers*); *Votes*, 3:2117-19, 2120, 2196-97; Isaac Norris, Sr., to Isaac Norris, Jr., 25 March 1734, Norris Papers, vol. 2; Debby Norris to Isaac Norris, Jr., 4 August 1734, ibid.; *Votes*, 3:2194, 2198, 2235-36; Charles Norris to Isaac Norris, Jr., 15 January 1734, Norris Papers, Isaac Norris Letterbook (hereinafter cited as INLB).

79. Stanley N. Katz, ed., *A Brief Narrative of the Case and Trial of John Peter Zenger, Printer of the New York Weekly Journal by James Alexander* (Cambridge, Mass., 1963).

80. Thomas Penn to John and Richard Penn, 14 January 1736, Penn Papers, unbound mss.

81. Thomas Penn to John and Richard Penn, 10 August 1736, TPLB, vol. 1.

82. For Assembly and Council proceedings on this issue, see *Votes*, 3:2302, 2305, 2307, 2309-14, 2310, 2315-16, 2317, 2338-39, 2340-46, 2347-52; *CR*, 4:22-23, 27-32, 34-40, 41-46.

83. Quoted in the *Gazette*, 24 December 1735.

84. Samuel Blunston to Thomas Penn, 9 April 1735, Cadwallader Coll., box 2, Thomas Penn Letters.

85. Thomas Penn to John Penn, 4 December 1739, Penn Papers, Small Letterbook.

86. Minutes of Donegal Presbytery, Presbyterian Historical Society, 1b (1736-40): 255 (hereinafter cited as PHS).

87. Francis Jennings, "The Indian Trade of the Susquehanna Valley," *Proceedings of the American Philosophical Society* 110 (1966): 406-24; idem, "Incident at Tulpehocken," *PH* 35 (1968): 335-55; Samuel Blunston to Thomas Penn, 20 February 1738, Gratz Coll.; idem, 3 March 1738, 25 March 1738, Lancaster County Misc. Papers, 1724-1772; James Logan to James Anderson, 22 January 1736, Logan Papers, vol. 10, Additional Letters and Business Papers.

88. John, Thomas, and Richard Penn to James Logan, 20 January 1732, TPLB, vol. 1.

89. Wolff, *Colonial Agency*, pp. 70-72.

90. See chapter 7.

CHAPTER 2

1. For a more complete treatment of some of the themes in this chapter, see *Journal of the Lancaster County Historical Society*, "King George's War and the Quakers: The Defense Crisis of 1739-1742 in Pennsylvania Politics" (forthcoming, 1978).

2. The four Quakers were Jonathan Robeson, William Monington, Job Goodson, and Morris Morris all members from Philadelphia County. For the religious composition of the Assembly 1729-54 see appendix I. 1.

3. William Allen to John Penn, 17 November 1739, 27 March 1741, PPOC, vol. 3; *Votes*, 3:2508, 2657.

4. William Allen to John Penn, 27 November 1741, PPOC, vol. 3.

5. *Votes*, 3:2657.

6. Ibid., pp. 2512, 2529-31, 2535-38, 2540-45; Governor Thomas to John Penn, 5 November 1739, PPOC, 3; John Penn to Governor Thomas, 2 August 1739, TPLB, vol. 3; *PA*, 1st ser. 1:577; *CR*, 4:350-51.

7. *PA*, 1st ser. 1: 581-83, 2nd ser. 7:238-39; *CR*, 4:395-97; *Votes*, 3:2564, 2570, 2587, 2609-10, 2619-20; John Kinsey's Opinion on the Enlisting of Servants, Penn Papers, Assembly and Provincial Council.

8. *Votes*, 3: 2594.

9. Ibid., pp. 2588-90, 2590-92, 2594-96, 2619, 2621, 4:2755; *PA*, 2nd ser. 7:238-39, 1st ser. 1:594-95, 616-19; Richard Peters to John Penn, 31 July 1740, Peters Papers, Richard Peters Letterbook (hereinafter cited as RPLB).

10. *Votes*, 3:2600-2604, 2617-27, 4:2742. Governor Thomas defended his enlistment of seven companies by referring to the Duke of Newcastle's orders, which instructed Thomas to raise "as great a number of men" as he "possibly could." *Votes*, 3:2599.

11. And several times in the course of the dispute the Assembly spokesmen stated that, while they would not appropriate money for wartime use, they could vote a gift to the king's use. *Votes*, 3:2594-96, 2619, 2658-59.

12. *PA*, 2nd ser. 7:238-39.

13. William Allen to John Penn, 27 March 1741, PPOC, vol. 3.

14. *Votes*, 3:2605-11, 2680-81; William Allen to John Penn, 27 March 1741, PPOC, vol. 3.

15. See the various exchanges between governor and Assembly during 1739-40 in *Votes*, vol. 3.

16. Governor Thomas to John Penn, 15 March 1739, PPOC, vol. 3; *Votes*, 3:2615-16, 2629-30.

17. William Moore, an Anglican who had been an outright advocate of defense preparations, met defeat in Chester County; Thomas Edwards, a Quaker turned Anglican, and Benjamin Jones, a Presbyterian, both of whom apparently had been too conciliatory, were rejected in Lancaster and Bucks Counties respectively. Israel Pemberton, Sr., to John Hunt, 8 November 1740, Pemberton Papers, vol. 3 (hereinafter cited as PemP); *Votes* 3:2663.

18. For the religious composition of the Assembly, see appendix I.1. Isaac Norris, Jr., to Robert Charles, 11 October 1740, INLB (1719-56).

19. Board of Trade Papers, Proprietaries, 15:T43; Samuel Blunston to Proprietor, 16 November 1740, Lancaster County Misc. Papers (1742-72); Richard Peters to John Penn, 31 July 1740, RPLB; John Reynell to Daniel Flexney, 31 July 1740, John Reynell Letter Book (1738-41), Coates-Reynell Papers; *PA*, 2nd ser. 7:238-39; "Logan-Story Correspondence, 1724-1741," Norman Penny, ed., *Friends' Historical Association Bulletin* 15 (1926): 84-90.

20. Richard Partridge to John Kinsey et al., 7 February 1741, PemP, vol. 3; Board of Trade Papers, Proprietaries, 15:T42; Thomas Penn to John and Richard Penn, 23 March 1741, Penn Papers, Small Letterbook; Thomas Penn to John Paris, 27 March 1741, PPOC, vol. 3.

21. Thomas Penn to John Penn, 23 March 1741, Penn Papers, Small Letterbook; John Penn to Governor Thomas, 7 March 1741, 21 June 1741, TPLB, vol. 1; John Penn

to John Kinsey, 15 March 1741, ibid.; Governor Thomas to John Penn, 25 March, 1741, PPOC, vol. 3.

22. Richard Peters to Proprietaries, 14 November 1741, RPLB; Richard Peters to John Penn, 20 November 1741, PPOC, vol. 3; William Allen to John Penn, 16 November 1741, ibid.; Governor Thomas to John Paris, 14 May 1741, ibid.; John Penn to Governor Thomas, 14 October 1741, TPLB, vol. 1; Board of Trade Papers, Proprietaries, 15:T54; Wolff, *Colonial Agency*, p. 95.

23. William Allen to Thomas Penn, 24 October 1741, PPOC, vol. 3.

24. Thomas Cookson to Conrad Weiser, 12 September 1741, Correspondence of Conrad Weiser, vol. 1 (1741-56); Richard Peters to Thomas Penn, 8 October 1741, RPLB; Minutes, Philadelphia Yearly Meeting, 1747-49, p. 55 (hereinafter cited as PYM); Friends Historical Library (hereinafter cited as FHL). For Weiser's letters, see "Two Addresses of Conrad Weiser to the German Voters of Pennsylvania," *PMHB* 23 (1899): 516-21; for Christopher Saur's replies, see "Answer to Conrad Weiser's Published Letter to the Germans," 29 September 1741, PPOC, vol. 3.

25. Governor Thomas to John Penn, 25 March 1741, PPOC, vol. 3; John Penn to Governor Thomas, 21 June 1741, TPLB, vol. 1.

26. William Allen to Thomas Penn, 24 October 1741, PPOC, vol. 3.

27. *Votes*, 4:2709.

28. For a sample of Penn's whiggish notions, see John Penn to Governor Thomas, 16 August 1742, TPLB, vol. 1. John Kinsey and his associates were certainly aware that differences of sentiment and opinion did exist between John and Thomas Penn. They probably did not know, however, how great those differences had been. Before the present crisis the two brothers had disagreed over the advisability of selling Pennsylvania and over whether Thomas Penn should become chief executive on Governor Gordon's death in 1736. On the latter issue John heeded the advice of James Logan and the London Quakers, despite Thomas's apparent willingness to shoulder the responsibility. John Penn to Thomas Penn, 4 February 1736, 10 October 1736, 6 June 1737, TPLP, vol. 1.; John and Richard Penn to Thomas Penn, 10 August 1736, ibid; John Penn to Andrew Hamilton, 17 February 1737, ibid.

29. Governor Thomas to John Penn, 27 October 1741, PPOC, vol. 3.

30. *Votes*, 4:2706-2707; Richard Peters to John Penn, 20 November 1741, PPOC, vol. 3; Richard Peters to John Penn, 20 October 1741, RPLB; Richard Peters to Proprietaries, 27 October 1741, ibid.

31. Richard Peters to John Penn, 20 October 1741, RPLB. Local law allowed the Governor to choose one of the two candidates who had received the greatest number of votes.

32. Richard Peters to John Penn, 20 November 1741, PPOC, vol. 3.

33. *Votes*, 3:2672-73, 2678-79, 4:2752-63, 2786-2803; *CR*, 4:496-498, 507-41.

34. *Gazette*, 17 June 1742; William Allen to Thomas Penn, 20 November 1742, PPOC, vol. 3; Richard Peters to Thomas Penn, 7 June 1742, 5 June 1742, RPLB.

35. Richard Peters to John Penn, 1 March 1742, 5 June 1742, RPLB; Richard Hockley to Thomas Penn, 1 March 1742, 27 May 1742, PPOC, vol. 3.

36. Richard Peters to Thomas Penn, 5 June 1742, Richard Peters to Proprietaries, 25 August 1742, RPLB; Isaac Norris, Jr. to Robert Charles, 21 November 1742, INLB (1719-56).

37. Richard Peters to Proprietaries, 17 November 1742, RPLB.

38. Until 1739 freeholders chose election inspectors in each county on the morning of election day. When the presiding election official called out the names of "substantial freeholders," eligible voters who supported the nomination moved to stand beside the nominee; if a majority of the voters present stood by him the candidate was elected. This procedure continued until the proper number of inspectors had been chosen. In Philadelphia this number was eight. Unfortunately, "disorderly persons, many of whom not being qualified to vote" had, on occasion "mixed themselves among the electors at the time of choosing inspectors, and (had) by their rude and disorderly behavior, disturbed the electors and created strife and quarrels." It often happened, too, that all inspectors were chosen from one part of the county and none were acquainted

with the qualifications of men who came from remote townships. Consequently, in 1739 the method of electing inspectors was changed. Each township, or ward in the case of Philadelphia, elected a candidate for inspector on September 25. On October 1 the inspectors were chosen by lot from among those candidates. After being in force for three elections, this law expired in May 1742, and the old procedure for choosing inspectors by view on election-day morning had to be revived. *Statutes at Large,* 4:77-80, 331-36; Richard Hockley to Thomas Penn, 1 November 1742, PPOC, vol. 3.

39. Richard Peters to Proprietaries, 17 November 1742, RPLB; William T. Parsons, "The Bloody Election of 1742," *PH* 36 (1969): 293. See also Sister Joan de Lourdes Leonard, "Elections in Colonial Pennsylvania," *WMQ,* 3rd ser. 11 (1954): 393-94. 393-94.

40. Richard Peters to Proprietaries, 17 November 1742, RPLB.

41. *Votes,* 2:2844.

42. The best contemporary description of the riot is in Richard Peter's letter of 17 November 1742 to the proprietors. The affidavits of numerous witnesses are published in *Votes,* 4:2957-3009. Two recent articles on the topic are Norman S. Cohen, "The Philadelphia Election Riot of 1742," *PMHB* 92 (1968): 306-19; William T. Parson, "The Bloody Election of 1742," *PH* 36 (1969): 290-306.

43. *Votes,* 4:2828-30, 2843-50.

44. Richard Peters to Proprietaries, 30 January 1743, RPLB; *Votes,* 4:2851-52, 2855, 2856, 2864, 2864-65, 2865-66; Richard Peters to Thomas Penn, 4 March 1743, RPLB; Isaac Norris, Jr., to Robert Charles, 22 January 1743, INLB (1719-56).

45. Governor Thomas to John Penn, 4 June 1742, 17 November 1742, PPOC, vol. 3; Richard Peters to Proprietors, 25 August 1742, 17 November 1742, RPLB; *Votes,* 4:2782, 2783-84.

46. John Penn to John Kinsey, 3 March 1742, TPLB, vol. 1; John Penn to Colonel Thomas, 19 May 1743, ibid.; Richard Partridge to John Kinsey, 17 February 1743, PemP, vol. 3; Thomas Penn to Colonel Thomas, 17 September 1742, 26 February 1743, TPLB, vol. 2; Thomas Penn to William Allen, 26 February 1743, ibid.; Thomas Penn to Richard Peters, 22 August 1743, Penn Papers, Saunders-Coates; Richard Hockley to Thomas Penn, 27 June 1742, PPOC, vol. 3; Richard Peters to John Penn, 30 August 1740, RPLB; Richard Peters to Proprietors, 17 October 1742, ibid.

47. Richard Peters to John Penn, 1 March 1742, RPLB; *Statutes at Large,* 4:360-94.

48. More than anything else, Richard Peters blamed the Philadelphia defense petition for bringing on the hostilities that culminated in the 1742 riot. Richard Peters to John Penn, 1 March 1742, RPLB.

49. *Votes,* 4:2777.

50. *CR,* 4:496-98, 507-41.

51. Richard Peters to John Penn, 1 March 1742, RPLB.

52. *Votes,* 4:2739.

53. For Logan's letter to the Philadelphia Yearly Meeting, advocating defensive war, see *PMHB* 4 (1882): 403-11.

54. Kinsey's fears may be traced in the Partridge-Kinsey correspondence, PemP. For example, see Richard Patridge to John Kinsey, 13 May 1743, 30 July 1743, 2 February 1745, 14 February 1745, PemP, vol. 3.

55. Richard Peters to Proprietors, 25 August 1742, RPLB; John Fothergill to Israel Pemberton, Jr., 8 April 1742, PemP, vol. 3.

56. Richard Peters to Thomas Penn, 4 March 1743, RPLB.

57. The eight dissenting votes were cast by James Morris, Joseph Trotter, Oswald Peele, Edward Warner, Robert Jones, John Watson, Joseph Shaw, and John Hall. Those who used their influence to promote accommodation were John Kinsey, Isaac Norris, Samuel Blunston, and Israel Pemberton, Sr. Richard Peters to Proprietaries, 30 January 1743, RPLB.

58. For example, Samuel Blunston convinced many that the reason the executive wanted a militia was to enforce land payments and ejectments. Richard Peters to

Proprietaries, 17 November 1742, RPLB. See also Isaac Norris, Jr., to Robert Charles, 12 May 1741, INLB (1719-56).

59. Minutes, PYM (1747-79), FHL, p. 55.

60. Richard Peters to Thomas Penn, 4 June 1743, 9 December 1743, RPLB; idem, 5 May 1743, Penn Papers, Additional Misc. Letters; *Votes*, 4:2913, 2901-2902, 2917-18, 2926-27, 2934-36. Thomas Penn approved of the Governor's low profile Thomas Penn to Colonel Thomas, 7 March 1745, TPLB, vol. 2.

61. Richard Hockley to Thomas Penn, 17 June 1743, PPOC, vol. 4; idem, 28 September 1743, Penn Papers, Additional Misc. Letters; Thomas Penn to Colonel Thomas, 8 February 1744, TPLB, vol.2.

62. Richard Peters to Thomas Penn, 3 October 1743, RPLB; William Allen to Thomas Penn, 3 October 1743, PPOC, vol. 3; Richard Hockley to Thomas Penn, 10 March 1744, ibid., vol. 4; Richard Peters to Thomas Penn, 13 June 1744, ibid. For Thomas Penn's reply to these charges, see Thomas Penn to William Allen, 5 February 1744, TPLB, vol. 2.

63. Richard Peters to Proprietaries, 20 October 1748, PPOC, vol. 4; Isaac Norris, Jr., to Robert Charles, 16 November 1748, INLB (1719-56). See chapter 8 for the 1747-48 defense crisis.

64. In 1749-50 five of the eight diehards (see note 57) who had voted against the 1743 settlement still had seats in the Assembly.

65. Richard Peters to Thomas Penn, 30 January 1751, PPOC, vol. 5.

66. idem, 17 November 1750, ibid.

67. idem, undated, ibid., vol. 6, p. 107; idem, 13 July 1750, ibid., vol. 5; Richard Peters to Proprietaries, 25 March 1748, ibid., vol. 4.

68. James Hamilton to Thomas Penn, 18 November 1750, PPOC, vol. 5; Thomas Penn to Richard Peters, 2 August 1749, Penn Papers, Saunders-Coates.

69. Richard Peters to Proprietaries, 29 April 1749, PvB (1740-56).

70. Ibid.; James Hamilton to Thomas Penn, 30 September 1749, Andrew and James Hamilton Papers, James Hamilton Letterbook (1749-83) (hereinafter cited as JHLB).

71. James Hamilton to Thomas Penn, 22 February 1750, PPOC, vol. 5.

72. Richard Peters to Thomas Penn, 4 February 1750, ibid.; *CR*, 5:503-505, 511.

73. *Votes*, 4:3362-63, 3435, 3437-38, 3443-47; Thomas Penn to James Hamilton, 26 September 1751, TPLB, vol. 3; James Hamilton to Thomas Penn, 5 February 1751, PPOC, vol. 5. Indian expenses had increased enormously since 1745, and Richard Peters admitted that the Assembly had "behaved well in Indian affairs" Richard Peters to Proprietaries, 27 July 1748, RPLB.

74. In the late 1730s Governor Thomas had lamented that "every disappointment in a bargain of land [had served] as a good reason for opposing the government." Governor Thomas to John Penn, 5 November 1739, PPOC, vol. 3.

75. Richard Peters to Proprietaries, 21 December 1754, ibid., vol. 6; Richard Peters to Thomas Penn, 16 May 1749, PPOC, vol.4; idem 16 March 1752, 12 June 1752, 20 June 1752, ibid., vol. 5.

76. Richard Peters to Thomas Penn, 12 June 1752, PPOC, vol. 5. In the same letters Peters described the situation as follows: "Your quitrents are shamefully in arrears; your ferries wrested out of your hands; your manor lands and appropriated tracts are settled as other parts of the province, promiscuously . . . the people of Marsh Creek [are] still in possession; the county of Cumberland [is] in great disorder—no jail in it, numbers in defiance of the law, being under recognizances are gone and going over the Blue Hills, others on their invitation joining them now grow too strong to be removed. . . . The sheriffs are the creatures of, and subservient to the people, the juries without virtue in proprietary disputes and no court of equity."

77. See chapter 6 for a discussion of justices of the peace.

78. James Hamilton to Thomas Penn, 29 April 1749, JHLB; idem, 18 March 1752, PPOC, vol. 5.

79. James Hamilton to Thomas Penn, 12 March 1750, JHLB.

80. The two Quakers were John Churchman and John Smith (James Hamilton to Thomas Penn, 22 February 1751, PPOC, vol. 5). For other refusals to accept the justice of the peace commission, see Taylor Papers, Correspondence, #3259.

81. Richard Peters to Thomas Penn, 18 March 1752, 18 April 1753, PPOC, vol. 6; Thomas Penn to Richard Peters, 24 February 1751, 18 March 1752, Penn Papers, Saunders-Coates; idem, 2 April 1753, TPLB, vol. 3; idem, 29 July 1751, Gratz Coll., Governors of Pennsylvania, case 2, box 33a.

82. Richard Peters to Thomas Penn, 3 February 1753, PPOC, vol. 6.

83. Richard Peters to Thomas Penn, 12 June 1752, ibid., vol. 5.

84. Thomas Penn to Richard Peters, 28 September 1751, Penn Papers, Saunders-Coates; James Hamilton to Thomas Penn, 24 October 1749, JHLB; Instructions from the Proprietary to Mr. Hamilton, 17 March 1748, PvB (1740-56).

85. James Hamilton to Thomas Penn, 18 March 1752, PPOC, vol. 5; Richard Peters to Thomas Penn, 29 April 1749, PvB (1740-56).

86. Thomas Penn to James Hamilton, 29 July 1751, Penn-Hamilton Correspondence (hereinafter cited as PHC).

CHAPTER 3

1. Isaac Norris, Jr., to Robert Charles, 16 November 1748, INLB (1719-56).

2. John Smith's Diary, 1 October 1747.

3. A. Tully, "William Penn's Legacy: Politics and Social Structure in Provincial Pennsylvania, 1726-1755" (Ph.D. diss., Johns Hopkins University, 1973), pp. 42-65.

4. Ibid.

CHAPTER 4

1. Estimates of Pennsylvania's population and the composition of it during this period can be no more than guesswork. My guesses are based on James T. Lemon's detailed calculations in *Best Poor Man's Country*, pp. 23, 126; Levi Oscar Kuhns, *The German and Swiss Settlements of Colonial Pennsylvania: A Study of the So-called Pennsylvania Dutch* (New York, 1901), pp. 30-59; Wayland F. Dunaway, *The Scotch Irish of Colonial Pennsylvania* (Chapel Hill, N.C., 1944), pp. 28-71; R. J. Dickson, *Ulster Emigration to Colonial America, 1718-1775* (London, 1966), pp. 19-59; Frank R. Diffenderffer, "The German Immigration into Pennsylvania through the Port of Philadelphia from 1700 to 1775," *Proceedings of the Pennsylvania German Society* 10 (1900):43-45, 100-105; William J. Hinke and Ralph B. Strassburger, eds., *Pennsylvania German Pioneers: A Publication of the Original Lists of Arrivals in the Port of Philadelphia from 1727 to 1808* (Norristown, Pa., 1934), 1: xxxi.

The five new counties were Lancaster (1729), York (1749), Cumberland (1750), Berks (1752), and Northampton (1752).

2. The following discussion of the changing cultural composition of Pennsylvania is based on the sources cited in note 1 and Theodore E. Schmauk "The Lutheran Church in Pennsylvania, 1638-1800," *Proceedings of the Pennsylvania German Society*, vols. 11 and 12 (1900 and 1901); William J. Hinke and James I. Good, ed., *Minutes and Letters of the Coetus of the German Reformed Congregations in Pennsylvania, 1747-1792, together with Three Preliminary Reports of John Philip Boehm, 1734-1744* (Philadelphia, 1903); C. Henry Smith, "The Mennonite Immigration to Pennsylvania in the Eighteenth Century," *Proceedings of the Pennsylvania German Society*, vol. 35 (1929); Albert B. Faust, *The German Element in the United States* (New York, 1909), vol. 1; H. M. J. Klein, "The Church People in Colonial Pennsylvania," *PH* 9 (1942):37-47; Selina G. Shulz, "The Schwenkfelders of Pennsylvania," ibid. 24 (1957): 292-321; Henry Harbaugh, *The Life of Reverend Michael Schlatter: His Travels and Labors among the Germans in Pennsylvania, 1716-1790* (Philadelphia, 1887); William J. Hinke, *Life and Letters of the Reverend John Philip Boehm, Founder of the Reformed Church in Pennsylvania, 1683-1749* (Philadelphia, 1916); Julius F. Sachse, *The German Sectarians of Pennsylvania* (Philadelphia, 1899), vol. 1; William S. Perry, ed., *Historical Collections*

Relating to the American Colonial Church, II: Pennsylvania (Hartford, Conn., 1871); Thomas Woody, *Early Quaker Education in Pennsylvania* (New York, 1920); Guy S. Klett, *Presbyterians in Colonial Pennsylvania* (Philadelphia, 1937); David M. Carson, "A History of the Reformed Presbyterian Church" (Ph.D. diss., University of Pennsylvania, 1964); Edwin S. Gaustad, *Historical Atlas of Religion in America* (New York, 1962); Albert Cook Meyers, *Immigration of the Irish Quakers into Pennsylvania, 1682-1750* (Lancaster, Pa., 1901); C. A. Hanna, *The Scotch-Irish, or, the Scot in North Britain, North Ireland, and North America*, 2 vols. (New York, 1902).

3. Sachse, *German Sectarians*, 1:442.

4. Lemon, *Best Poor Man's Country*, pp. 42-70. See figs. I and II.

5. Ibid. See figs. III and IV.

6. Ibid., pp. 13-24, 49-61, 71-117.

7. For sample petitions see *Votes*, 3:1924, 4:3235.

8. Lemon, *Best Poor Man's Country*, pp. 18-23; Klett, *Presbyterians in Colonial Pennsylvania*, pp. 87-126; Harold D. Eberlein and Cortlandt Van Dyke Hubbard, *The Church of Saint Peter in the Great Valley, 1700-1942* (Richmond, Va., 1944), pp. 1-35; Schmauk, "The Lutheran Church in Pennsylvania," pp. 235-43, 277n.; Harbaugh, *Schlatter*, pp. 70-71; Hinke, *Boehm*, pp. 83-85; Carson, "A History of the Reformed Presbyterian Church," pp. 18, 21-22; Klein, "The Church People in Colonial Pennsylvania," p. 38. In his *Historical Atlas of Religion in America*, Edwin S. Gaustad enumerated the following congregations in 1750: Anglicans 19, Baptists 29, Lutherans 73, Presbyterians 56, Reformed 64, Roman Catholic 11, Dutch Reformed 7. With the fifty Quaker meetings that existed in 1750, the total stands at 309. Not included, however, were Mennonites, Schwenkfelders, and a number of other sectarian groups. With these included, the number of congregations or comparable units at mid-century would total at least 350. For the number of Quaker meetings in 1750 see Woody, *Early Quaker Education*, p. 270.

9. Other causes for disciplinary action were defamation of character, breaking marriage provisions, disrespect for the session, fornication, bastardy, propositioning, quarreling, purposely damaging a neighbor's property, fighting, slander, harboring runaway servants, mistreating servants, selling goods on the Sabbath, and breaking a contractual obligation. Faggs Manor, Pa., New Londonderry Congregation, Records of the Session (1740-93); PHS; Second Presbyterian Church of Philadelphia, Consistory Book (1744-98), PHS, pp.1-20.

10. Records of Donegal Presbytery, 1a (1732-35): 84-85, 89-90, 124, 135-137, 1b (1736-40): 220, PHS; Richard Webster, *A History of the Presbyterian Church* (Philadelphia, 1857), pp. 121-22, 134-36; Klett, *Presbyterians*, pp. 93-94, 116-26, 172-77. Enforcing discipline was difficult because supply ministers, not knowing the congregation, would often administer the sacraments to everyone who pressed forward. Martin E. Lodge, "The Crisis of the Churches in the Middle Colonies," *PMHB* 95 (1971): 209.

11. Hinke, *Boehm*, pp. 137-38, 166-67, 286; Henry M. Muhlenberg, *The Journals of Henry Melchior Muhlenberg*, trans. and ed. Theodore G. Tappert and John W. Doberstein (Phildelphia, 1942), 1:83-84, 174, 193, 211-12, 221; Harbaugh, *Schlatter*, pp. 70-83, 203-204; Hinke and Good, *Minutes and Letters of the Coetus*, pp. 42-44, 64. The Classis of Amsterdam sent the Rev. Michael Schlatter to Pennsylvania in 1746 to organize the German Reformed Church. Henry M. Muhlenberg, who came to Pennsylvania in 1742 from Halle, Germany was the chief organizer of the German Lutheran Church.

12. Hinke, *Boehm*, pp. 88-89; Muhlenberg, *Journals*, 1:118-19, 265; Michael Schlatter, "Diary of the Reverend Michael Schlatter," ed. William J. Hinke, *Journal of the Presbyterian Historical Society* 3 (1905): 119, 169; Dietmar Rothermund, "The German Problem of Colonial Pennsylvania," *PMHB* 84 (1960): 20-21.

13. *Gazette*, 11 March 1731, 30 August 1739, 21 December 1742; John Smith's Diary, 16 January 1747, 12 August 1748; *Votes*, 3:2334; Peter Kalm, *The America of 1750: Peter Kalm's Travels in North America*, trans. and ed. A. B. Benson (New York, 1937), 1:212; Abbot E. Smith, *Colonists in Bondage: White Servitude and Convict Labor in America, 1607-1776* (Chapel Hill, N. C., 1947), p. 51; William H. Egle, ed., *Notes and*

Queries, 1st and 2nd ser. 1: 20, 2:3; *PA,* 1st ser. 2:364; Stevenson W. Fletcher, *Pennsylvania Agriculture and Country Life, 1640-1840* (Harrisburg, Pa., 1950), 1:437-58.

14. For an example of a Pennsylvania family that maintained if not increased its cohesiveness despite distance, see Randolph Shipley Klein, "The Shippen Family: A Generational Study in Colonial and Revolutionary America" (Ph.D. diss., Rutgers University, 1972).

15. Such was the case in Philadelphia, at least, where individuals who wanted to join civic and recreational clubs tended to join those composed of their peers. Daniel R. Gilbert, "Patterns of Organization and Membership in Colonial Philadelphia Club Life, 1725-1755" (Ph.D. diss., University of Pennsylvania, 1952), pp. 12-16, 123-24.

16. For example, ibid., pp. 17, 22, 24-25, 117, 184, 188; Judy M. DiStefano, "A Concept of the Family in Colonial America: The Pembertons of Philadelphia" (Ph.D. diss., Ohio State University, 1970), pp. 136-66.

17. Kenneth A. Lockridge, *A New England Town: The First Hundred Years* (New York, 1970), pp. 1-90.

18. Ibid., pp. 102, 117, 167-69; Zuckerman, *Peaceable Kingdoms,* pp. 17-18, 50, 107-13, 116-19, 188, 197-98; Bruce E. Steiner, "Anglican Officeholding in Pre-Revolutionary Connecticut: The Parameters of New England Community," *WMQ,* 3rd ser. 31 (1974): 388-406. The best short summary of declension in community organization and behavior in New England is Edward M. Cook, Jr., "Social Behavior and Changing Values in Dedham, Massachusetts, 1700-1775," *WMQ,* 3rd ser. 27 (1970): 546-80.

19. Lockridge, *A New England Town,* pp. 16-17; Susan M. Forbes, "As Many Candles Lighted: The New Garden Monthly Meeting, 1718-1774" (Ph.D. diss., University of Pennsylvania, 1972), pp. 18-27, 148-51.

20. Not that personal rivalries and contention failed to appear; they did, and when they did they were as likely to take place between members of a minority group as between representatives of different nationalities. Lemon, *Best Poor Man's Country,* pp. 22-23, 59, 82, 116; Minutes, Sadsbury Monthly Meeting, FHL, 1739, p. 10, 1750-51, pp. 55-59 (hereinafter cited as MM); Muhlenberg, *Journals,* 1:93, 264; Forbes, "As Many Candles Lighted," p. 127.

21. *Statutes at Large,* 4:312, 347; Franklin Ellis and Samuel Evans, *History of Lancaster County, Pennsylvania* (Philadelphia, 1883), pp. 215-17.

22. Ford, "Germans and other Foreign Stock," pp. 7-8, 10-11; Morton L. Montgomery, *History of Berks County in Pennsylvania* (Philadelphia, 1886), pp. 493, 495-98. Emmanuel Carpenter served Lancaster County as a justice of the peace after moving westward from Germantown in the early 1730s. Apparently he had been influenced by the type of attitude Daniel Pastorius displayed when he advised young Germans to "remember that your father was naturalized . . . [and that] each of you [are] *Anglus Natus* and Englishmen by birth" (quoted in Harry M. and Margaret B. Tinkcom, *Historic Germantown: From the Founding to the Early Part of the Nineteenth Century* [Lancaster, Pa., 1955], pp. 17-18), for Carpenter changed his name from the German Zimmerman to the English equivalent. On Carpenter see *Journal of the Lancaster County Historical Society* 24 (1920): 138-68.

Conrad Weiser and Edward Smout were also justices of the peace. Both had lived in the province for some time, both were well-to-do, and both had performed important services for the province—Weiser in Indian affairs and Smout during the Maryland boundary dispute. On Weiser see Paul A. Wallace, *Conrad Weiser, 1696-1760: Friend of Colonist and Mohawk* (Philadelphia, 1945). The best measure of the Anglican Smout is in his will, Lancaster County Will Book A, Lancaster County Court House (hereinafter cited as LCCH), p. 196. See also Thomas Penn to Richard Peters, 1 March 1745, Gratz Coll. , Governors of Pennsylvania, case 2, box 33a. A fourth German justice of the peace was Simon Adam Kuhn, a prominent German Lutheran physician who moved to Lancaster from Germantown in 1740, served for some time as chief Burgess of Lancaster Borough, and cooperated closely with members of the English establishment. On Kuhn see Alexander Harris, *A Biographical History of Lancaster County* (Lancaster, Pa., 1872) pp. 355-56; and more fully Jerome Wood, Jr., "Connestoga Crossroads: The Rise of Lancaster, Pennsylvania, 1730-1789" (Ph.D. diss., Brown University, 1969), pp. 45-46.

Martin Mylin, elected county commissioner in 1749, was one of the German-Swiss Mennonites who first settled in Lancaster County. The most revealing thing about Mylin was that in 1740-41 he built a large, showy home on his farm in Lampeter Township that became a local landmark known as "the palace." Mylin died a rich man, with personal assets alone totalling nearly £1800. I. Daniel Rupp, *History of Lancaster County* (Lancaster, Pa., 1844), pp. 286-87; Lancaster County Inventories (1751), LCCH.

The only personal possession that these men had that set them off from their English or Scotch-Irish counterparts were German books. See, for example, J. B. Nolan, ed., "Conrad Weiser's Inventory," *PMHB* 56 (1932):265-69.

23. For a more extended treatment of the tensions German immigration precipitated prior to 1755, see Tully, "William Penn's Legacy," pp. 42-61.

24. For a detailed discussion of the effects of the Great Awakening, see ibid., pp. 63-86.

25. Faggs Manor, Pa., New Londonderry Congregation, Records of the Session (1740-93) PHS, 3 January 1744.

26. Lemon, *Best Poor Man's Country*, pp. 23, 28, 69, 123, 222-24; James G. Lydon, "Philadelphia's Commercial Expansion," *PMHB* 91 (1967): 404. For a general discussion of the growth of Philadelphia's trade during the eighteenth century, see Arthur L. Jensen, *The Maritime Commerce of Colonial Pennsylvania* (Madison, Wis., 1963), pp. 1-10; Marc Egnal, "The Changing Structure of Philadelphia's Trade with the British West Indies, 1750-1775," *PMHB* 99 (1975):156-62.

27. The export ratio is based on figures for wheat, flour, and flaxseed only. Lemon, *Best Poor Man's Country*, p. 28.

28. Address of the settlers in Springtown Manor to Governor Thomas, April 1744, Society Miscellaneous Collection, Springtown Manor, Pa.; John Penn to Richard Penn, 10 March 1735, TPLB, vol. 1; James Logan to Hannah Penn, 1 January 1726, JLLB (1716-43); Isaac Norris, Jr., to Robert Charles 31 December 1754, INLB (1719-56). James Logan to Amos Strettel, 15 September 1728, JLLB (1717-28); Hinke, *Boehm*, p. 286; Dickson, *Ulster Immigration*, pp. 1-60; Smith, *Colonists in Bondage*, pp. 317-23.

29. Frederick B. Tolles, *Meeting House and Counting House: The Quaker Merchants of Colonial Philadelphia, 1682-1763* (Chapel Hill, N. C., 1948), pp. 43-44; Nash, *Quakers and Politics*, pp. 56-58.

30. Lydon, "Philadelphia's Commercial Expansion," pp. 402-403; Tolles, *Meeting House and Counting House*, pp. 86-88, 90-91.

31. Jensen, *Maritime Commerce*, pp. 3-5; Nash, *Quakers and Politics*, pp. 55-57; James T. Lemon and Gary B. Nash, "The Distribution of Wealth in Eighteenth-Century America: A Century of Change in Chester County, Pennsylvania, 1693-1802," *Journal of Social History* 2 (1968): 17. For the organization of trade by Philadelphia merchants, see Harry D. Berg, "The Organization of Business in Colonial Philadelphia," *PH* 10 (1933): 157-77; and, briefly, Lydon, "Philadelphia's Commercial Expansion," p. 405. For a superb treatment of "the Quaker economic ethic," see Tolles, *Meeting House and Counting House*, pp. 51-62.

32. Lydon, "Philadelphia's Commercial Expansion," pp. 401-18.

33. For a detailed consideration of land quality, availability, and usage, see Lemon, *Best Poor Man's Country*, pp. 33-40, 42-70, 180-83.

34. This is not to exclude the importance of cultural and kinship ties as reasons for Pennsylvania's remarkable record of immigration.

35. From 1717 to 1738 the price of unsettled Maryland land was forty shillings for one hundred acres; after the latter date it jumped to fifty-two shillings per hundred. The standard quitrent for most of the second quarter of the eighteenth century was four shillings per hundred. Clarence P. Gould, *The Land System in Maryland, 1720-1765* (Baltimore, 1913), pp. 10, 55.

36. *Statutes at Large*, 5:10. The Loan Office came into existence with Pennsylvania's first currency act in 1723 and continued to operate throughout this period.

37. What evidence remains indicates that public access to loans was relatively easy. *Statutes at Large*, 3:328; *Votes*, 5:3834; Thomas Penn to John and Richard Penn, 11 June 1738, Penn Papers, Small Letterbook.

38. *Votes*, 4:3519, 5:3834.

39. John Swift to John White, 20 September 1747, John Swift Letterbook.

40. *Votes*, 4:3520. For Hamilton's activities see ibid., 3:2196-97.

41. James Logan to John Penn, 10 November 1740, JLLB (1716-43); *Votes*, 3:2570. On the Loan Office providing capital, see *Franklin Papers*, 1:142, and Penn Papers, Assembly and Provincial Council, p. 55.

42. Lydon, "Philadelphia's Commercial Expansion," p. 408; Lemon, *Best Poor Man's Country*, p. 10.

43. Lemon, *Best Poor Man's Country*, pp. 7-9, 12-13, 94-96.

44. Ibid., pp. 69, 96. For contemporary comment see *Votes*, 4:3520; Benjamin Franklin, "A Modest Enquiry into the Nature and Necessity of a Paper Currency," *Franklin Papers*, 1:151; Gottlieb Mittelberger, *Journey to Pennsylvania*, trans. and ed. Oscar Handlin and John Clive. (Cambridge, Mass., 1960), p. 90; John Swift to John White, 10 December 1748, John Swift Letterbook.

45. Lemon, *Best Poor Man's Country*, pp. 7-8.

46. Tully, "William Penn's Legacy" pp. 96-104.

47. Tolles, *Meeting House and Counting House*, pp. 51-62; Lemon, *Best Poor Man's Country*, pp. 6, 19-22.

48. For an extreme form of this argument, see Lemon, *Best Poor Man's Country*, pp.4-7 and passim.

49. For evidence of this see Christopher Saur's interpretation of the German immigrants' experiences (*Pennsylvania Berichte*, 1 March 1749). The Scotch-Irish had felt many of the same kinds of pressures as the Germans. Dickson, *Ulster Immigration*, pp. 1-60. Historians have tended to cite the listed occupations of immigrants as husbandman or artisan as proof that they were men of skill and means who were upwardly mobile prior to immigration. It would seem, however, that the relative youth of Pennsylvania's immigrants indicates that, although many came from families whose status was that of yeoman or artisan and although their parents educated them for occupations at that level, the family could not provide all children with the resources they needed to set out on their own in an occupation at that status level. Hence, although the move to Pennsylvania eventually produced upward mobility for many, as long as they remained in Europe, many of these same people were probably downwardly mobile.

50. Sigmund Diamond, "Values as an Obstacle to Economic Growth: The American Colonies," *Journal of Economic History* 27 (1967): 561-75.

51. Address of the Settlers in Springtown Manor to Governor Thomas, April 1744, Society Miscellaneous Collection, Springtown Manor, Pa.

52. Alan Tully, "Economic Opportunity in Mid-Eighteenth Century Rural Pennsylvania," *Histoire sociale [Social History]*: 9(1976): 118-23.

53. Lemon, *Best Poor Man's Country*, pp. 29-30, 150-51, 216-17. The major change during this period was the founding of a number of towns "to foster the expansion of the economy, to maintain order, and to sustain social values." Lemon, *Best Poor Man's Country*, p. 118; see, generally, pp. 118-149, 221-23.

54. Tully, "Economic Opportunity in Mid-Eighteenth Century Rural Pennsylvania," pp. 124-128.

55. Lemon and Nash, "The Distribution of Wealth in Eighteenth-Century America," p. 11.

56. "Our method of assessments is by certain imaginary rates or valuation of estates, but is, properly speaking, a ratio or proportion of one man's estate to another. Thus, one man is rated at £20, another at £40 and another at £100 when, perhaps, their yearly incomes may sometimes be twice as much and at other times not half so much; for the necessary expenses of one shall induce the mitigation and the contrary of the other. . . ." (Lewis Evans, A brief Account of Pennsylvania . . . [1753].)

57. A Book for the Poor of the Township of East Caln, 1735-1755, Chester County Historical Society (hereinafter cited as CCHS).

58. For an example of a man with capital coming from Ireland, see William Pim's Account Book, CCHS. Pim became one of the largest property holders in East Caln, a justice of the peace, and an influential member of the Society of Friends.

59. See, for example, *Mercury*, 7 August 1729.

60. Tolles, *Meeting House and Counting House*, pp. 65, 104-105; *Gazette*, 19 November 1730. For the social effects of a loss of wealth, see John Swift to John White, 20 September 1749, John Swift Letterbook.

61. For the commendability of the pursuit of wealth, see *Mercury*, 17 April 1729. For a rare dissenting view, see *Gazette*, 22 August 1751. One of the best descriptions of the "work ethic" as it appeared among members of the provincial elite is a letter Edward Shippen (of Lancaster) wrote to his son Edward on 20 March 1754. *PMHB* 30 (1906): 85-90.

62. Thomas Story to James Logan, 28 June 1734, "Logan-Story Correspondence," p. 45. After studying Quaker disownments in eighteenth-century Pennsylvania, Jack D. Marietta concluded that, of disownments for matters of "pride and vanity," more than 80 percent came after 1755 and most of the remainder before 1710. "Ecclesiastical Discipline in the Society of Friends, 1682-1776" (Ph.D. diss., Stanford University, 1968), pp. 148-49.

63. The observations made in this paragraph are based on Tolles, *Meeting House and Counting House*, pp. 109-143, and my own reading of the manuscript sources for Philadelphia society. The best single source is John Smith's Diary. On the relatively "sober" nature of Philadelphia society, see John Swift to Governor Bedford, 22 March 1748, John Swift Letterbook.

64. Tolles, *Meeting House and Counting House*, p. 132.

65. J. G. A. Pocock described and pointed out the central importance of the ideology in English thought in his essay "Machiavelli, Harrington, and English Political Ideologies in the Eighteenth Century," *WMQ*, 3rd ser. 22 (1965): 547-83.

66. To use the criterion of "merchant" would either be too restrictive or, if interpreted to include everyone who dabbled in a commercial venture, too broad.

67. Tolles, *Meeting House and Counting House*, p. 97; Jerome H. Wood, Jr., "The Town Proprietors of Lancaster, 1730-1790," *PMHB* 96 (1972): 346-68; Norman S. Cohen, "William Allen—Chief Justice of Pennsylvania, 1704-1780" (Ph.D. diss., University of California, Berkeley, 1966), pp. 43-44.

68. John Swift to John White, 22 July 1748, John Swift Letterbook; Chester County Inventories #646, #1887, #3674, Chester County Court House (hereinafter cited as CCCH).

69. Mrs. Thomas Potts James, *Memorial of Thomas Potts, Jr.* (Cambridge, Mass., 1874); Rutter and Potts Families Newspaper Clippings File, CCHS; Mildred Goshow, "The Hockley Family of Chester County." (unpublished ms.).

70. Martin, *Bench and Bar*, pp. 241, 292, 256.

71. Ibid., p. 16.

72. Owen was a member of the Assembly and three times sheriff of Chester County. Chester County Will Book C, CCCH, p. 339. For some of Wharton's interests see *Gazette*, 28 May 1747. Also J. Smith Futhey and Gilbert Cope, *History of Chester County* (Philadelphia, 1881), p. 374.

73. For evidence on the economic activities and life style of the county leaders, see Chester County Inventories #1887, #2612, #1714, #1413, #1603, #1412, #1487, #394, CCCH; Chester County Will Book C, CCCH, pp. 334, 329, 418; Samuel Blunston's Inventory of Estate, Griffith-Paschall Coll. To compare descriptions of plantations owned by James Hamilton, Edward Horne, and one suitable for a "gentleman or storekeeper" with the seats of county leaders David Lloyd, Joseph Harvey, and Mark Watson, see *Gazette*, 1 April 1736, 15 April 1736, 6 October 1744, 25 October 1744, 22 October 1747, and 1 January 1751.

CHAPTER 5

1. This discussion is based on Edward Shils's model of deference. Shils argues that deference is an "act of appreciation or derogation" and that personal proximity to the centers of power in society—whether they be political, religious, military, etc.— determines the degree of deference demanded and accorded. The centers of power are awe-inspiring because they create order not only by ensuring coherence and predictabili-

ty, but also by establishing a social order that is in harmony with a greater moral order. In a society there will be a greater degree of deference when the political, religious, military, economic, and individual elites are composed of the same people, or members of the same kinship groups, than when society's power centers are occupied by different personnel. Edward Shils, "Deference," in J. A. Jackson, ed., *Social Stratification* (Cambridge, Mass., 1968), pp. 104-32; "Centre and Periphery" in *The Logic of Personal Knowledge: Essays in Honour of Michael Polanyi* (London, 1961), pp. 117-30; "Charisma Order and Status," *American Sociological Review* 30 (1965): 199-213; "The Concentration and Dispersion of Charisma," *World Politics* 11:1-19.

2. There were exceptions among appointees to the Provincial Council and to other offices as well. For example, Speaker of the Assembly John Kinsey held the office of attorney general from 1738 to 1741, and William Logan, a close friend of the three Pembertons—Israel Junior, James, and John—was appointed to the Provincial Council in 1747. Martin, *Bench and Bar*, pp. 27, 167.

3. After conducting her study of the Philadelphia Corporation, Judith M. Diamondstone concluded that "in the aggregate the members gave the Corporation a proprietary slant." From 1722 to 1755, 67 percent of the admissions were Anglican, Presbyterian, and nominal or dismissed Quakers. In the late 1720s and early 1730s, when society had yet to be openly divided by the political split between proprietary and Quaker groups, leading Quakers such as Isaac Norris, Jr., were admitted. After 1742, however, those Quakers who had been active in Corporation affairs no longer took part. Judith M. Diamondstone, "The Philadelphia Corporation, 1701-1776" (Ph.D. diss., University of Pennsylvania, 1969), pp. 231-37, 323-67. On the overlapping membership in the Corporation and Provincial Council, see ibid., p. 276. More generally on the Council, see James Laverne Anderson, "The Governor's Councils of Colonial America, A Study of Pennsylvania and Virginia, 1660-1776" (Ph.D. diss., University of Virginia, 1967). On kinship connections see Diamondstone, "Philadelphia Corporation," pp. 255, 258-59, 264, 267-68; Darold D. Wax, "The Negro Slave Trade in Colonial Pennsylvania (Ph.D. diss., University of Washington, 1962), pp. 73-75. For an example of informal socializing see Richard Peters to Proprietaries, 14 November 1741, RPLB; Gilbert, "Philadelphia Club Life," pp. 17, 175, 184-85.

4. Gilbert, "Philadelphia Club Life," pp. 14-17, 169-84.

5. The Keithian divisions of the late 1720s were not along these lines, and the paper currency dispute did not break out openly until the summer of 1754.

6. Debby Norris to Isaac Norris, 3 November 1733, Norris Papers, Family Letters vol. 1; John Smith's Diary, 29 August 1747, 30 November 1747, 31 December 1747, 26 December 1749.

7. Charles P. Keith, *Provincial Councillors of Pennsylvania who Held Office Between 1733 and 1776* (Philadelphia, 1883), pp. 185-93.

8. Nash, *Quakers and Politics*, p. 231; Diamondstone, "Philadelphia Corporation," pp. 209-16, 284-88.

9. Chester R. Young, "The Evolution of the Pennsylvania Assembly 1682-1748," *PH* 35 (1968): 147-68.

10. Lewis B. Namier and John Brooke, *The History of Parliament. The House of Commons, 1754-1790,* (New York, 1964), 1:177-84; Robert Zemsky, *Merchants, Farmers and River Gods: An Essay in Eighteenth Century Politics* (Boston, 1971), pp. 3-4.

11. "Democracy and the American Revolution," pp. 165-90.

12. For a definition of "independence" see chapter 4, for a definition of "virtue" see chapter 7. "Capacity" connoted mental ability, aptitude, and integrity. For a good example of the kind of qualities attributed to the ideal candidate, see *Mercury,* 25 September 1729.

13. See appendix II.1.

14. See appendices II.1 and II.2.

15. For example, see Robert Jordan to Isaac Norris, Jr., 3 July 1735, Norris Papers, vol. 2.

16. On the value of education, see *Gazette,* 21 November 1754; James Logan to

William Logan, February 1731-32, JLLB (1731-32); John Penn to Thomas Penn, 4 June 1737, TPLB vol.1; Woody, *Early Quaker Education*, pp. 26-46; Lawrence A. Cremin, *American Education: The Colonial Experience* (New York, 1972), p. 469. On the literary tastes of Philadelphia society, see Tolles, *Meeting House and Counting House*, pp. 144-204. For a listing of books held by a member of the country elite, see Joseph Brinton's Inventory, Chester County Inventory #1413, CCH.

17. *PMHB* 22 (1898): 386-87.

18. Richard Peters to Thomas Penn, 5 June 1742, RPLB.

19. There is no way of knowing exactly how many Quakers were in Pennsylvania. My estimate of one-third the population is for 1730, of one-sixth for 1755. Similarly, there is no conclusive evidence on how many Quakers settled in Lancaster County. In 1741 spokesmen for the Philadelphia quarterly meeting stated that not more than twenty Quakers had taken part in the Lancaster elections of that year. Minutes, PYM (1747-79), FHL, p. 55. The estimate of "less than 100 Quakers" in Lancaster is based on Isaac Norris, Jr.'s letter to Robert Charles, 5 October 1755, INLB (1719-56).

20. With the exception of Philadelphia County between 1726 and 1728, when political leaders were split into two factions. During these years the Keithians attracted the support of most of the non-Quaker Philadelphians, but they also had the backing of numerous city Quakers. See chapter 7.

21. Except for 1743 in Bucks County. Isaac Norris, Jr., to Robert Charles, 1 October 1743, INLB (1719-56).

22. *Votes*, 3:2657; *PA*, 2nd ser. 8:94-95; John Smith's Diary, 1 October 1747, 2 October 1749, 24 September 1750, 27 September 1750, 2 October 1750, 2 October 1752; John Taylor to William Moore, 20 September 1738, Taylor Papers, Correspondence (1723-50); Richard Peters to Proprietaries, 20 October 1748, PPOC, vol. 4; John Smith to Elizabeth Hudson, 10 October 1750, Correspondence of John Smith (1740-70); Isaac Norris, Jr., to Robert Charles, 7 October 1754, INLB (1719-56).

23. For a few isolated examples of writers questioning the assumptions on which political practices stood, see *Gazette*, 8 December 1737; *Mercury*, 21 December 1731; *A Dialogue Showing What's Therein To Be Found* (Philadelphia, 1725).

24. John Smith's Diary, 24 September 1750; John Taylor to William Moore, 20 September 1738, Taylor Papers, Correspondence (1723-50); *PMHB* 22 (1898): 386-87; John Smith to Richard Partridge, 7 January 1754, Correspondence of John Smith (1740-70); John Smith to James Logan, Jr., 13 October 1750, ibid.

25. *PMHB* 22 (1898): 386-87.

26. Ibid.; John Taylor to William Moore, 20 September 1738, Taylor Papers, Correspondence (1723-50). There was, of course, a final appeal in the case of election disputes to the Assembly, but, in the three cases of contested elections between 1726 and 1755, ballot counts were upheld. See note 35.

27. Richard Peters to Thomas Penn, 2 October 1756, PPOC, vol. 8. See appendix I.1.

28. See chapters 1, 2, 4, and 7; Isaac Norris, Jr., to Robert Charles, 1 October 1743, 7 October 1754, INLB (1719-56).

29. The opposition slate of candidates was short one person. Presumably this was to leave the voter some semblance of choice. Probably the division in Bucks County in 1743 followed lines similar to the 1740 and 1742 splits, but there is no direct evidence of this.

30. 1740 Bucks County election results:

John Hall	450	Thomas Marriot	343
Mark Watson	436	Joseph Kirkbride	341
John Watson	428	Christian Van Horne	328
Abraham Chapman	428	Benjamin Jones	311
Benjamin Field	410	Lawrence Growdon	309
Thomas Canby	401	Simon Butler	228
Mahlon Kirkbride	390	Hugh Watson	186
Jeremiah Langhorne	344		

Benjamin Jones and Joseph Kirkbride were defeated incumbents. Norris added the comment that "these who failed were all of their ticket except Thomas Marriot." Jeremiah Langhorne, the man who beat out Marriot, was too ill to take his seat. Isaac Norris, Jr. to Robert Charles, 11 October 1740, INLB (1719-56).

1742 Bucks County election results:

Mahlon Kirkbride	569	Joseph Kirkbride	459
Mark Watson	561	Lawrence Growdon	445
John Watson	558	Benjamin Jones	435
Abraham Chapman	558	Christian Van Horne	434
John Hall	557	Ennion Williams	431
Benjamin Field	557	John Moreland	428
Joseph Shaw	542	Simon Butler	424
Garrat Vansant	533	Richard Walker	419

Isaac Norris, Jr.'s Journal, *Taylor's Almanac* (1742), Library Company of Philadelphia (hereinafter cited as LCP).

1740 Philadelphia County election results:

Thomas Leech	1822	William Allen	807
John Kinsey	1097	William Branson	756
Robert Jones	1089	William Monington	751
Isaac Norris	1088	William Rawle	747
Edward Warner	1087	George Boone	740
James Morris	1072	Samuel Lowe	731
Joseph Trotter	1070	Joseph Maddox	731
Owen Evans	1070		

Isaac Norris to Robert Charles, 11 October 1740, INLB (1719-56).
    31. 1742 Philadelphia County election results:

Thomas Leech	1793	William Allen	336
John Kinsey	1786	Jonathan Robeson	334
Robert Jones	1786	Nicholas Scull	304
Isaac Norris	1775	Joseph Brientall	102
Edward Warner	1773		
Owen Evans	1767		
James Morris	1494		

Isaac Norris, Jr.'s Journal.
    32. 1742 Lancaster County election results:

Samuel Blunston	1480	James Hamilton	360
John Wright	1479		
Thomas Lindley	1470		
Anthony Shaw	1469		

1742 Chester County election results:

James Gibbons	960	John Parry	80
John Owen	960		
Samuel Levis	957	"the rest about 40 and under"	
Jeremiah Starr	957		
Thomas Chandler	922		
Joseph Harvey	874		

William Hughs	859
Thomas Tatnall	842

Isaac Norris' Journal.

33. 1740 Lancaster County election results:

Thomas Lindley	988	James Mitchell	148
John Wright	984	James Hamilton	103
Thomas Ewing	977	Thomas Edwards	81
Anthony Shaw	684	Edward Shippen	51
		Samuel Smith	10

Isaac Norris, Jr., to Robert Charles, 11 October 1740, INLB (1719-56). From Isaac Norris's description of the 1740 election in Chester County and from the context of politics in that area, it appears unlikely that opposition politicians sponsored a complete slate. William Moore was the most prominent candidate. Ibid.

There is no evidence extant that indicates whether the group of Philadelphia county politicians who opposed the Keithians between 1726 and 1728 put forward a full ticket or not. On Keithian politics see chapters 1 and 7; for the 1741 Lancaster election, see chapter 2.

34. John Smith's Diary, 2 October 1747, 3 October 1749, 2 October 1750; Samuel Noble to John Smith, 3 October 1741, Correspondence of John Smith (1740-70).

35. *Register of Pennsylvania*, 5 (1830):21. In the 1748 Bucks County election and again in Lancaster the following year, other controversies occurred. In the former case, John Hall (a Quaker) had been one of the eleven candidates who failed election to the eight-seat county delegation. (Of those who succeeded seven were Quakers and one Presbyterian.) In the Lancaster dispute, one Presbyterian and three Quakers had been elected from among one Presbyterian and four Quaker candidates. James Wright, a successful Quaker candidate, and James Webb, the unsuccessful candidate, combined their efforts to have Quaker Peter Worral removed from the Assembly. *Votes*, 4:3279-80, 3222, 3225; Richard Peters to Proprietaries, 8 December 1749, PPOC, vol. 4; Richard Peters to Proprietaries, 25 November 1748, RPLB.

36. When, six months after the 1732 Lancaster election, one of the incumbents, George Stuart, died, the loser, John Wright, was elected to the vacancy. *Votes*, 3:2164, 2172.

37. Ibid., p. 2011; John Smith's Diary, 1 October 1750, 2 October 1751. Isaac Norris, Jr., best articulated the ideal values governing political behavior: "My own inclination for many years have been strongly bent upon retreat and the public station I suffer myself to hold arises from a duty I apprehend every member of society owes to the public when that duty becomes binding upon him by the voluntary call of others without any interposition or acts of our own. . . ." Isaac Norris, Jr. to John Fothergill, 25 May 1755, INLB 1719-56. John Smith's Diary, 24 September 1750, 28 September 1750; William Allen to John Penn, 24 October 1741, PPOC, vol. 3.

38. It is unlikely that men of great provincial reputation, such as Andrew Hamilton, John Kinsey, Isaac Norris, and Jeremiah Langhorne, had campaigned for themselves, but these political leaders did use their influence to procure what they regarded as a favorable group of candidates.

39. Richard Peters to the Proprietaries, 17 November 1742, RPLB; Isaac Norris, Jr., to Robert Charles, 11 October 1740, INLB, 1719-56; *Votes*, 4:2956-3014.

40. *Register of Pennsylvania*, 5 (1830): 21.

41. For examples of general statements of political beliefs, see *To the Freeholders of the Province of Pennsylvania* (Philadelphia, 1742), and *A Letter from a Gentleman in Philadelphia* (1742). For examples of solicitation and personal attacks, see *Gazette*, 29 September 1737; *Mercury*, 13 September 1733, 20 September 1733, 27 September 1733, 25 September 1735; Paul Veritt, *To My Friends in Pennsylvania* (Philadelphia, 1738). For a listing of some of the main polemical tracts of the late 1720s, see Wendel, "The Keith-Lloyd Alliance," *PMHB* 92 (1968): 300.

42. *Advice to the Freeholders and Electors of Pennsylvania* (Philadelphia, 1735); John Smith's Diary, 3 October 1749, 1 October 1750, 2 October 1750; John Taylor to William Moore, 20 September 1738, Taylor Papers, Correspondence (1723-70); *PMHB* 22 (1898): 386-87.

43. John Taylor to William Moore, 20 September 1738, Taylor Papers, Correspondence (1723-50); Richard Peters to Proprietaries, 17 November 1742, RPLB.

44. Richard Peters to Thomas Penn, 5 June 1742, RPLB.

45. Elections were held at the county seats on the first of October or, if the first was a Sunday, on the following day. Voters cast one ballot for assemblymen (each ballot to contain the same number of names as the county had House seats), one ballot for sheriff and coroner (each ballot to contain the names of two nominees for each position), and one ballot for county commissioner and assessors (each ballot to contain the name of one person for the former position and six for the latter). Philadelphia City residents elected six city assessors at the same time as they elected two burgesses to sit in the Assembly. City elections took place the day after the county elections.

Prior to 1727, the officer who presided over the voting activities could be the sheriff, his deputy, the coroner, or any two freeholders chosen on election-day morning by the assembled electors. These men were aided by an unspecified number of clerks that they were to appoint. In 1727 the Assembly passed legislation that required the presiding officer or officers to conduct elections among the assembled voters, prior to the opening of the polling station, for inspectors who were to take the place of the appointed clerks. Inspectors were to ensure the orderly conduct of the election and to administer the oath or affirmation to freeholders who were not known to be qualified but who claimed a right to vote.

After receiving complaints about how the choosing of inspectors was often disorderly and how those not qualified to vote often participated in the choosing of inspectors, the Assembly passed a new law in 1739 governing election procedure. On September 25 of each year, the constable or overseers of the poor in each township were to conduct an election in which a freeholder available for inspector was to be chosen. Each county was divided into eight "districts" by the court of quarter sessions, and the name of each township representative was placed in the proper district box. On election-day morning the presiding officer supervised the drawing of one name from each district, the individual chosen to serve as inspector. In the city of Philadelphia the same procedure was carried out on September 25 within each of the ten wards. On election day four names were to be drawn from among the ten, the four to serve as inspectors at the county election; the remaining six were to serve as inspectors for the city election the following day. This legislation lapsed after three years, and the 1742 election was carried on under the old arrangement in which inspectors were chosen openly on election-day morning. The new legislation was again put into effect in 1743, and through 1755 this, or very similar legislation, governed election procedures. *Statutes at Large*, 2:212-21, 4:11-12, 77-80, 331-36, 375-81, 5:16-22, 153-58.

46. The numbers of county taxables are approximations derived from the Harrington and Greene figures. The numbers of Philadelphia taxables are guesses based on the 1749 count of houses in the May 18 edition of the *Gazette* and on the trend of population growth in the city during that period. Estimates of voting figures are based on the assumption that each voter submitted a complete ticket *Votes*, 3:2162-63. In one situation—the city of Philadelphia, 1741—I used the totals in the vote for sheriff to determine the number of tickets cast for assemblymen. The validity of this procedure is borne out by the agreement of that figure with those from other years and by John Smith's method of calculating the number of city voters. The 1742 total for Philadelphia City is the maximum possible, given the total votes of the two winners.

47. John Smith to Elizabeth Hudson, 10 October 1750, Correspondence of John Smith (1749-70).

48. Richard Peters to Proprietaries, 8 December 1749, PPOC, vol. 4; *Register of Pennsylvania*, 5 (1830): 21-22. On corrupt practices see Leonard, "Elections in Colonial Pennsylvania," pp. 385-401.

49. *Advice to the Freeholders and Electors of Pennsylvania; Mercury*, 21 December 1733.

50. At the present time there is no way of determining just how restrictive Pennsylvania's franchise was. The sufferage requirements through the years 1726-55 were that an elector be a native or naturalized citizen, twenty-one years old, resident in the province for two years, and possessing a fifty-acre freehold with at least twelve acres cleared or fifty pounds in personal property. Two conclusions are obvious: there were variations in the numbers who could meet these tests from county to county and township to township, and as time progressed a greater percentage of the population could qualify on grounds of personality alone. In the three older counties I would estimate that no more than 40 percent of the adult males could have failed to meet property requirements. It is impossible to even hazard a guess about residents of the city of Philadelphia. *Statutes at Large*, 2:212-21. For an early effort to get at this problem, see Albert E. McKinley, *The Suffrage Franchise in the Thirteen English Colonies in America* (Philadelphia, 1905), pp. 273-99; for other more recent remarks based on evidence from the 1760s and 1770s, see Chilton Williamson, *American Sufferage: From Property to Democracy, 1760-1860* (Princeton, 1960), pp. 3-61.

51. *Advice and Information to the Freeholders and Freemen of the Province of Pennsylvania* (Philadelphia, 1727), p. 1.

52. Only a very few people protested that their representatives kept too much secret and that constituents should be given more information and assert more control. For example, see *Mercury*, 31 December 1733; *Votes*, 4:3030.

53. *Franklin Papers*, 3:14-17; *Gazette*, 9 August 1750; John Churchman, *An Account of the Gospel Labours and Christian Experiences of . . . John Churchman* (Philadelphia, 1778), pp. 96-98. See also the meetinglike pronouncement on Peter Worral's character by several leading Assembly members *Gazette*, 27 September 1750.

54. See appendix II.3.

55. See appendix II.4. In Lancaster there were pockets of political power, such as in Hempfield and Lancaster, and these changed somewhat over time. Overall, the Assembly's refusal to grant equal representation to backcountry counties meant that the original three far outweighed the others.

56. For example, John Wright, Arthur Patterson, Joseph Pennock, Thomas Cummings, John Crosby, William Moore, Samuel Smith, and William Allen. Several others who had come early to Pennsylvania and prospered with the country continued to be active politically in the 1720s and 1730s. For example, Thomas Canby, Edward Farmer, Edward Horne, Thomas Rutter, Thomas Potts, John Swift, John White, and Joseph Kirkbride, Sr.

57. For example, George Ashbridge, Jr., Peter Dicks, James Junior and Joseph Gibbons, Samuel Levis, Jr., Evan Lewis, John Owen, John Taylor, Nathaniel Pennock, Jeremiah and Moses Starr, William Webb, Thomas Worth, Francis Yarnall, Jeremiah Langhorne, Joseph Junior, and Mahlon Kirkbride, Abraham Chapman, Thomas Marriot, John and Mark Watson, John Junior and James Wright, James Webb, Samuel Blunston, and Calvin Cooper.

58. Governor Thomas to John Penn, 27 October 1741, PPOC, vol. 3.

59. See appendix II.5. In order to measure the distribution of power in the Assembly, I carried out a committee analysis from 1727-28 to 1754-55. Depending on the nature of their duties, I assigned committees the standing of either major or minor ranking and tabulated appointments of each type. Major committee appointments averaged seventy per Assembly year and minor appointments fifty-five. The men I have designated as leaders were the handful who clearly dominated appointments to major and minor committees. The number varied slightly from year to year but averaged approximately 30 percent of the total House membership. On major committees these legislative leaders controlled an average of 70 percent of the appointments (the median figure was 69 percent and outside limits were 88 percent and 57 percent), and on minor committees they controlled an average of 55 percent (the median figure was 57 percent and outside limits were 80 percent and 26 percent). On committee organization see Sister

Joan de Lourdes Leonard, "The Organization and Procedure of the Pennsylvania Assembly, 1682-1776," *PMHB* 72 (1948): 236-38.

60. There were, of course, numerous reasons for the Philadelphia bias: as the seat of government, Philadelphia was the center of political activities; the metropolis generally produced and attracted the most ambitious individuals; Philadelphians were, as a rule, more sophisticated and better equipped to handle the business of government; city residents had no need to absent themselves from governmental affairs if their private businesses required a few hours' attention; because of the pressure of political opposition in Philadelphia City residents felt that they were most acutely aware of the dangers to Assembly rights and usually became personally involved when controversies with executive supporters broke out.

61. Seniority alone was, apparently, not an important consideration. Long service bought nothing but anonymity for such men as Garrat Vansant, Thomas Chandler, and Owen Evans.

62. The sixteen were Samuel Blunston, James Wright, Joseph Harvey, George Ashbridge, Jr., John Owen, Israel Pemberton, Sr., Jeremiah Langhorne, Joseph Kirkbride, Jr., Mahlon Kirkbride, Abraham Chapman, Lawrence Growdon, Job Goodson, John Kinsey, Thomas Leech, Isaac Norris, Jr., and James Morris.

63. The obligation to perpetuate a tradition of leadership in public affairs was one that many acknowledged. For example, see Joseph Shippen, Jr., to William Shippen, Jr., 17 May 1755, Shippen Family Papers, Misc. Volumes, Letterbook of Joseph Shippen, Jr. (1754-84).

64. Pennsylvania's tradition of political professionalism was virtually as old as the province itself. The forerunners of these leaders were men like Thomas Lloyd, David Lloyd, and James Logan.

65. For example, see Richard Peters to John Kinsey, 25 November 1748, RPLB; *CR*, 5:90-92.

66. Donald L. Kemmerer, *Path to Freedom: The Struggle for Self-Government in Colonial New Jersey, 1703-1776* (Princeton, 1940), pp. 128-32.

67. *Statutes at Large*, 4:304-408. Martin, *Bench and Bar*, p. 27. For Kinsey's position vis-à-vis the proprietor in 1739, see Richard Peters to Proprietaries, 10 April 1739, RPLB.

68. The importance of these patronage positions may be inferred from Richard Peters to Thomas Penn, 9 October 1743, RPLB. Currency signers received a flat rate for every thousand bills signed, trustees earned £110 per annum and excise collectors kept 7½ percent in Philadelphia, and 10 percent in the other counties, of what they collected *Statutes at Large*, 4:413, 5:15; *Votes*, 3:2411.

69. On Kinsey's power as chief justice see James Hamilton to Thomas Penn, 18 November 1750, PPOC, vol. 5. Despite an Assembly resolution that Loan Office officials should be replaced every four years, Kinsey occupied the position of acting trustee from 1738 until his death in 1750. In December of 1733 a group of petitioners requested that since "the important station of a trustee of the General Loan Office is attended with such influence and power upon the persons and estates of the inhabitants of this province and upon their votes in elections . . . it is highly unreasonable they should sit or act as representatives in the General Assembly." The point was that there were numerous ways the acting trustee could favor or, alternatively, harass the present or potential mortgagor. If a waiting list for loans existed, one man could be favored before another; if a number of quotas were outstanding, certain ones could be chosen against which to institute legal proceedings; if a man wanted to use Loan Office funds to purchase proprietary land, there were numerous ways the acting trustee could expedite or retard the transaction. *Votes*, 3:2009, 2196, 2197, 2201, 4:2910-11, 3250, 5:3713, 4021; PPOC, 4:151.

70. The Journals of the House of Representatives contain a complete record of the petitions read and tabled by the Assembly. Most petitions other than those that required an act of the legislature fell into one of two categories, requests for place or for some benefit—usually monetary—for effort expended, service rendered, damages or costs incurred.

71. See appendix II.6.

72. *Votes*, 3:1921, 1924, 2314-15, 4:3237-38, 3477-78; *Statutes at Large*, 4:121-22, 122-23, 131-34, 291-96, 5:100-101, 161-78.

73. *Votes*, 3:1914, 1917, 1929, 2482; *Statutes at Large*, 4:98-116, 147-50, 337-38.

74. *Votes*, 3:1914, 1917; *Statutes at Large*, 4:98-116. See chapter 8.

75. *Votes*, 3:2261, 2262-63, 2288, 2296, 2297, 2298, 2299-2300, 2300-2304, 2323, 2324, 2327, 2305, 2306, 2307, 2308-14, 2315, 2316, 2317, 2321, 2323-24, 2529, 2534-38, 2538-39, 2540-54, 2567-68.

76. Ibid., pp. 2138, 2140, 4:2926, 2930, 3477, 3488.

77. Ibid., 3:1846, 1925-26.

78. Ibid., pp. 2246, 2247, 2249-50.

79. Ibid., pp. 2487, 2490, 2500, 2503-2504.

80. Ibid., pp. 1861, 1867, 1921, 1924, 4:3476; James Pemberton to John Pemberton, 2 February 1751, PemP, vol. 6.

81. *Votes*, 3:2494, 2533-40, 4:2831, 2854, 2868, 2870-71, 2910.

82. Ibid., 3:2454-55, 2831, 4:3126-27, 3238, 3399, 3477-78, 5:3630.

83. *Statutes at Large*, 4:154-56, 157-63, 189-94, 197-208, 229-30, 238-48, 248-57, 266-77, 296-99, 338-91, 5:5-6, 7-15, 16-22, 22-27.

84. *Votes*, 3:2054, 2085; *Statutes at Large*, 4:171-84, 211-15.

85. For example, *Votes*, 3:2048-49, 2262, 2264, 2296, 2303, 4:3307, 3397, 3399, 3539, 3564, 3565, 3571.

86. *Franklin Papers*, 4:193; Isaac Norris, Jr., to Robert Charles, 22 June 1743, INLB (1719-56); *CR*, 3:391; Richard Peters to Thomas Penn, 5 June 1742, RPLB; John Smith's Diary, 10 May 1746; Samuel Emlen, Jr., to James Pemberton, 31 May 1749; Israel Pemberton, Jr., to James Pemberton, 13 June 1749, PemP, vol. 5.

87. For example, some of the leading Quakers in Chester Monthly Meeting were George Ashbridge, Thomas Cummings, Joseph Harvey, and Caleb Cowpland. In Sadsbury John Wright, Anthony Shaw, Calvin Cooper, Peter Worral, and James Webb were continually involved in meeting affairs. (Minutes, Chester MM, Sadsbury MM.).

88. Provincial leaders acknowledged the existence of an instructive aspect in their relationships with dependents and social inferiors. They were "to propagate civility, good sense, reason and good manners . . . wherever they lived; they were to be as 'a city set upon a hill whose light cannot be hid.'" Isaac Norris, Jr., to Susanna Wright, 18 April 1728, Norris Papers, Family Letters, vol. 2.

89. *Votes*, 3:2718, 5:3696; *PA*, 2nd ser. 7:238-39.

CHAPTER 6

1. Lemon, *Best Poor Man's Country*, pp. 65, 99. After the Assembly set up Lancaster County in 1729, Chester contained approximately 600,000 acres.

2. *Votes*, 3:1924, 4:3235, 3255.

3. *PA*, 6th ser. 14:263.

4. The smallest number of justices of the peace appointed for any one county was twelve, the largest thirty-one. *CR*, 5:3, 378, 600, 7:769.

5. The best discussion of local government agencies is Clair W. Keller's "Pennsylvania Government, 1701-1740: A Study of the Operation of Colonial Government" (Ph.D. diss., University of Washington, 1967). For the functions of justices of the peace and an outline of the court system see pp. 166-73, 202-205.

6. Three or more judges could also hold "special and private sessions" as courts of judicature. *Statutes at Large*, 4:86.

7. Ibid., 3:255-56, 4:7-8, 65. Prior to 1736 their authority over actions for debt was limited to those not exceeding forty shillings. Ibid., 3:63-64, 4:291, 339, 371.

8. Ibid., 3:246, 4:161, 246, 316, 403.

9. Ibid., 2:85, 238, 251-53, 4:15, 153-54, 275, 5:167.

10. Ibid., 2:231, 3:306-40, 358, 4:19-20, 22-23.

11. Keller, "Pennsylvania Government," pp. 204-207.

12. *Ibid.*, pp. 211-21; *Statutes at Large*, 4:10-26; Journal of the Philadelphia County Commissioners (1726-50); Journal of the Lancaster County Commissioners (1729-1755), Lancaster County Historical Society (hereinafter cited as LCHS).

13. Keller, "Pennsylvania Government," pp. 204-207.

14. Ibid., pp. 278-93, 314-16; Jerome Wood, Jr., "Conestoga Crossroads," pp. 60-74, 99-105. Of course, the Assembly could pass laws that specifically applied to urban residents.

15. Judith M. Diamondstone, "Philadelphia's Municipal Corporation, 1701-1776," *PMHB* 90 (1966):183.

16. Ibid., p.187. Annual elections brought out twenty to thirty common councilmen in the 1730s and 1740s, and thirty to forty in later years.

17. Ibid., pp. 194-96.

18. Keller, Pennsylvania Government," pp. 169-70.

19. Ibid., pp. 273-78.

20. Bristol was the county seat for Bucks until 1724, when Newton took over that role.

21. Lewis Evans, "A Brief Account of Pennsylvania . . . " (1753); Keller, "Pennsylvania Government," pp. 307-19; Wood, "Conestoga Crossroads," pp. 37-74, 99-105.

22. Keller, "Pennsylvania Government," pp. 310-14; Wood, "Conestoga Crossroads," pp. 37-42. Bristol had two burgesses, five councilmen, and two assessors; Chester, four burgesses; and Lancaster, two burgesses and six assistants. Wood argues, and Keller implies, that the town franchises were liberal.

23. Martin, *Bench and Bar*, pp. 57-58, 71, 73-74, 83; Ellis and Evans, *History of Lancaster County*, pp. 215-17; J. Smith Futhey and Gilbert Cope, *History of Chester County* (Philadelphia, 1881), pp. 374-75.

24. Richard Peters to John Penn, 20 October 1741, RPLB.

Some of the justices, led by John Wright of Lancaster, had been among those who whipped up popular feeling against the governor after he had encouraged the enlistment of servants in 1740. For Wright's statement on learning that he had been stripped of the post of chief magistrate for Lancaster County, see John Wright, *The Speech of John Wright, Esq.: One of the Magistrates of Lancaster County to the Court and Jury On His Removal From the Commission of the Peace at the Quarter Sessions Held at Lancaster for the Said County* (Philadelphia, 1741).

A second reason why Penn was determined to make some changes in the commissions was that, at the autumn sitting of the county assize in Chester County, a non-Quaker juror could not be qualified, because all of the judges present were Quakers who refused to administer the oath. John and Richard Penn to Thomas Penn, 20 November 1740, TPLB, vol. 1; John Penn to Thomas Penn, 26 November 1740, ibid.

25. Thomas Penn to John and Richard Penn, 23 March 1741, Penn Papers, Small Letterbook.

26. Although the proportion of Quakers was lower. In 1729 twelve justices of the peace were probably Quakers, in 1730 thirteen of sixteen, in 1738 fourteen of seventeen, in 1741 eleven of eighteen, in 1745 ten of eighteen, in 1749 twelve of seventeen, in 1752 thirteen of eighteen. For a listing of the justices of the peace, see Futhey and Cope, *History of Chester County*, p. 364.

27. In Chester County the proportion of justices of the peace who served as assemblymen dropped from six of fourteen in 1729 to three of eighteen in 1752.

28. For an argument somewhat along these lines, see Clair W. Keller, "The Pennsylvania County Commission System, 1712-1740," *PMHB* 93 (1969): 381-82.

29. John Taylor et al. to William Allen, Taylor Papers, Correspondence (1723-50), #3259.

30. Samuel Finley to Richard Peters, 15 November 1755, Roberts Collection, Quaker Collection, Haverford College Library.

31. John Taylor et al. to William Allen, Taylor Papers, Correspondence (1723-50), #3259.

32. For example, see Lewis Evans, "A Brief Account of Pennsylvania . . . " (1753).

33. These calculations are based on an analysis of the 1730, 1740, and 1751 tax lists for Chester County.

34. Samuel Finley to Richard Peters, 15 November 1755, Roberts Collection, Quaker Collection, Haverford College Library.

35. Ibid.

36. John Taylor to Richard Peters, 10 September 1742, Taylor Papers, Correspondence (1723-50).

37. *Statutes at Large*, 3:297.

38. Ibid., 2:272; Keller, "Pennsylvania Government," p. 226.

39. Keller, "Pennsylvania Government," pp. 215-17.

40. Ibid., pp. 226-27; Ellis and Evans, *History of Lancaster County*, p. 215; Futhey and Cope, *History of Chester County*, p. 375.

41. Ellis and Evans, *History of Lancaster County*, p. 215; Futhey and Cope, *History of Chester County*, p. 375; Martin, *Bench and Bar*, p. 103.

42. *Statutes at Large*, 4:235; Futhey and Cope, *History of Chester County*, p. 376.

43. The names of the newly elected county commissioners and assessors for Philadelphia County were listed in the *Gazette* in early October. Those for Lancaster County are in the Lancaster County Commissioners' Book, LCHS. For Chester County see Futhey and Cope, *History of Chester County*, pp. 376-77.

44. Christopher Saur, "Answer to Conrad Weiser's Published Letter to the Germans," 29 September 1741, PPOC, vol. 3.

45. James Logan to Governor Thomas, 1 October 1741, JLLB (1731-32, 1741-42).

46. *PMHB*, 22 (1898): 386.

47. *Statutes at Large*, 2:132.

48. Isaac Norris, Jr., to Robert Charles, 26 October 1741, INLB (1719-1756).

49. *PMHB*, 22 (1898): 386-87.

50. Futhey and Cope, *History of Chester County*, p. 376. Samuel Nutt and George Ashton were former Quakers; I could not identify John Party, Jr. with any certainty. Attendance at the Chester Quarterly Meeting and the Philadelphia Yearly Meeting is listed in the appropriate minutes.

51. This figure is based on the relative position of the officeholders on the one of three tax lists (1730, 1740, and 1751) closest to the mid-point of their term in office. I left out from all calculations three men whom I could not positively identify.

52. All but three of the sheriffs, coroners, and county commissioners came from within a sixteen-mile radius of Chester. These three were commissioners.

53. For example, see John Smith to Elizabeth Hudson, 10 October 1750, Correspondence of John Smith (1740-79).

54. Richard Peters to John Penn, 20 October 1741, RPLB.

55. *Gazette*, 16 August 1744.

56. Ibid., 23 August 1744.

57. Ibid., 1 October 1747, 27 September 1750, 26 September 1751, 28 September 1752, 27 September 1753, 26 September 1754. The reason for the failure to observe the customary practice of allowing an elected sheriff three successive terms was that Thomas Griffith, who was elected in 1750, failed to discharge his post satisfactorily. His shortcomings must have been noticeable in his first year of office, for in 1751 he was challenged by other candidates. Although he successfully withstood this attempt to unseat him, Griffith was removed from office in March of 1752 for neglect of duty and contempt of court and was replaced by Samuel Morris. Apparently some felt that his was merely an interim appointment, for at least one opposition slate ran against Morris in October 1752, and, since 1753 was the regular year for contested elections, Morris faced opposition then, too. When he was reelected in that year, some residents felt that he should be replaced in the fall of 1754, for by that time he had served two and one-half years. Morris was again successful in that election, and he left office in the fall of 1755. *CR*, 5:561-62; Martin, *Bench and Bar*, p. 99.

58. *Gazette*, 26 September 1751, 28 September 1752, 26 September 1754.

59. The passage of an "Act Preventing Bribery and Corruption in the Election of Sheriffs and Coroners," in 1752 serves as corroborative evidence that outward solicitation

for votes by candidates for those offices had increased during the late 1740s and early 1750s. The preamble charged that candidates "too frequently" made it "their practice to engage persons to vote for them by giving them strong drink, and using other means inconsistent with the design of voting freely at elections," fined those who engaged in bribery and treating, and disqualified any candidate who was personally convicted of such action. *Statutes at Large*, 5:159-61.

60. Private Sessions Docket, Court of Quarter Sessions, Chester County, CCHS.

61. Whereas all townships were served by one constable and two overseers of the poor, some had one and some two supervisors of the highway.

62. James Logan to Proprietaries, 30 April 1729, JLB (1726-32).

63. A Book For the Poor of the Township of East Caln, CCHS; Private Sessions Docket, Court of Quarter Sessions, Chester County, CCHS.

64. A Book For the Poor of the Township of East Caln, CCHS; East Bradford Township Book, CCHS; Goshen Town Book, CCHS; John Taylor to Joseph Brinton and Caleb Pierce, 21 October 1745, Misc. Mss., CCHS.

65. My conclusions on officeholding patterns at the township level are based on analyses of local tax lists, the appointments in the Private Sessions Docket of the Chester County Court of Quarter Sessions, and nominations for office recorded in the Book For the Poor For the Township of East Caln, both CCHS.

66. Chester, 64 percent; Upper and Lower Darby, 68 percent; East and West Fallowfield, 80 percent Goshen, 62 percent; Kennett, 76 percent; East and West Nanmeal, 84 percent; Tredyffrin, 66 percent.

67. Diamondstone, "Philadelphia Corporation," pp. 232-34.

68. Ibid., pp. 234-37; Richard Peters to John Penn, 20 October 1741, RPLB.

69. Diamondstone, "Philadelphia Corporation," pp. 230-31, 258-59, 264, 272.

70. Wood, "Conestoga Crossroads," pp. 37-48; Keller, "Pennsylvania Government," pp. 305-19.

71. Wood, "Conestoga Crossroads," pp. 37-48; Keller, "Pennsylvania Government," pp. 305-19. Wood notes that almost all Lancaster burgesses were in the top 4 percent of the town property holders (ibid., p. 44).

72. See generally *Statutes at Large*, vol. 2.

73. See appendix III.1.

74. *Statutes at Large*, 2:67, 163, 4:215-16, 5:108-11.

75. *Minutes of the Common Council of Philadelphia, 1704-1776* (Philadelphia, 1847), pp. 313-14, 414-15; Minutes of the Corporation of Lancaster, LCHS, 8 February 1743, 30 May 1743, 16 February 1745, 31 October 1750, 29 January 1751.

76. Minutes of the Corporation of Lancaster, LCHS, 28 November 1744, 30 May 1752, 30 November 1752.

77. *Minutes of the Common Council of Philadelphia*, pp. 287, 295, 363, 367, 368; Keller, "Pennsylvania Government," pp. 279-86, 291-94, 314.

78. John Smith's Diary, 21 August 1749; *CR*, 4:284; *PA*, 2nd ser. 2:553-54.

79. Keller, "Pennsylvania County Commission System," pp. 375, 377-78.

80. Cited in William R. Steckel, "Pietist in Colonial Pennsylvania: Christopher Saur, Printer, 1738-1758" (Ph.D. diss., Stanford University, 1949), p. 129.

81. Namier and Brook, *House of Commons*, 1:177-84.

82. Minutes of the Lancaster Corporation, LCHS, 8 February 1743, 23 October 1743, 28 September 1744, 9 October 1744, 25 January 1746, 1 February 1746. On Philadelphia see Keller, "Pennsylvania Government," pp. 287-89.

83. Lemon, *Best Poor Man's Country*, p. xv; Samuel B. Warner, *The Private City: Philadelphia in Three Periods of Growth* (Philadelphia, 1968), pp. 3-21.

CHAPTER 7

1. James Logan, "The Charge Delivered From the Bench to the Grand Inquest at a Court of Oyer and Terminer, and General Jail Delivery, Held For the City and County of Philadelphia, April 13, 1736," in Wilson Armistedd, ed., *Memoirs of James Logan* (London, 1851), pp. 122-23, 120-22, 123-30; *Gazette*, 20 June 1734, 8 April 1736, 21

March 1738, 5 December 1749; *Mercury*, 27 January 1730; *Votes*, 3:1861; *My Dear Fellow Travellers* (Philadelphia, 1740), p. 3; Richard Peters, *The Two Last Sermons Preached at Christ Church in Philadelphia* (Philadelphia, 1737), pp. 10-14.

2. Many spokesmen resorted to Natural Law and to a personal intervening God at the same time. *Mercury*, 10 July 1729; *Gazette*, 6 July 1749. Even the Natural Law spokesman, James Logan, left room for an independent "Divine influence." Armistedd, *James Logan*, p. 139.

The most significant observation about the sectarian literature in Pennsylvania, and also about Anglican and some German church literature, is the optimism of the writings as compared to the gloomy tracts of "New Light" Presbyterians. Pennsylvania was no New England—"that dark Presbyterian Country" (Mary Weston to Isaac Pemberton, Jr., 24 August 1750, PemP, vol. 6)—where preoccupation with sin and grace obscured the comfort afforded by a benevolent deity. The Quaker allegiance to consensualism and the success they had in promoting harmony among Friends, as well as between Friends and their non-Quaker neighbors, reinforced the perfectionist strain. The conditions of peace, tolerance, and prosperity that characterized the provincial experience performed a similar function.

3. For example, James Logan brought a personal God into direct communication with man by positing a "Divine influence" which "pacifies, annimates, and strengthens" the affections. Armistedd, *James Logan*, p. 139.

4. *Mercury*, 18 September 1729. See also *Mercury*, 20 March 1729, 27 January 1730, 22 February 1732, 8 June 1732; *Gazette*, 1 April 1736; Joseph Morgan, *The Nature of Riches Showed From the Natural Reason of the Use and Effects Thereof* (Philadelphia, 1732), pp. 5, 10.

5. *Gazette*, 5 September 1751; *Mercury*, 18 September 1729, 27 January 1730.

6. *Mercury*, 18 September 1729.

7. Ibid., 18 September 1729, 27 January 1730, 10 February 1730; James Logan to Samuel Blunston, 11 January 1736, Autograph Collection of Charles Thomas Jenkins, FHL; John Penn to Colonel Thomas, 15 March 1740; Penny, "Logan-Story Correspondence," p. 57; *Gazette*, 1 April 1736, 28 January 1752.

8. *Mercury*, 6 April 1732, 5 February 1734; Tolles, *Meeting House and Counting House*, pp. 56-57; Samuel Chew, *The Speech of Samuel Chew Esq., Delivered From the Bench to the Grand Jury of the County of Newcastle, November 21, 1741* (Philadelphia, 1741), pp. 3-4; James Logan, *The Latter Part of the Charge Delivered From the Bench to the Grand Inquest at a Court of Oyer and Terminer and General Jail Delivery, Held For the City and the County of Philadelphia, September 24, 1733* (Philadelphia, 1733); Archibald Cummings, *The Character of a Righteous Ruler* (Philadelphia, 1736), p. 5.

9. *Gazette*, 21 March 1738, 5 December 1749; *Mercury*, 18 September 1729, 25 September 1729; *Letters Between Theophilus and Eugenio on the Moral Depravity of Man and the Means of His Restoration* (Philadelphia, 1747), pp. 11-13; John Penn to John Kinsey, 15 March 1741, TPLB, vol. 1.

10. *Letters Between Theophilus and Eugenio*, pp. 1-5; *Mercury*, 18 September 1729, 27 January 1730, 23 March 1732, 6 April 1732; *Gazette*, 5 September 1751, 28 January 1752; Logan, *The Charge Delivered From the Bench to the Grand Inquest . . .;* Armistedd, *James Logan*, pp. 120-30; Churchman, *Gospel Labors*, pp. 2-3.

11. *Votes*, 3:2506; *Gazette*, 30 March 1738. See also Penn Papers, Assembly and Provincial Council, p. 45; Francis Roule, *A Just Rebuke* (Philadelphia, 1726), p. 25; *Gazette*, 24 December 1735; *Mercury*, 20 April 1738; William Fishbourne, Sr., "Some Remarks on Ye Settlement of the Province of Pennsylvania to the year 1739," Etting Coll., Misc. Mss.; John Wright, *The Speech of John Wright Esq. . . . ,* p. 2.

12. *Gazette*, 24 December 1735; John Wright, *The Speech of John Wright Esq. . . . ,* pp. 3-4; *Votes*, 4:2728, 5:3709; *CR*, 4:541-42, 547-48; *Mercury*, 8 April 1736, 13 May 1736, 17 June 1736, 22 July 1736; Richard Peters to Thomas Penn, 12 June 1752, PPOC, vol. 5.

13. Young, "The Evolution of the Pennsylvania Assembly," pp. 147-68; Nash, *Quakers and Politics;* Lokken, *David Lloyd.*

14. Governor Thomas to John Paris, 14 May 1741, PPOC, vol. 3; Richard Peters to Proprietaries, 17 October 1742, RPLB; Thomas Penn to John and Richard Penn, 23

March 1741, Penn Papers, Small Letterbook; John and Richard Penn to Thomas Penn, 10 August 1736, TPLB, vol. 1.

15. Since the founding of the Loan Office, the interest payments on mortgages and the income from the excise produced considerably more revenue than was needed to meet the operating costs of that office and to cover the specific public expenditures funded by the paper currency. James H. Hutson estimates that the Assembly's annual "unrestricted" income approached £6,000 in 1755. James H. Hutson, "Benjamin Franklin and Pennsylvania Politics, 1751-1755: A reappraisal," *PMHB* 93 (1969): 322. Since the size of the excise revenue depended on the volume of liquor retailed, it is likely that this total was somewhat lower during the 1740s.

16. See appendix IV.1.

17. See appendix IV.1 and Root, *Relations of Pennsylvania with the British Government*, pp. 288-90; Richard Peters to Proprietaries, 29 April 1749, RPLB.

18. Richard Peters to Proprietaries, 19 November 1747, RPLB.

19. Thomas Penn to James Hamilton, 6 June 1749, 31 July 1749, PHC; Thomas Penn to Richard Peters, 2 August 1749, Penn Papers, Saunders-Coates; Wolff, *Colonial Agency*, pp. 129-35; Richard Partridge to John Kinsey, 17 February 1748, 4 March 1748, 11 March 1748, 23 March 1749, 3 May 1749, 30 May 1749, 6 June 1749, PemP, vol. 4; *Gazette*, 18 May 1749, 25 May 1749; *Votes*, 4:3234, 3277-79, 3283-84, 3284-85; *CR*, 5:397.

20. *Votes*, 4:3500-3501.

21. Ibid.; Thomas Penn to James Hamilton, 31 July 1749, PHC; Thomas Penn to James Hamilton, 29 July 1752, PPOC,vol. 5. Penn's formal instructions already included orders to establish a chancery court and regular militia if possible.

James Hamilton to Thomas Penn, 18 March 1752, ibid. In his letter Hamilton carefully pointed out that public disclosure of such instructions would throw the country into "a flame." Since the excise and currency acts that provided an income of £6,000 per annum for the Assembly ran until 1756, the contest would likely be a long one, during which Penn could expect little revenue and placemen could expect the loss of their salaries.

22. Additional Instructions to Lieutenant-Governor James Hamilton from Thomas and Richard Penn, 30 May 1752, Penn Papers, Large Misc. Folio Vol.

23. Thomas Penn to James Hamilton, 13 July 1752, PHC. See also Thomas and Richard Penn to James Hamilton, 24 October 1752, ibid.

24. *Votes*, 4:3544, 3546; Richard Peters to Thomas Penn, 7 February 1753, PPOC, vol. 6; James Hamilton to Proprietaries, 9 February 1753, PPOC, vol. 7; Thomas and Richard Penn to James Hamilton, 28 March 1753, PHC; Thomas Penn to James Hamilton, 2 April 1753, Etting Coll.

25. *Votes*, 4:3593-3603; To James Hamilton, Additional Instruction for His Government and Conduct Therein, 1 November 1753, Penn Papers.

26. *Votes*, 5:3649-50.

27. Ibid., pp. 3637-43, 3653-54, 3682-83, 3686-87, 3697-99; James Hamilton to Thomas Penn, 17 April 1753, PPOC, vol. 5; 13 July 1752, PHC; Hutson, "Franklin and Politics," pp. 332-33.

28. Thomas Penn to James Hamilton, 31 May 1754, 10 June 1754, TPLB, vol. 3; Altered Clauses and Additional Causes in the Instructions to Mr. Morris for Government, 21 May 1754, Penn Papers, Assembly and Provincial Council; Thomas Penn to Robert Hunter Morris, 9 July 1754, 17 October 1754, TPLB, vol. 4; Robert Hunter Morris to Thomas Penn, 26 October 1754, 26 December 1754, PPOC, vol. 6; *Votes*, 5:3771-80, 3874, 3917, 3922. For details of the controversy under Morris, see Hutson, "Franklin and Politics," pp. 338-63.

29. *Votes*, 5:3928-29, 3933. From July through November of 1755 the Assembly and governor were deadlocked over Morris's refusal to authorize taxation of proprietary land. Thomas Penn resolved this particular conflict by presenting a gift of £5,000 to the province for defense.

30. A hint of what Penn had in mind when he left Pennsylvania appeared in a Richard Peters letter that asked if Governor Thomas should concur in renewing the Excise Act if no share in the disposition of the proceeds was given to the executive. Richard Peters to Thomas Penn, 17 October 1742, RPLB.

31. Thomas Penn to James Hamilton, 29 January 1754, 17 November 1754, PHC; Robert Hunter Morris to James Hamilton, 2 June 1754, Society Misc. Coll.; Thomas Penn to Richard Peters, 31 July 1754, TPLB, vol. 3; Wolff, *Colonial Agency*, pp. 146-47, 150, 156; Richard Peters to Thomas Penn, 12 February 1753, PPOC, vol. 6; Thomas Penn to Richard Peters, 29 June 1753, TPLB, vol. 3. See also Thomas Penn to Robert Hunter Morris, 26 February 1755, Gratz Coll., Governors of Pennsylvania, case 2, box 33a.

32. Richard Peters to Proprietaries, 29 April 1749, RPLB.

33. Richard Peters to Proprietaries, 11 May 1748, 29 April 1749, RPLB; James Hamilton to Thomas Penn, 22 February 1750, PPOC, vol. 5; James Hamilton to Thomas Penn, 30 September 1749, JHLB; *CR*, 5:456-57, 505, 506-507; Thomas Penn to James Hamilton, 31 July 1749, 29 July 1751, PHC.

34. Richard Peters to Proprietaries, 21 March 1753; James Hamilton to Thomas Penn, 26 November 1753, PPOC, vol. 6. The most colorful contemporary description of the state of the prerogative in Pennsylvania is in James Hamilton's letter to Thomas Penn on 18 March 1752, ibid., vol. 6.

35. James Hamilton to Thomas Penn, 7 July 1753, ibid., vol. 6.

36. Thomas Penn to James Hamilton, 30 March 1751, TPLB, vol. 3; *Votes*, 4:3504, 5:3671; Thomas Penn to James Hamilton, 22 February 1749, PHC.

37. In November 1753 Richard Hockley could still wonder at the chief executive's determination to resign. "That gentleman has had the most easy administration that has been here for many years." Richard Hockley to Thomas Penn, 14 November 1753, PPOC, vol. 6.

38. Wolff, *Colonial Agency*, p. 156; Hutson, "Franklin and Politics," pp. 335-36; Isaac Norris, Jr., to Robert Charles, 7 October 1754, INLB (1719-56).

39. *Votes*, 5:3761, 3771-72. The £20,000 vote was to be funded by the same process as the two earlier votes to the King's use under Hamilton—a ten-year excise. Morris implied that he would accept such a gift funded on a five-year excise.

40. After trying, through the governor, to solicit contributions from the proprietors to help cover the rising cost of Indian affairs, and receiving no for an answer, the Assembly drew up a representation, in August 1751, directly requesting such aid. Penn blew up when he received it, calling those who had sent it a "set of mean dirty politicians" who hoped to "show the people their great zeal for their interest." What contributed a great deal to the proprietor's anger was the repeated refusal of the Assembly to accept his 1749 offer of £400 plus £100 per annum toward the construction and maintenance of a fort in the west, provided the Assembly furnish the remainder. After he had cooled somewhat, Penn sent a reply to Hamilton, which the governor received in April 1753. When the chief executive sent it to the Assembly during the May session, nothing was said. The assemblymen kept it tucked away until December 1754, when they published it along with a point-by-point rebuttal. *Votes*, 4:3362-63, 3435, 3437-38, 3443-47, 5:3808-26; Thomas Penn to Richard Peters, 18 March 1752, Peters Papers, Letters of Thomas Penn to Richard Peters, 1752-72; Thomas Penn to James Hamilton, 26 October 1752, TPLB, vol. 3; James Hamilton to Thomas Penn, 17 April 1753, Penn Papers, Additional Misc. Letters, vol. 2; Richard Peters to Thomas Penn, 1 June 1753, PPOC, vol. 6; Theodore Thayer, *Israel Pemberton, King of the Quakers* (Philadelphia, 1943), pp. 57-59.

41. Robert Charles to Thomas Penn, 3 September 1753, PPOC, vol. 6; Issac Norris, Jr., to Robert Charles, 7 October 1754, 28 April 1755; Isaac Norris, Jr., to Richard Partridge and Robert Charles, 12 January 1755, INLB (1719-56).

42. James Logan to John Penn, 17 November 1734, Logan Papers, vol. 10, Additional Letters and Business Papers; Isaac Norris, Sr., to Richard Miles, 22 May 1727, INLB (1719-30); Charles Norris to Isaac Norris, Jr., 25 March 1734, Norris Papers, vol. 2.

43. James Logan to John Penn, 17 November 1734, Logan Papers, vol. 10, Additional Letters and Business Papers.

44. Although Keith drew considerable support from the growing Anglican community in Philadelphia, it is not at all clear that any meaningful religious polarization took place along with the rough urban-rural dichotomy. There is no evidence that Anglicans in outlying areas promoted Keithian candidates, while in the city the former governor attracted Baptist, German Church, and Quaker support as well

as an Anglican following. Without a broad base of popular support that transcended religious cleavages, Keithian partisans could not have been so disruptive. Wendel, "Keith-Lloyd Alliance," pp. 289-305.

45. *PA*, 2nd ser. 7:95-97; James Logan to John Penn, 17 October 1726, Patrick Gordon to John Penn, 18 October 1726, PPOC, vol. 1; Wendel, "The Keith-Lloyd Alliance," pp. 289-305.

46. James Logan to John Penn, 17 October 1726, PPOC, vol. 1; Patrick Gordon to John Penn, 18 October 1726, ibid.; Wendel, "Keith-Lloyd Alliance," pp. 301-302.

47. For the place of the Reemitting Act in relationship to other paper money legislation, see appendix IV.1.

48. Patrick Gordon to John Penn, 25 October 1727; Patrick Gordon to John Penn, 12 December 1726, PPOC, vol. 1.

49. Patrick Gordon to Proprietaries, 28 June 1728, ibid., vol. 2; Patrick Gordon to John Penn, 1 May 1728, ibid.; "Proceedings of the Assembly on Sir William Keith's Coming to England For Electing a Member to Serve in his Place," ibid., p. 5; James Logan to John Penn, 8 April 1728, JLLB (1716-43). The Keithians probably organized the petition in favor of more paper currency which was presented to the Assembly on 26 January 1728. *Votes*, 3:1867; Patrick Gordon to John Penn, 1 May 1728, PPOC, vol. 2.

50. See appendix IV.1.

51. *Votes*, 3:1874.

52. Ibid., pp. 1877, 1879-80, 1887; Morris Morris was the sole Philadelphia representative who refused to follow his associates William Monington, Edward Horne, John Swift, Job Goodson, Lodwick Christian Sprogle, Thomas Rutter, Thomas Tress, and John Kearsley from the House.

53. Ibid., pp. 1879-80; *CR*, 3:298-301. Daniel Williamson, a representative from Chester, had died, and Christian Van Horne of Bucks was unable to attend the House because of illness.

54. A group of whites had murdered three Indians. *Votes*, 3:1880-1881; James Logan to John Penn, 15 May 1728, JLLB (1716-43).

55. *Votes*, 3:1882.

56. The only business they attended to was to appropriate a hundred pounds for the purchase of gifts to be distributed among the Indian chiefs whose tribesmen had been murdered. Ibid.,p. 1888.

57. Ibid., pp. 1881-82, 1892, 1897.

58. *CR*, 3:300-301; Edward Horne et al., *A Defense of the Legislative Constitution* (Philadelphia, 1728), p. 6; *Remarks on the Late Proceedings of Some Members of Assembly at Philadelphia* (Philadelphia, 1728), pp. 1-3; *The Proceedings of Some Members of Assembly at Philadelphia, April 1728, Vindicated from the Unfair Reasoning and Unjust Insinuations of a Certain Remarker* (Philadelphia, 1728); *A Letter From a Gentleman in Philadelphia to His Friend in Bucks* (Philadelphia, 1728), pp. 2-3. By the time the August session of the Assembly had ended, there had been no change in the fundamental issue, but each group had modified its demands slightly because of what had transpired in the past four months. The eight dissidents wanted to have the entire Assembly record expunged, a concession that would erase the Assembly's stated opinion that their position in the "ex officio" order was wrong and which would amount to a tacit admission of illegality by the Lloydians. The Bucks and Chester County representatives had dredged up two depositions that charged Keith with subversive activities and wanted to have the Philadelphia members join with them in formally expelling Keith from the House on the strength of this evidence before ordering a new election to fill his seat. *Votes*, 3:1890-92, 1895-96; *A Letter Occasioned By the Perusal of a Paper Lately Published* (Philadelphia, 1728); Morris Morris, *Morris Morris's Reasons For His Conduct in the Present Assembly in the Year 1728* (Philadelphia, 1728).

On the question of the Speaker's power to order the sheriff "ex officio" to prepare an election, there was no doubt the Keithians were wrong. There were no precedents for such actions in the English House of Commons, and the ones sighted by the eight from Pennsylvania's past proved exactly the opposite. On more general grounds, the old established rule that the House was judged of its own election procedure was clearly applicable. *Votes*, 3:1805-1806, 1879; *Remarks on the Late Proceedings of Some Members of the Assembly at Philadelphia; The Proceedings of Some Members of Assembly . . . ; A Letter From a Gentleman in Philadelphia . . .* , pp. 1-3; Edward Horne et al., *A Defense of the Legislative Constitution* (Philadelphia, 1728), pp. 6, 8; *To the Honorable Patrick Gordon, Lieutenant Governor of Pennsylvania, The Representative of the Assembly of the Said Province* (Philadelphia, 1728), p. 4.

59. *Copies of Some Original Papers and other Proceedings Relating to the Late Differences in the House of Representatives of the Province of Pennsylvania* (Philadelphia, 1728); *CR*, 3:300-301.

60. In an uncharacteristically perceptive comment, Patrick Gordon hinted at the psychological lift the dispute gave to the Keithians. Patrick Gordon to the Proprietaries, 28 June 1728, PPOC, vol. 2.

61. James Logan to John, Thomas, and Richard Penn, 30 April 1729, ibid.; James Logan to Joshua Gee, 14 December 1726, JLLB (1716-43); James Logan to John, Thomas, and Richard Penn, 29 July 1728, ibid.; *PMHB* 34 (1910): 122-23; Isaac Norris, Sr., to John Penn, 30 April 1729, INLB (1719-30). James Logan and David Barclay contended that the pressure exerted by the ten Philadelphia representatives was responsible for the new issuance of paper money. It seems unlikely, however, that the county members, whose constituents had little to lose and much to gain by the easing of credit, would have been any less ardent. But regardless of where the center of agitation for more currency was, there certainly were no dissenting voices. See James Logan to John Penn, 18 October 1728, JLLB (1726-32); David Barclay to John Penn, 27 October 1728, PPOC, vol. 2.

62. For the easing of tension after the 1728 election, see Isaac Norris, Sr., to Joseph Pike, 28 October 1728, INLB (1719-30). On the riots, see *Votes*, 3:1909-10, 1940, 1963-64; *CR*, 3:340, 351-52.

63. *Advice and Information to the Freeholders and Freemen of the Province of Pennsylvania* (Philadelphia, 1727); *Some Necessary Precautions Worthy to be Considered by all the English Subjects in the Election of Members to Represent Them in General Assembly* (Philadelphia, 1727?); *Conspiracy of Cataline: Recommended to the Serious Consideration of the Author of "Advice and Information to the Freeholders and Freemen of the Province of Pennsylvania"* (Philadelphia, 1727?); Sir William Keith, *A Modest Reply to the Speech of Isaac Norris, Esq., Delivered From the Bench in the Court of Common Pleas, Held For the City and County of Philadelphia, the 11th day of September 1727* (Philadelphia, 1727); *A Letter From a Gentleman in Philadelphia . . .*

64. *A Revisal of the Intrigues of the Triumvirate with the Rest of the Trustees of the Proprietor of Pennsylvania* (Philadelphia, 1729); *A View of the Scandal Lately Spread in Some Printed Libels Against the Government of Pennsylvania* (Philadelphia, 1729).

65. *Remarks Upon the "Advice and Information to the Freeholders and Freemen of the Province of Pennsylvania"* (Philadelphia, 1727); *To My Respected Friend Isaac Norris* (Philadelphia, 1727); *To Morris Morris, On the Reasons Published for his Conduct in Assembly in the Year 1728* (Philadelphia, 1728).

66. The social standing of the Keithians was comparable to that of their opponents. On the two Keithian clubs, see Wendel, "The Keith-Lloyd Alliance," pp. 299-300.

CHAPTER 8

1. Richard Peters to Thomas Penn, 3 October 1744, RPLB.

2. In John Smith's Diary and the Pemberton Papers, it is possible to see the intimate and constantly changing nature of group relations in one general circle of Quaker society. For mention of other groups, see John Smith's Diary, 9 June 1748.

3. "Plainness in speech and apparel, in our salutations and conversations are by some slighted and called small things, yet however small or trivial such may esteem them our elders and worthies have considered and experienced them not only as duty in

aiming to conduct their lives and manners according to the primitive simplicity of the Gospel, but as a kind of barrier against the conversation of the loose, vicious and immoral part of mankind" (Friends' Book of Advices [1682-1763], Bradford MM, CCHS, p. 28; see also Frederick B. Tolles, *Quakers and the Atlantic Culture* (New York, 1960), pp. 76-77.

4. Generally on Quaker beliefs, see Howard Brinton, *Friends For Three Hundred Years: The History and Beliefs of the Society of Friends Since George Fox Started the Quaker Movement* (New York, 1952), pp. 15-58.

5. *Ibid.*, pp. 126-43. There was a strong potential for equalitarianism in Quaker beliefs and meeting organization, but, although some of it was actualized in the form of mutuality that existed among meeting members, and by the common use of simple forms of address in conversation, its translation into practice during the second quarter of the eighteenth century was retarded by the existence of relatively high levels of deference. On the acceptance of rank, see Tolles, *Meeting House and Counting House*, pp. 109-13. Simplicity, too, was not a strong point among Quakers during this period. Ibid., pp. 113-43; Tolles, *Quakers and the Atlantic Culture*, pp. 83-88.

6. Tolles, *Meeting House and Counting House*, pp. 65, 80.

7. Friends' Book of Advices, Bradford MM, CCHS, p. 1.

8. Brinton, *Friends For Three Hundred Years*, p. 100.

9. Ibid., pp. 106-16. If division existed and a decision was necessary, the meeting would appoint a committee to settle the matter. Ibid., p. 107.

10. Tolles, *Meeting House and Counting House*, pp. 109-13; Sydney V. James, *A People Among Peoples: Quaker Benevolence in Eighteenth Century America* (Cambridge, Mass., 1963), p. 11.

11. When as prominent a man as John Smith reacted to French threats to Philadelphia shipping in the spring of 1748 by starting a private subscription to allow the Council to outfit a privateer, his peers soon convinced him such an act was "not expedient." Smith lamented his "folly in attempting to set on foot a scheme without consulting Friends about it." John Smith's Diary, 25 May 1748, 1 June 1748.

12. William Fishbourne, Sr., "Some Remarks on Ye Settlements of the Province of Pennsylvania to the Year 1739," Etting Coll., Misc. Mss.; Isaac Norris to Richard Partridge, 16 June 1744, INLB (1735-55).

13. Jerry M. Frost, "The Quaker Family in Colonial America: A Social History of the Society of Friends" (Ph.D. diss., University of Wisconsin, 1968), p. 153; Edith Verlenden Paschall, "The Founders of the Darby Library: Written for the 200th anniversary, 1743-1943," Mss. Darby Library. On the relative size of Quaker families, see Robert V. Wells, "A Demographic Analysis of Some Middle Colony Quakers in the Eighteenth Century" (Ph.D. diss., Princeton University, 1969), pp. 46, 53-56.

14. Although there was a definite tendency for members of one monthly meeting to marry others within that same meeting, what intermarriage did take place, along with a reasonably high rate of geographic mobility, did extend kinship ties beyond the bounds of any one geographic area. On mobility see Wells, "Some Middle Colony Quakers," pp. 38-39. Also see the marriage and removal certificates for any of the Pennsylvania monthly meetings.

15. For a note on city and country Quakers, see appendix V.1.

16. The function of ministers and elders may be observed in any representative Friend's journal, in the Pemberton Papers, or in John Smith's Diary. For example, see John Churchman, *Gospel Labors*, pp. 25-26, 31-32, 36-39, 40-45, 59-60; Israel Pemberton, Jr., to John Pemberton, 6 July 1751, 21 July 1751, PemP, vol. 7. For biographical notes on the above, and other elders and ministers, see A. M. Gummere, ed., *The Journal and Essays of John Woolman* (New York, 1922), pp. 511-92.

17. The structure of Quaker organization was pyramidal in shape, with four distinct levels of participation. Preparative meetings were the smallest and most basic unit of organization; Friends met at that level primarily for purposes of worship. At the second level, several preparatory meetings fell within the compass of one monthly meeting. In addition to holding meetings for worship, the members of the monthly meeting divided themselves according to sex, and held separate men's and women's

business meetings. Within the ambit of the business meetings fell all matters that touched the general welfare of members. They supervised the care of the poor, made decisions on matters of discipline, gave or denied permission to marry, processed applications of removal, and certified Quaker ministers. On the third level, representatives from member monthly meetings attended a quarterly meeting. The functions of the quarterly meeting were relatively simple: tendering advice on request to monthly meetings, deciding appeals from the monthly meeting decisions on discipline, and both transmitting information gathered from the lower levels up to the yearly meeting and passing down advice given out by the yearly meeting.

Once a year, at the end of September, delegates from the quarterly meetings, and such other Friends as decided to attend, assembled for the yearly meeting. The meeting set out statements clarifying Quaker testimonies (urged the monthly meetings to pay attention to a variety of general problems), reported to the London Yearly Meeting, appointed a publication committee to oversee Quaker tracts, arranged for the procurement and distribution of religious literature, and considered any matter that members felt concerned the society as a whole. For elaboration on this, see Howard H. Brinton, *Guide to Quaker Practice* (Wallingford, Pa., 1952); L. Hugh Doncastle, *Quaker Organization and Business Meetings* (London, 1958); *The Inventory of Church Archives: Society of Friends in Pennsylvania* (Philadelphia, 1941).

18. In the ensuing discussion I have replied on the sociological models expounded by Robert A. Dentler and Kai T. Erikson in "The Functions of Deviance in Social Groups," *Social Problems* 7 (1959): 98-107, and Erikson's *Wayward Puritans: A Study in the Sociology of Deviance* (New York, 1966).

19. For a summary of quarter sessions records, see appendix III.1. For evidence of justices of the peace fining those charged for drinking and swearing, see William Pim, His Book for Recording Assignments of Servants (1739-51), CCHS.

20. Tolles, *Meeting House and Counting House*, p. 233.

21. Goshen MM, 1732, p. 150; H. O. Gillette, ed., *Minutes of the Philadelphia Baptist Association, 1717-1807* (Philadelphia, 1851), p. 27; Perry, *Historical Collections,* 2:215; Frost, "Quaker Family," pp. 370-71.

22. Minutes, Chester MM, 1747, FHL, p. 20.

23. Friends' Book of Advices, Bradford MM, CCHS, p. 34. The meaning of "public reading" was decided in each case by the monthly meeting. In most instances the reading took place at the breakup of the first day's meeting of the preparative meeting to which the repentant sinner belonged. In other cases it might be ordered to be read at several preparative meetings. On the necessity of personal appearance see Minutes, Chester MM, 1743, FHL, p. 340.

24. Friends' Book of Advices, Bradford MM, CCHS, pp. 74-78.

25. Ibid., pp. 63-66.

26. Ibid., p. 55.

27. Minutes, Bradford MM, 1741, FHL, p. 24; Minutes, Chester MM, 1740, FHL, pp. 281-82.

28. For an extreme example, see the patient dealing with Thomas Hughes, who, when faced with the charge of fighting, "would not tarry to answer the charge." Minutes, Nottingham MM, 1733, FHL, p. 39.

29. "Dealing" with an individual was the process by which the meeting attempted to persuade that person that his actions had been wrong and that he should publicly acknowledge them as such. The Quaker allegiance to peace and unanimity required such a process. No matter how intolerable the crime, that procedure could not be discarded. When the Chester Monthly Meeting inquired of the quarterly meeting "whether it not better have a rule established among us that such as are guilty of fornication and all great crimes should be testified against without dealing with," the representatives of the quarterly meeting replied with a decisive no. Minutes, Chester MM, 1740, FHL, p. 310; Minutes, Chester Quarterly Meeting, 1740, FHL, p. 143 (hereinafter cited as QM.)

30. Minutes, Bradford MM, 1743-44, FHL, pp. 1-10, 42-43.

31. Minutes, Kennett MM, FHL, 1733, pp. 276-82, 1735, pp. 307-18; Minutes, Bradford MM, 1741, FHL, pp. 24-26.

32. Minutes, Concord MM, 1741, FHL, pp. 323, 325.

33. For the concern for sincerity, see Minutes, Goshen MM, 1740, FHL, p. 242. For a case where the benefit of the doubt went against the deviant, see Minutes, Sadsbury MM, 1746, FHL, p. 78. For the reverse situation, see Minutes, Concord MM, 1754, FHL, p. 412.

34. This figure is based on the three sample meetings in appendix V.2. Relative to Quaker membership, the number of disciplinary actions and percentage of disownments was certainly lower between 1725 and 1755 than after 1755, and probably lower than during the first three decades of the colony's existence. Marietta, "Ecclesiastical Discipline," pp. 173-209.

35. Minutes, Chester MM, 1753, FHL, p. 93. When John Morris was about to be dealt with, he apparently said that he had "disowned" them "long ago." Minutes, Bradford MM, 1740, FHL, p. 20.

36. Minutes, Chester MM, 1753, FHL, p. 97.

37. These were the specific provisos of the testimony against Mary Hunt, who was being disowned for bastardy and the concealment of the father's identity. Minutes, Darby MM, 1748, FHL, p. 314.

38. Friends' Book of Advices, Bradford MM, CCHS, pp. 84-90.

39. Minutes, Sadsbury MM, 1745, FHL, p. 38; Minutes, Bradford MM, 1755, FHL, p. 90; Minutes, Chester QM, 1751, FHL, pp. 201, 205.

40. Minutes, Concord MM, 1745, FHL, p. 348; Minutes, Chester QM, FHL, 1750, p. 199, 1751, p. 200.

41. Minutes, Bradford MM, 1752, FHL, pp. 63-69.

42. Minutes, Concord MM, 1728, FHL, p. 235; Minutes, Chester QM, 1752, FHL, pp. 207-208. If, by transgressing Quaker discipline in concert, a group of men threatened the peace and stability of the monthly meeting, the matter might be passed on immediately to the quarterly meetings. Minutes, Sadsbury MM, 1751, FHL, pp. 55-58.

43. Friends' Book of Advices, Bradford MM, CCHS, pp. 175-76; Minutes, PYM, 1743, FHL, p. 434.

44. Conversely, requests for disciplinary rulings were often cast in specific terms. "Where a young man having been born of believing parents and educated in the principles of friends until he arrives at the eighteenth year of his age, and afterwards his father puts him apprentice to one of another persuasion and about the twenty-first or second year of his age he joins himself to another society and marrys a young woman belonging to Friends by a priest, whether such a young man ought not to be denied if he do not condemn the same and join himself to the Friends again?" Minutes, Chester MM, 1734, FHL, p. 213.

45. Minutes, Chester MM, 1732-1733, FHL, pp. 181-92.

46. Brinton, *Friends For Three Hundred Years,* pp. 119-120, 140.

47. Frost, "Quaker Family," pp. 163-65.

48. Marietta, "Ecclesiastical Discipline," pp. 129-30.

49. For example, in a trip to Lancaster, Mary Pemberton, Daniel Stanton, and others stayed at George Ashton's, whose father had left the Society of Friends. George, Jr., was an officer in a Chester County regiment of the 1747-48 Association. Mary Pemberton to Israel Pemberton, 26 August 1754, PemP, vol. 10.

50. Churchman, *Gospel Labors,* p. 58.

51. Marietta, "Ecclesiastical Discipline," pp. 148-49.

52. Tolles, *Quakers and the Atlantic Culture,* pp. 80-88.

53. Minutes, PYM, FHL 1706, p. 107, 1707, p. 113; Friends' Book of Advices, Bradford MM, CCHS, p. 71.

54. Friends' Book of Advices, Bradford MM, CCHS, pp. 71-72.

55. Minutes, Chester MM, 1732, FHL, p. 175.

56. Minutes, Goshen MM, 1732, FHL, p. 126.

57. Minutes, Nottingham MM, 1732, FHL, p. 28.

58. Minutes, Chester QM, 1731, FHL, p. 123.

59. Minutes, PYM, 1732, FHL, p. 360; Friends' Book of Advices, Bradford MM, CCHS, p. 72.

60. I have relied mainly on Hermann Wellenreuther's article, "The Political Dilemma of the Quakers," *PMHB* 94 (1970): 135-72, for the history of the peace testimony prior to 1726.

61. Ibid., pp. 147-55.

62. Ibid. When members of the Darby Monthly Meeting refused to pay the 1711 war tax, the Concord Quarterly Meeting ordered the Darby members to "proceed against all such offenders." Minutes, Chester QM, 1712, FHL, p. 55.

63. Isaac Norris, Jr., to Robert Charles, 31 March 1741, INLB (1719-56); Richard Peters to John Penn, 20 October 1741, RPLB; *PMHB* 4 (1882): 403-11; Isaac Sharpless, *A History of Quaker Government in Pennsylvania* (Philadelphia, 1898), 1:225-27; Minutes, PYM, 1741, FHL, p. 425.

64. *CR,* 4:765-66; *Votes,* 4:3025, 3027-28, 3036, 3038, 3042-43, 3064, 3071, 3093, 3094-95, 3097, 3102; Notes on Assembly Debates, *Franklin Papers,* 3:15-17.

65. *CR,* 5:90-92.

66. Ibid., pp. 89-93, 98, 114-18; *Votes,* 4:3141, 3146-48, 3162-65.

67. *Franklin Papers,* 3:183-204, 214-16, 221n.; John Smith, *The Doctrine of Christianity As Held By the People Called Quakers* (Philadelphia, 1748); Samuel Smith, *Necessary Truth or Seasonable Considerations For the Inhabitants of the City and Province of Pennsylvania In Relation to the Pamphlet Called "Plain Truth"* (Philadelphia, 1748).

68. *Votes,* 4:3183-85; *CR,* 5:250, 276-77.

69. *Franklin Papers,* 3:185; "Plain Truth," ibid., p. 199; Richard Peters to Proprietaries, 29 November 1747, ibid, p. 217; *CR.* 5:91-92, 250-51, 274-76.

70. Ibid., p. 250.

71. John Smith, *The Doctrinne of Christianity . . .;* John Smith's Diary, 25 May 1748.

72. John Smith's Diary, 1 June 1748.

73. Ibid., 28 May 1748.

74. John Kinsey's death in 1750, apparently, occasioned some division among Friends over who should succeed him in his various offices. The chief justiceship, of course, was an appointive position (it went to William Allen) but the position of clerk of the yearly meeting, Speaker of the Assembly, and acting trustee of the Loan Office were all in Quaker hands. The first went to Israel Pemberton, Jr., the second to Isaac Norris, Jr., and the third to James Morris. (Morris only served a few months before his death, and then Charles Norris, Isaac's brother, succeeded him.) Tradition has it that Quakers were badly divided between backers of Isaac Norris, Jr., and Israel Pemberton, Jr., for political leadership. Certainly there was personal and family rivalry between the two, and undoubtedly there were differences in outlook and philosophy, although their disagreement on the peace principle had to await the crisis of 1755 before it was articulated, but it is doubtful that Quakers as a group were badly divided between backers of the two men. Richard Peters and James Hamilton, who were the source of most information along this line (for example, James Hamilton to Thomas Penn, 13 October 1750, PPOC, vol. 5; Richard Peters to Thomas Penn, 13 July 1750, ibid.) were, I suspect, a trifle myopic because of their Philadelphia situation. While Pemberton undoubtedly had numerous friends in Philadelphia, and although he was not without influence in the country, there is no evidence to suspect he had anything like the political interest that Norris, a full-time politician, had among the county leaders. The proof lies in Charles Norris' appointment to what was the most important patronate position in the province, without there being a hint of opposition from Pemberton, and Pemberton's failure—it is possible that he was defeated rather than he chose to resign—to sit in the Assembly for more than one year (1750-51).

75. Root, *Relations of Pennsylvania With the British Government,* pp. 293-96.

76. Thayer, *Pennsylvania Politics,* pp. 25-47.

77. *Votes,* 5:3701-2, 3705, 3708-13.

78. Ibid., pp. 3637-44; *CR,* 6:200-202.

79. *Votes,* 5:3686-87, 3690, 3692-95, 3697.

80. Ibid., pp. 3728, 3758-59, 3766.

81. Ibid, p. 3841; Minutes, PYM, FHL, 1755, p. 61. This phrase had come to mean that the legislature would vote a sum of money to the king's use, on the monarch's demand, as a token of loyalty in time of war. Later, Quaker reformers used it in a different sense. For example, see *Votes*, 5:4102.

82. On the background of the Quaker reform movements, see Richard Bauman, *For the Reputation of Truth: Politics, Religion and Conflict among the Pennsylvania Quakers, 1750-1800* (Baltimore and London, 1971), pp. 9-46.

When Catherine Payton and other concerned Friends addressed the Quaker assemblymen, in early 1755, on the difficulties that lay ahead of them in fulfilling their obligations as Quakers, their instructions were suitably vague. Catherine Phillips, *Memoirs of the Life of Catherine Phillips* (Philadelphia, 1798), pp. 141-42. See also the Epistle penned by John Woolman and signed by a number of representatives of the Philadelphia yearly meeting for ministers and elders in March 1755. John Woolman, *The Journal and Essays of John Woolman*.

83. *Votes*, 5:4102; *PA*, 1st ser. 2:487-88.

For elaboration on the divisions among Friends, see Bauman, *Reputation of Truth*, pp. 30-31, 44-46, 69-70; Jack D. Marrietta, "Conscience, the Quaker Community, and the French and Indian War," *PMHB* 95 (1971): 15-16.

EPILOGUE

1. Zemsky, *Merchants, Farmers, and River Gods*, p. xii; Sirmans, *Colonial South Carolina*, pp. 223-24; Robert M. Weir, " 'The Harmony We Were Famous For': An Interpretation of Pre-Revolutionary South Carolina Politics," *WMQ*, 3rd ser. 26 (1969): 473-501; Greene, "Changing Interpretations of Early American Politics," p. 177. See also Jack P. Greene, "The Growth of Political Stability: An Interpretation of Political Development in the Anglo-American Colonies, 1660-1760," in *The American Revolution: A Heritage of Change*, ed. John Parker and Carol Urness (Minneapolis: James Ford Bell Library, 1975), pp. 26-52.

2. Among the works I found most helpful in dealing with the problem of political stability were Lewis Coser, *The Functions of Social Conflict* (New York, 1956); Harry Eckstein, *The Evolution of Political Performance: Problems and Dimensions*, Sage Professional Papers in Comparative Politics (Beverley Hills, Calif., 1971); and Eckstein, "Authority Relations and Governmental Performance: A Theoretical Framework," *Comparative Political Studies* 2 (1969-70): 269-325.

3. Seymour Martin Lipset, *Political Man, The Social Basis of Politics* (New York, 1960), p. 64.

4. For example, see John M. Murrin, "Review of Michael Kammen, 'People of Paradox: An Inquiry Concerning the Origins of American Civilization,' " *WMQ*, 3rd ser. 30 (1973): 494; "Anglicization and Identity: The Colonial Experience, the Revolution, and the Dilemma of American Nationalism" (paper read at the Annual Convention of the Organization of American Historians, Denver, Colo., April 1974), pp. 17-18.

5. Bernard Bailyn, "Politics and Social Structure in Virginia," in James M. Smith, ed., *Seventeenth Century America* (Chapel Hill, N. C., 1959), pp. 112-15; Bailyn, *Origins of American Politics*, pp. 88-92; Michael Kammen, *People of Paradox: An Inquiry Concerning the Origins of American Civilization* (New York, 1972), pp. 31-56.

6. For example, see Guy Frégault, *La Civilisation de la Nouvelle-France, 1713-1744* (Montreal, 1969); W. S. Macnutt, *The Atlantic Provinces: The Emergence of a Colonial Society, 1712-1857* (Toronto, 1965), pp. 103-270.

BIBLIOGRAPHICAL ESSAY

§

The most important sources for this book are the manuscript holdings of a number of archives in Pennsylvania, foremost among which are the holdings of the Historical Society of Pennsylvania. The collections there, that I found the most useful are the following: Bucks County Miscellaneous Papers (1682-1745), Cadwalader Collection, Chester County Papers (1684-1847), Dreer Collection, Etting Collection, Gratz Collection, Andrew and James Hamilton Papers, Lancaster County Miscellaneous Papers (1724-72), Logan Papers, Norris Papers, Pemberton Papers, Penn Papers, Penn-Hamilton Correspondence (1748-70), Pennsylvania Miscellaneous Papers, Peters Papers, Smith Manuscripts, and Taylor Papers. Because of the voluminous nature of the better known of these collections, the researcher can easily be overwhelmed. The metropolitan bias—the interpreting of Pennsylvanian society through Philadelphians' eyes, the generalizing about the provincial experience on the strength of the Philadelphia example—is one that has deeply permeated historical writings on colonial Pennsylvania, largely because of exclusive reliance on such collections as the Penn Papers or Pemberton Manuscripts.

In order to avoid this pitfall I have used as many collections as possible that deal with outlying areas or with county figures. More importantly, I have spent long days at the Lancaster and Chester County Historical Societies and the appropriate courthouse, working through the manuscripts, local histories, and genealogical files that are there. Only by working out in the counties, with county material, is it possible to get a sense of what went on in rural Pennsylvania and of the kinds of relationships that existed between hinterland and metropolis.

Much of Pennsylvania history must have to do with members of the Society of Friends, and so, Quaker archives were particularly important. I used microfilm copies of the records of the Quaker meetings in Pennsylvania and a variety of other manuscript sources at Friends Historical Library at Swarthmore College. Equally valuable was the Quaker Collection at the Haverford College Library.

Several other depositories also held useful material. The Presbyterian Historical Society has a good collection of religious documents. The American

Philosophical Society holds manuscripts of some of the prominent public figures of the time. And, although the Library Company of Philadelphia had given most of its manuscript collections to the Historical Society of Pennsylvania by the time I researched this book, there were still one or two important items in its care. So, too, were there a few records of interest at the Philadelphia City Archives. Finally, the Bucks County Historical Society and the Bucks County Court House made available some worthwhile sources on local figures.

Second in importance to the manuscripts I used were the published primary sources. Samuel Hazard's edition of the *Pennsylvania Archives* (9 ser., Philadelphia and Harrisburg, 1852-1935), holds a vast store of information; I made particular use of the eighth series, which contains the proceedings of the Pennsylvania Assembly. Two other basic sources that are best used in conjunction with this are Samuel Hazard's edition of the *Minutes of the Provincial Council of Pennsylvania* . . . (16 vols., Philadelphia, 1838-53), and James T. Mitchell and Henry Flander's edition of the *Statutes at Large of Pennsylvania from 1682 to 1801* . . . (vols. 2-5, Harrisburg, 1896-1911). Journals such as the *Pennsylvania Magazine of History and Biography, Pennsylvania History,* the *Journal of the Presbyterian Historical Society, Friends Historical Association Bulletin* (becomes *Quaker History*), *Papers and Addresses of the Lancaster County Historical Society* (becomes *Journal of . . .*), *Proceedings of the Pennsylvania German Society, Pennsylvania Folklife,* and the *Mennonite Quarterly Review* often include important documents or excerpts from worthwhile documents in the various articles. Consequently, I used these journals much as I would any primary source. The same is true of Samuel Hazard's *Register of Pennsylvania* (16 vols., Philadelphia, 1828-36) and William H. Egles's *Notes and Queries* (Lancaster, Pa., 1894-1900).

There are a few sets of published papers and journals that cover the second quarter of the eighteenth century. The best known of these are the first six volumes of Leonard W. Labaree, ed., *The Papers of Benjamin Franklin* (vols. 1-19 to date, New Haven, 1959-); Henry Melchior Muhlenberg, *The Journals of Henry Melchior Muhlenberg,* ed. and trans. Theodore G. Tappert and John W. Doberstein, (vol. 1, Philadelphia, 1942); and Gottlieb Mittelberger's *Journey to Pennsylvania,* ed. and trans. Oscar Handlin and John Clive (Cambridge, Mass., 1960). There is other material of this sort included in many of the nineteenth- and early twentieth-century biographies of important Pennsylvanians. So, too, are there published minutes of several governmental and religious bodies. The most important of these are the *Minutes of the Common Council of the City of Philadelphia* (Philadelphia, 1847) and the *Records of the Presbyterian Church in the United States of America* (Philadelphia, 1904).

Needless to say newspapers are essential sources in any attempt to deal with political events and public attitudes. The *American Weekly Mercury,* the *Pennsylvania Gazette,* and the *Pennsylvania Journal* all contributed to my knowledge of Pennsylvania life. Along with these I read the Philadelphia publications listed in the Evans Collection and supplemented them with a few additional pamphlets housed in the Library Company of Philadelphia.

As any historian of colonial America must be, I am deeply indebted to those who have gone before. There are, of course, a whole series of general works on the colonies as well as studies of provinces other than Pennsylvania that have played an important part in my thinking. But to deal with them —beyond what I have said in the Prologue—would be to go too far afield.

The period of prerevolutionary Pennsylvania history with which I have dealt has attracted less attention from political historians than any other. Nevertheless, there are a number of books and articles that I found particularly helpful. Roy N. Lokken, *David Lloyd, Colonial Lawmaker* (Seattle, 1959); Gary B. Nash, *Quakers and Politics: Pennsylvania, 1681-1726* (Princeton, 1968; Frederick B. Tolles, *James Logan and the Culture of Provincial America* (Boston, 1957); and Thomas Wendel, "The Keith-Lloyd Alliance: Factional and Coalition Politics in Colonial Pennsylvania," *Pennsylvania Magazine of History and Biography* 92 (1968): 289-305, were important in helping me come to terms with early eighteenth-century politics and society. Once I moved beyond the time limits of these studies, however, there was little to replace them. Burton Alva Konkle's biography *The Life of Andrew Hamilton, 1676-1741* (Philadelphia, 1941) is a disappointment, as is Theodore Thayer's treatment of Israel Pemberton's early public career in his *Israel Pemberton, King of the Quakers* (Philadelphia, 1943).

Three articles are of some help in dealing with the early 1740s. Norman S. Cohen, "The Philadelphia Election Riot of 1742," *Pennsylvania Magazine of History and Biography* 92 (1968): 306-19, and William S. Parson, "The Bloody Election of 1742," *Pennsylvania History* 36 (1968): 290-306, provide useful information on the hotly contested Philadelphia County election of 1742. Hermann Wellenreuther, "The Political Dilemma of the Quakers in Pennsylvania, 1681-1748," *Pennsylvania Magazine of History and Biogrpahy* 94 (1970): 135-72, is a very important rethinking of the Quaker pacifist position, and his comments about the defense crisis of 1739-42 merit close consideration.

Theodore Thayer's book *Pennsylvania Politics and the Growth of Democracy, 1740-1776* (Harrisburg, 1953) does include useful summaries of events during the 1740s but it is not until the end of that decade that historians have begun a really intensive study of prerevolutionary politics. Then there is an embarrassment of riches. William S. Hanna's *Benjamin Franklin and Pennsylvania Politics* (Stanford, Calif., 1964) brings Thomas Penn into focus as no earlier historian had been able to do. James H. Hutson's *Pennsylvania Politics, 1746-1770. The Movement For Royal Government and Its Consequences* (Princeton, 1972) provides an important if rather narrow view of Pennsylvania politics between 1746 and 1755. Hutson's article "Benjamin Franklin and Pennsylvania Politics: A Reappraisal", *Pennsylvania Magazine of History and Biography* 93 (1969): 303-71, is important, for it sets out clearly and accurately the reasons for executive-legislative tensions in the early and mid 1750s. Other pieces that are useful in sorting out the politics of the early fifties are the first two chapters of Benjamin F. Newcomb, *Franklin and Galloway: A Political Partnership* (New Haven 1972); John J. Zimmerman, "Benjamin Franklin and the Quaker Party, 1755-56," *William and Mary Quarterly*, 3rd ser. 17 (1960): 291-

313; Ralph L. Ketcham, "Conscience, War, and Politics in Pennsylvania, 1755-1757," ibid. 20 (1963): 416-39; and Jack D. Marietta, "Conscience, the Quaker Community, and the French and Indian War," *Pennsylvania Magazine of History and Biography* 95 (1971): 3-27.

There is one additional book that deserves note in relationship to the politics of the 1740s and 1750s. This is Dietmar Rothermund's *The Layman's Progress: Religious and Political Experience in Colonial Pennsylvania, 1740-1770* (Philadelphia, 1961). Although he takes in much more in the way of social and religious themes than many other political studies, one of Rothermund's major concerns is the configuration of provincial politics. And he does have some perceptive insights into the workings of the Pennsylvania world. The book must, however, be used carefully, for Rothermund's model of declension for Pennsylvania society, and his tendency to slip into erroneous positions, makes it, at times, a very misleading book.

A number of the foregoing books and articles include important analyses of, and comments about, the structural features of Pennsylvania politics. In addition, there are three articles worth special attention. These are Sister Joan de Lourdes Leonard, "The Organization and Procedure of the Pennsylvania Assembly, 1682-1776," *Pennsylvania Magazine of History and Biography* 72 (1948): 215-39, 376-412; and, by the same author, "Elections in Colonial Pennsylvania," *William and Mary Quarterly*, 3rd. ser. 11 (1954): 385-401; and Thomas Wendel, "The Speaker of the House, Pennsylvania, 1701-1776," *Pennsylvania Magazine of History and Biography* 97 (1973): 3-21.

There is another important group of books that deal largely with politics. These are writings that are concerned not only with political events and the means of organizing and controlling political power in Pennsylvania, but also in the structure of imperial relationships. Mabel P. Wolff, *The Colonial Agency of Pennsylvania, 1712-1757* (Philadelphia, 1933); Winfred T. Root, *The Relationship of Pennsylvania with the British Government, 1696-1765* (New York, 1912); and William R. Shepherd, *History of Proprietary Government in Pennsylvania* (New York, 1896), all belong in this category, and they all contain important material that cannot be found elsewhere. Two helpful articles that also deal with proprietary affairs and the relationship between London and Philadelphia are Nicholas B. Wainwright's "The Missing Evidence: Penn versus Baltimore," *Pennsylvania Magazine of History and Biography* 80 (1956): 227-35, and "Tale of a Runaway Cape: The Penn-Baltimore Agreement of 1732," ibid. 87 (1963): 251-93.

In addition to the realms of provincial politics and imperial relationships, there is also that of local government. Studies of local government in Pennsylvania are not as numerous as one would hope. The best sources are the old information-packed county histories, a few unpublished doctoral dissertations, and two articles, Judith M. Diamondstone, "Philadelphia's Municipal Corporation," *Pennsylvania Magazine of History and Biography* 90 (1966):183-201, and Clair W. Keller, "The Pennsylvania County Commission System, 1712-1740," ibid. 93 (1969): 372-82.

As everyone knows, the Quakers were at the center of political affairs in Pennsylvania throughout the first half of the eighteenth century. Because of that and the nature of William Penn's "Holy Experiment," numerous historians have focused on the Quaker experience. The following are those "Quaker" studies that are most valuable: Isaac Sharpless, *A Quaker Experiment in Government* (Philadelphia, 1898), and *Political Leaders of Provincial Pennsylvania* (New York, 1919); Frederick B. Tolles, *Meeting House and Counting House: The Quaker Merchants of Colonial Philadelphia* (Chapel Hill, 1948), and *Quakers and the Atlantic Culture* (New York, 1960); Sydney V. James, *A People Among Peoples: Quaker Benevolence in the Eighteenth Century* (Cambridge, Mass., 1963); Richard Bauman, *For the Reputation of Truth: Politics, Religion, and Conflict among the Pennsylvania Quakers, 1750–1800* (Baltimore, 1971); J. William Frost, *The Quaker Family in Colonial America: A Portrait of the Society of Friends* (New York, 1973); Jack C. Marietta's aforementioned article, his "Wealth, War and Religion: The Perfecting of Quaker Asceticism, 1740–1783," *Church History*, 43 (1974): 230–41, and his "Quaker Family Education in Historical Perspective," *Quaker History* 63 (1974): 3–16; Hermann Wellenreuther's aforementioned article and his *Glauge und Politik in Pennsylvania, 1681–1776: Die Wandlungen der Obrigkeitsdoktrin und des Peace Testimony der Quaker* (Cologne, 1972).

Understandably, no other religious group in Pennsylvania has drawn the same attention as the Quakers. There are, however, several important studies of the Great Awakening that do throw light not only on that event, but also on the more general conditions of the different religious groups in the colony. Charles H. Maxson, *The Great Awakening in the Middle Colonies* (Chicago, 1920), is still the standard reference work, although it is badly outdated. Leonard J. Tinterud, *The Forming of An American Tradition: A Re-examination of Colonial Presbyterianism* (Philadelphia, 1949), is an indispensable piece of work. Four worthwhile articles are Dietmar Rothermund, "Political Factions and the Great Awakening," *Pennsylvania History* 26 (1959): 317–31; Martin E. Lodge, "The Crisis of the Churches in the Middle Colonies," *Pennsylvania Magazine of History and Biography* 95 (1971): 195–220; William H. Kenny, III, "George Whitefield, Dissenter Priest of the Great Awakening, 1739–41," *William and Mary Quarterly*, 3rd ser. 26 (1969): 75–93; and John B. Frantz, "The Awakening of Religion among the German Settlers in the Middle Colonies," ibid. 33 (1976): 266–88. In themselves these modern studies are thin, but when combined with the standard nineteenth- and early twentieth-century studies of Pennsylvania denominations and church leaders, they provide important insights into the colony's condition of religious diversity.

Despite the obvious cultural diversity—which was the other side of the religious diversity—of Pennsylvania, there are few modern works that deal effectively with the interaction of the different national groups. Helpful information may be found in James G. Leyburn, *The Scotch-Irish: A Social History* (Chapel Hill, N.C., 1962); James O. Knauss, "Social Conditions among the Pennsylvania Germans as Revealed in German Newspapers Published in America", *Proceedings of the Pennsylvania German Society* 29 (1922): 1–211; Dietmar Rothermund, "The German Problem of Colonial Pennsylvania," *Pennsylvania Magazine of History and Biography* 84 (1960): 3–21; and Samuel E. Weber, *The Charity School Movement in Colonial Pennsylvania* (Philadelphia, 1905).

Economic affairs in Pennsylvania have not received the same attention political topics have. Harry D. Berg's "The Organization of Business in Colonial Philadelphia," *Pennsylvania History* 10 (1943): 157–177, and James G. Lydon's "Philadelphia's Commercial Expansion 1720–1739," *Pennsylvania Magazine of History and Biography* 91 (1967): 401–418, are helpful on the structure of trade in Philadelphia. Francis P. Jennings has some worthwhile comments on the hinterland in his article "The Indian Trade of the Susquehanna Valley," *Proceedings of the American Philosophical Society* 110 (1966): 406–424. Stevenson W. Fletcher's *Pennsylvania Agriculture and Country Life, 1640–1840* (Harrisburg, 1950), is helpful in gaining entrance to the rural life of preindustrial Pennsylvania.

Finally, two books merit special mention. One is James T. Lemon's *The Best Poor Man's Country: A Geographical Study of Early Southeastern Pennsylvania* (Baltimore and London, 1972)—an invaluable work, for it touches on so many economic and social themes. The second is Joseph E. Illick's *Colonial Pennsylvania: A History* (New York, 1976). This is a sound introduction to so many of the important issues in the history of provincial Pennsylvania.

INDEX

§

§

THE JOHNS HOPKINS UNIVERSITY PRESS

This book was composed in Baskerville text and display type by
Jones Composition Company from a design by Susan Bishop.
It was printed on 50-lb. Publisher's Eggshell Wove paper and
bound in Joanna Arrestox cloth by The Maple Press Company.

Library of Congress Cataloging in Publication Data

Tully, Alan.
    William Penn's legacy.

    (The Johns Hopkins University studies in historical and political science; 95th ser., 2)
    Bibliography: p. 245.
    Includes index.
    1. Pennsylvania—Politics and government—Colonial period, ca. 1600-1775.
2. Pennsylvania—Social conditions. I. Title. II. Series: Johns Hopkins University.
Studies in historical and political science; 95th ser., 2.

F152.T89   320.9′748′02   77-4548
ISBN 0-8018-1932-6